Short Order Cooking

Short Order Cooking

Lendal H. Kotschevar, Ph.D

Distinguished Professor
School of Hospitality Management
Florida International University
North Campus
North Miami, Florida

VAN NOSTRAND REINHOLD
_____ *New York*

Library of Congress Catalog Card Number 90-33447
ISBN 0-442-00404-4

Printed in the United States of America

Van Nostrand Reinhold
115 Fifth Avenue
New York, New York 10003

Van Nostrand Reinhold International Company Limited
11 New Fetter Lane
London EC4P 4EE, England

Van Nostrand Reinhold
480 La Trobe Street
Melbourne, Victoria 3000, Australia

Nelson Canada
1120 Birchmount Road
Scarborough, Ontario M1K 5G4, Canada

16   15   14   13   12   11   10   9   8   7   6   5   4   3   2   1

Library of Congress Cataloging-in-Publication Data

Kotschevar, Lendal Henry, 1908–
    Short order cooking / by Lendal H. Kotschevar.
       p.   cm.
    Includes bibliographical references.
    ISBN 0-442-00404-4
    1. Short order cooks.   2. Cookery—Vocational guidance.
I. Title.
TX943.K68   1990   90-33447
641.5'72'023—dc20   CIP

Contents

Preface

The foodservice industry accounts for about a sixth of our gross national product each year. It is one of our biggest employers, but predictions are that in the future it will be faced with a serious lack of people to fill its jobs. Already it is feeling the pinch and is aggressively recruiting the elderly, teenagers, the handicapped, retrainees, and other previously unsought workers to fill waiting jobs. Despite these efforts, however, the situation will worsen. The number of workers available to fill jobs will decrease, competition from other industries also needing workers from a narrowing market will intensify, and the foodservice industry will require more workers as it grows and expands.

As this scenario of high worker demand unfolds, the industry must prepare would-be workers for the various available jobs. Hiring the untrained and providing them with on-the-job training is no longer considered the most desirable way to go. Using educational training facilities to prepare those who aspire to work in the industry is considered today the most practical, most efficient, and least expensive way to produce workers. Coupling such education with some job experience while learning produces a worker who can step into a job and perform adequately much more quickly.

Short Order Cooking is written to assist in teaching job competence to people who want to become short order cooks. This is usually a good entry-level position in the cooking profession, from which workers can move into cooking positions of greater pay, responsibility, and job competency. It is therefore a very important area of instruction, since the basic knowledge acquired here can be applied in later positions and can last a lifetime.

Because individuals using this text will probably be graduating to higher positions than short order cook later in their careers, the subject matter is not limited to the specific job skills and knowledge required in short order cooking; thus, safety, sanitation, nutrition, and the basic principles of cooking are discussed in some detail. The purpose is to develop a well-rounded worker who possesses the technical skills needed to do the job and has a broad understanding of what the job is and why things are done in a certain way. A person who knows how to do a job certainly can succeed at that job, but one who knows the principles behind the "how" can do a better job and will have a greater feeling of accomplishment, satisfaction, and job security in doing it. It all goes back to the old adage: "The guy who knows 'how' will always have a job, but the one who knows 'why' will be boss of that guy."

The author of this book came into the cooking profession via the job of short order cook and rose from there to become a chef and eventually an educator; for him, the knowledge and skills he learned as short order cook provided a solid block of support throughout his professional lifetime. He therefore sincerely hopes that those who use this book will enjoy the best of success and progress in moving into greater and greater job competency.

CHAPTER ONE

The Job and the Workplace

□ The Job

The job of short order cook is challenging and difficult. Basically, the work revolves around preparing foods to order, which means that most of the food is not ready to serve until ordered, when it is promptly cooked. Most of the orders are prepared from scratch. Thus, for breakfast one might see a short order cook prepare hotcakes, fried eggs, grilled breakfast meats, and French toast all at the same time. For lunch the short order cook may be preparing at one time a ham sandwich, an order of grilled liver and onions, a hamburger with french fries, and an order of deep-fried breaded shrimp. At dinner simultaneous orders might call for french fries, grilled steak, poached salmon, and oyster stew. Some preliminary work can be done so that only last-minute preparation is needed for some items—as, for example, having a hotcake or waffle batter already mixed and having potatoes for hash browns steamed, cut up, and ready for frying.

In addition, some short order jobs require that the individual not only cook the food but also take orders from patrons and serve. When this occurs, the operation is usually a small one. In a large operation, cooking alone constitutes a complete job.

In 1977 the U.S. Department of Labor published the fourth edition of the *Dictionary of Occupational Titles*, which lists job titles and duties for over 20,000 jobs. The following two job titles and job descriptions are given for short order cooks:

313.361-022 COOK, SHORT ORDER (hotel & rest.) I
Prepares and cooks to order foods requiring only short preparation time. May carve meats and fill orders from steamtable. May prepare sandwiches [SANDWICH MAKER (hotel and rest.)]. May prepare salads. May prepare beverages [COFFEE MAKER

1

(hotel & rest.)]. May serve meals to patrons over counter. May be designated according to type of food prepared as HAMBURGER-FRY COOK (hotel & rest.). When cooking is limited to frying foods on grill, may be designated as COOK, GRIDDLE (hotel & rest.).

313.671-010 COOK, SHORT ORDER (hotel & rest.) II
Prepares food and serves restaurant patrons at counters or tables. Takes order from customer and cooks foods requiring short preparation time. Completes order from steamtable and serves customer. Accepts payment or writes charge slip. Carves meats, makes sandwiches, and brews coffee. Usually found in small establishments, such as lunch counters and snack bars.

Characteristics Needed to Do the Job

Short order cooking requires a number of special talents, as well as knowledge, skill, and stamina. A person with a good sense of humor and an even temperament who works well with others is needed. Yet one can have all these things and still lack job competence because of a lack of experience. Practice over a period of time builds competence, raising the level of job performance.

Let us examine a bit more closely some of the specific characteristics needed to properly perform the job of short order cook.

Knowledge A wide range of information is needed, including knowledge about the use and care of tools, utensils, and equipment and about the nature and handling of the foods used. Foods react differently in their preparation: eggs coagulate, baking powders give off carbon dioxide, starch gelatinizes (thickens), and fat smokes when it gets too hot. The short order cook has to know how to handle foods in order to elicit the desired reactions from them. And since foods have different reactions when combined, the short order cook needs to know what these reactions are to produce the right finished item.

For example, blueberries in a hotcake leavened by baking soda turn a dirty purple, but blueberries in a hotcake leavened by baking powder acquire an appetizing red; this is because soda (which is alkaline) turns the color pigment in these berries a dirty purple, while baking powder (which is neutral or slightly acidic) turns it red. Foods also react differently depending on how they are handled. Beef is red because it contains a red pigment called *myoglobin*. Myoglobin turns a dull gray when meat is cooked, but it turns to this "done" color much faster when acid is present. Thus, the short order cook must be aware that a steak marinaded in an acidic medium cooks to a "done" color faster than does a plain steak, and the cook must not grill such a steak as long as usual if the steak is ordered rare.

A wide variety of preparation methods must be learned, and many of these are critical to the quality of the product obtained. Thus, for example, too much stirring of a waffle batter makes for tougher waffles. Knowing proper techniques also speeds work and makes it easier. It is easy work when you know how but tough work when you do not.

Mise en Place Getting lined up—or practicing what the French call *mise en place*—is an essential element of success for a short order cook. Lining up means getting everything in readiness so that, when orders come in, the work proceeds rapidly, sequentially, and in good order. *Mise en place* also involves keeping the workplace cleaned up. Working in a mess delays work and causes quality problems. An example of good *mise en place* would be to preblanch french fries so that the cooking time is 2½ minutes instead of 7 or 8 minutes. For breakfast, eggs, bacon, and other commonly ordered items should be on hand so that the short order cook does not have to walk to the refrigerator to get them. Everything else likely to be needed should be in readiness so that the cook works only at getting the orders out and does not have to stop and do a lot of preparation work.

The key meaning of *mise en place* is "organize." This involves organizing tasks, time, food, tools, and utensils. Organizing tasks means knowing the job, knowing the menu, knowing and using good sanitary procedures, knowing how to think clearly, knowing one's place in the organization and the contribution one must make to it, and having good personal hygiene and working habits. By being alert and organizing the work properly, one will not lose control and fail to do a proper job in times of stress.

Organizing time means knowing how long it takes to prepare items, so that steaks or chicken come out as needed to accompany other foods being served to guests at the same time.

Organizing food, tools, and utensils means arranging a workplace in which all the things needed are on hand and the work moves along in an efficient and expeditious manner. Equipment, tools, and utensils must be kept clean and in good working order. Recipes must be organized and, during use, placed where they are easy to read.

Motor Skills It takes good muscle and eye control to work successfully as a short order cook. Clumsiness has no place in this job. The cook's movements must be well coordinated and dexterous. Motions must be made quickly and precisely. The cook must be deft and skilled in handling a range of tools and foods at the same time. In rapid sequence, eggs may have to be flipped over in the pan, hotcakes turned on the grill, the basket of a deep-fat fryer of potatoes lifted, and a side order of hash browns dished—all while the cook keeps an eye on the waffle iron to note when it stops steaming (the signal that the waffle is done). Few other workers in the kitchen are required to do so many skillful manipulations so rapidly.

Stamina A short order cook needs to have good physical endurance, since the energy expended is considerable and the cook has little if any chance to sit or intersperse more restful jobs. It is "go-go-go," first in lining up and then in pushing orders out fast during the meal hour. Usually, a work shift has two meals in it—a breakfast and a lunch or a lunch and a dinner. This requires two lining-up periods and two meal periods during which a large number of orders are taken and filled. This work requires a person with stamina, who can stand in there and slug it out!

Tension and strain are undoubtedly significant factors in producing fatigue. Studies have shown that tension and strain can be as tiring as actual physical effort. As cooks grow more experienced, they learn to conserve energy, keeping enough in reserve to get through the final rush period in good shape.

Heat can also contribute to fatigue, and many short order units are hot. Thus, the job is not for someone who lacks stamina. But this does not mean that strength is a key demand. Few tasks in short order work require brawn, and as a result a physically unimposing person can handle the job. Endurance is the quality that counts.

Stability Because the pressure is often substantial and the work must move quickly, a short order cook must be even-tempered and able to remain calm and collected while seeing that orders are properly produced and are put out in sequence and on time. The waitstaff or other workers may also be under pressure; and in the rush to see that things go right, tempers may flare. However, this is all a part of the job. To someone on the outside looking in, it can be amusing because one sees how the workers are reacting and sometimes bringing about situations that never should have arisen. To those who are experienced on the job and know how such spats can develop, it is all in a day's work. While at the moment there may be sharp tension, the show has to go on: there's no time for extended tantrums. Then, when the shift is over, everything is forgotten and people are friends again.

Sometimes conflicts arise because a short order cook plays favorites, and other employees, knowing they are being given second-class treatment, resent it. Whatever the reason underlying such a situation arising, its existence is not proper and can only bring about problems for the short order cook. The best way to avoid trouble is to treat all personnel alike. Orders should come out in the order in which they are placed or as required for service needs.

At times during peak periods, orders may stack up. Too many orders come in for even the best cook to keep pace with them. This translates into problems for the waitstaff, who may have patrons glaring at them. But here, too, it is all part of a day's work. At such times, trying to rush may lead to more mistakes and slower production time than if one had simply continued to work at a smooth and steady pace. Indeed, it is a pleasure to watch an experienced cook handle an overflow of orders, plodding along working steadily and evenly with never a false motion, keeping things moving while gradually reducing a difficult situation to manageable size. While the motions are fast, they are accurate and smooth; and even though the short order cook knows that orders are backed up, there is no loss of composure and hence no catastrophe. In the vernacular of the kitchen, the worst response would be to "climb a tree," meaning to panic. Under such stress, an important asset is a sense of humor—the ability to rise above the strain and see the situation realistically.

Experience An experienced pianist, typist, or other technician knows the way around. In any craft, some of the things one must do become almost automatic responses. Proficiency in this case comes from practice in doing things over and over again. The precision, skill, and seeming effortlessness exhibited by an experienced short order cook at work are a joy to behold. A novice who has a thorough basic knowledge of what the job entails—good skill, stamina, stability, and so on—will still not work as easily and effortlessly, and as a result will find the job difficult and tiring. Only after a lot of practice does the work fall into a pattern and flow smoothly and evenly; this is the point at which a cook can achieve peak production. Short order cooking upholds the old adage, "practice makes perfect."

If possible, therefore, students in short order cooking should learn by doing the actual work as well as by reading and taking classes. While books and classroom study are essential for a thorough knowledge of the job, concurrently working at the job reinforces this knowledge and develops skills. By doing the job, students also learn how to organize the work so that it proceeds in an orderly and expeditious manner.

Good Personal Hygiene A short order cook must know and follow the rules for achieving good safety and sanitation. High standards in personal hygiene (including good grooming) must be followed, especially where the short order cook meets the patrons, takes their orders, serves the food, makes out the checks, and even takes the cash. It is essential that the cook know how to manage all of these tasks with professional accomplishment.

Versatility Although the job of a short order cook is fundamentally one of preparing items to order, there are many variations on what the job entails, depending on the nature of the foodservice operation. Some operations are so limited in short order work that one cook does everything: short orders, vegetables, roasts, and other preparations. In this case, the short order job loses its identity, and the work is merged into other work. In some systems, the short order cook is also the vegetable cook; in others, the job may consist of short order preparation and dishup. The duties are usually determined on the basis of what combination of tasks yields a complete job.

Short order cooks may have different names but still primarily do short order cooking. For instance, because so many items are either deep-fried or sautéed, the cook may be called a *fry cook*. Or if the work largely consists of cooking breakfast orders, the cook may be called a *breakfast cook*. But whatever the name, the work is essentially the same.

Given the diversity of the job, a person training for short order cooking must not only be familiar with short order cooking as strictly defined but must be versatile enough to handle related work. Consequently, this book briefly describes how to perform some of these other functions.

In some cases, items come preprepared, so the cook need not know how to get them ready for service from scratch. This category may include batter mixes and frozen or breaded foods. A punch of a microwave button may suffice to heat up a portion of frozen hollandaise sauce in a few seconds. However, since one never knows what the working situation will be, this book also covers the preparation of most items—even french-fried potatoes—from scratch so that the novice entering a job where the newer convenience items and appliances are not used will not be at a loss about how to prepare them.

The key for anyone aspiring to be a short order cook is to be versatile in order to be able to adjust to present conditions. We are living in an age in which norms are difficult to establish because change comes unexpectedly and rapidly, and what may once have been a normal situation is suddenly no longer so. Change is so prevalent that it is difficult to predict what a job may encompass when the student cook gets it. A good, solid foundation, however, will enable one to make adaptations as needed.

☐ The Workplace

Short order cooking is a specialized method of preparing foods to order. The preparation must be fast and good. How well the job is done depends on the equipment available and whether it is placed and used in a way that allows work to be done efficiently.

Equipment Arrangement

Some of the equipment used in a short order section is fairly standard for all such units. Standard items are a griddle, an open or sealed hot top, and perhaps a broiler, a deep-fat fryer, and a microwave. Additional equipment needs usually include a waffle iron and a refrigerator. A workspace and a storage area for food, tools, and utensils are also needed. A salamander can replace a broiler when the demand for broiled foods is low. Other equipment needs depend upon specific needs of the section.

Equipment placement is important for making work easier and for achieving good results. Speed of getting the work done is also a factor. It is seldom possible to have all of the equipment arranged in such a way that a short order cook can just stand in one place and do all the work.

Usually the shortest length of a line of short order equipment is about 72 inches, with equipment arranged in front and in back of the cook. Thus, a 12-inch deep-fryer, 36-inch griddle, 12-inch open hot plate, and 12-inch three-container steam table (as shown in Fig. 1-1a) require a space 72 inches long. A back shelf can be positioned over this equipment to hold some food supplies, dishes, and utensils. Opposite is a 72-inch work surface with a 30-inch refrigerator underneath, and with utensil and equipment storage under the remainder of the work area, as shown. The 32-inch work surface gives room for a cutting board, food supplies, and equipment such as a waffle iron or microwave. An enclosed heated dish storage space is included on this 72-inch work surface so that waitstaff and short order cooks can reach in and get dishes. Figures 1-1b and 1-1c show L-shaped and U-shaped arrangements of equal quantities of equipment.

When two short order cooks are working side by side, it is possible to keep each worker in one place, as in the arrangement shown in Figure 1-1a, with each only having to turn back and forth between the front and back areas. To avoid overcrowding, more space would have to be provided in the arrangement shown in Figures 1-1b and 1-1c if two workers were placed in them.

Once a kitchen is planned, little can be done to correct problems caused by poor equipment placement. Some limited rearrangement of small equipment may be possible, but the major pieces cannot be moved without complete remodeling. When a short order cook inherits a misplanned unit, a study should be made to see what can be done to mitigate the problem. Perhaps small equipment, food supplies, utensils, or other elements can be rearranged to improve the situation; it is often

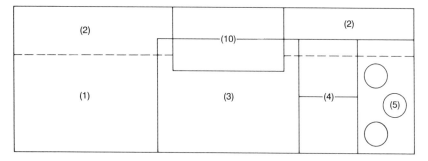

1. Work and supply table with refrigerator under
2. Shelf over
3. Griddle with pot and pan storage under (an oven could be under instead)
4. Hot plate with storage under
5. Food warmer (steam table) with storage under
6. Sink
7. Cutting board on work table with storage under
8. Work table space
9. Plate-warming section that can be opened on both sides
10. Salamander over griddle

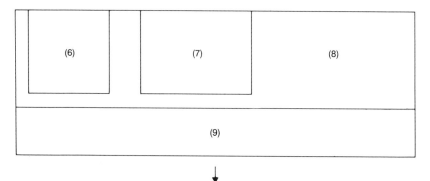

(a)

FIGURE 1-1. Three different equipment arrangements for a short order section: (a) A parallel arrangement, front and back, with the arrow indicating the direction of service to the waitstaff. The flow of work here is good, moving from the supply table over the refrigerator and then across the complete sequence of preparation to the steam table, before foods are moved across the aisle to be given final preparation for service personnel. (b) An L-shaped arrangement, but with a faulty flow of work (left to right), which forces the short order cook to crisscross and backtrack in doing work. L-shaped arrangements, if well planned, can be very efficient and time-saving. (c) A U-shaped arrangement with fairly good work flow, except that foods coming from the refrigerator for use must move in a direction opposite to the desirable one. It might be better to situate the refrigerator under the worktable here.

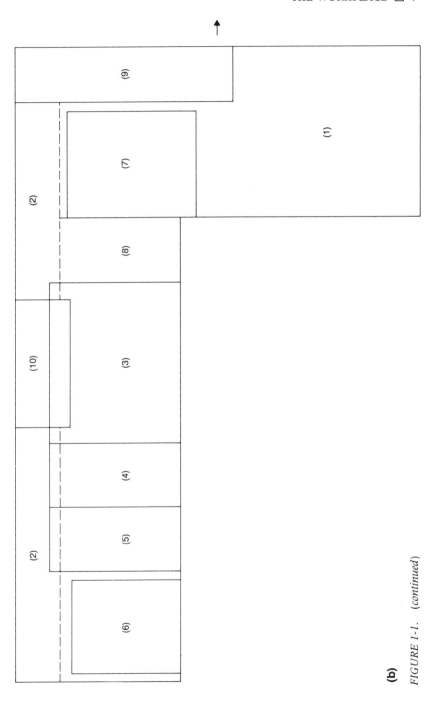

(b)

FIGURE 1-1. (*continued*)

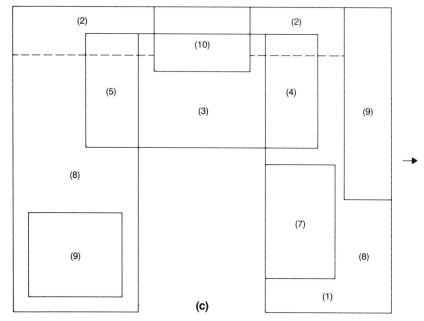

FIGURE 1-1. (continued)

amazing to see how ingenious some workers are in overcoming such difficulties. By doing so, the cook eliminates extra work factors and makes it possible to do a lot more work in a given time. The work may also be easier.

Developing Good Work Patterns

People's work patterns are developed largely by habit. Many people work in whatever way comes naturally. Some develop good work habits, while others do not. The good short order cook works efficiently, saving time and energy by making motions that require the least effort and by organizing work correctly. The poor short order cook expends energy needlessly because of wasteful motions and because of unnecessary wandering about. A good short order cook always seems to be working easily and smoothly: the motions made are deft and quick and there is little crisscrossing or backtracking of motions.

Studies have been made to identify the easiest and most efficient way to do work, and certain rules have been compiled that allow work to be completed more efficiently, easily, and quickly. The following subsections summarize the most important information from these studies.

The Work Center

The basic area where a short order cook works is called a *work center*. The ideal work center for the average male is an area of 69 inches by 26 inches of horizontal work space and an area of 69 inches by 58 inches of vertical space; the vertical space begins about 30 inches from the floor. The ideal work-area measurements are about 10 percent less for the average woman. See Figure 1-2.

For best work effort, it is desirable (although seldom possible) to confine a cook to a work center. The average maximum reach is 26 inches for a man and 23½ inches for a woman. In planning work, it is desirable that no reach exceed this. Otherwise, the body will be pulled out of position, requiring greater time and effort to do the work. The average normal reach in the horizontal area is 14 inches for a man and 12½ inches for a woman. This area is where the most frequently used tools, utensils, and supplies should be placed. Less commonly used items can be placed in the maximum reach area. Thus, the average man has a maximum reach from side to side of 69 inches, and a similar combined normal reach of 46 inches, while the average woman has a maximum from side to side of 62 inches and a combined normal reach of 41½ inches.

In the vertical work area, the average maximum reach upward for a man is 88 inches and again 69 inches left to right, whereas for the average woman the figures are 79 and 62 inches, respectively. The lowest reach is 30 inches for the average man and 27 inches for the average woman. To reach down lower than this requires additional time and body motion which translates into extra effort. The same is true for one reaching up over 88 (or 79) inches. More time and effort are required when a worker reaches outside this area.

Cooks should try to arrange their work so that all motions are made within the normal and maximum work areas. Of course, this is the ideal result, and in many instances it is violated because the equipment required to do the job takes more space than can be filled into the optimum dimensions of a work area. Vertical space is often underused, which is unfortunate; with good planning, shelves and other vertically situated units can save a lot of mileage, energy, and time. Figure 1-3 shows a work area that has been set up for a worker to chop vegetables. This arrangement conforms to normal and maximum reach requirements. The flow of work is from left to right, and the cook does not move out of the work area. Note the drop delivery method used to avoid picking up the vegetables after chopping them.

Work Heights Working at a table or other workplace that is the wrong height can be tiring because the body is thrown out of position and put under strain. Often work heights are set at 34 inches for women and 35

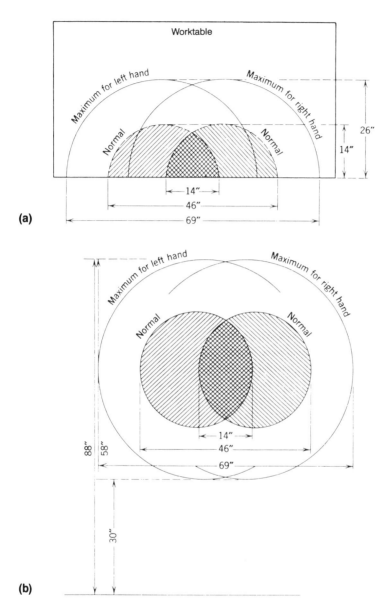

FIGURE 1-2.   Maximum and normal work areas for a man: (a) Horizontal plane. (b) Vertical plane. All dimensions are 10 percent less for women.

FIGURE 1-3. A work center for chopping vegetables that conforms to normal and maximum reach requirements. The flow of work is from left to right. Note that with a sweep of the knife the cook can pan the cut vegetables into the container in the sink, thus eliminating the need to pick up, carry, and deposit them. This is called "drop delivery." (*Photo by Michael Upright*)

inches for men. This may be satisfactory for some, but for a person who is taller or shorter than average it is not. For taller cooks, the work height may be better at 36 inches for women and 38 inches for men; and for shorter ones, optimum heights may be below these standard measurements. A short order cook doing handwork such as making sandwiches should have the work height at 2 to 4 inches below the elbow (see Fig. 1-4). When a cook works with a tool, such as a long-handled ladle for serving soup, the work height should be such that the cook can stand erect at the work surface with hands flat on the surface and arms straight but not stretched (see Fig. 1-5).

Work Flow Another important factor is to see that proper work flow is observed. In Figure 1-6a the flow is from left to right: the cook reaches for cutlets, drops them into flour, gives the pan a shake to coat the cutlets, removes the cutlets, and drops them into the egg wash to moisten them, again removes the cutlets, drops them into a pan of crumbs, and shakes the pan to cover the cutlets with crumbs, thus breading them. Figure 1-6b shows two carts used next to the worker, which helps to bring the breading process into a good work-center arrangement.

FIGURE 1-4. Checking for proper work height when a worker is using a knife or similar tool. The work surface should be 2 to 4 inches below the elbow. (*Photo by Michael Upright*)

FIGURE 1-5. Checking for proper work height when a worker is using a tool such as a whisk or a serving spoon. The cook should be able to stand erect and place the hands flat on the surface. (*Photo by Michael Upright*)

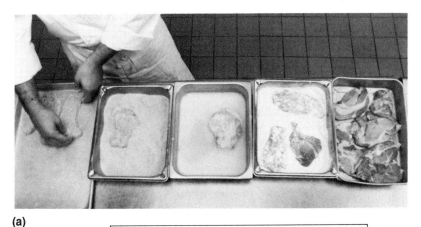

(a)

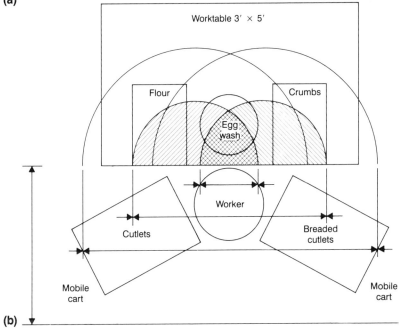

(b)

FIGURE 1-6. Organizing a work center for a multistep task (breading cutlets): (a) A cook breading pork cutlets. The work flow is from left to right, with the worker standing in the middle, reaching for the cutlets, flouring them, dipping them into the egg wash, breading them, and finally placing them in a pan to dry a bit before sautéing. (*Photo by Michael Upright*)
(b) A schematic drawing of the same operation but this time two carts are brought in to hold the unbreaded and the breaded cutlets making it unnecessary for the worker to extend the reach as shown in (a).

For right-handed short order cooks, work is more easily done if the flow is from left to right. Therefore, a desirable arrangement might be for a right-handed short order cook at one meal to have food supplies stored on the griddle's left so that they can be taken by the left hand, put onto the griddle, cooked, and then dished onto plates stored on the right. Using mobile equipment sometimes makes it easier to arrange proper flow.

When related work centers are put together, the result is a *section*, such as a baking section or a pot-and-pan section. Proper flow through the entire section is highly desirable, just as it is through each work center.

Storage Four important rules have been developed to govern the storage of items.

1. *Store at the point of first use*. Thus, instead of storing clean pots and pans on a rack somewhere in the kitchen center, it is better to have them delivered by the pot-and-pan workers to each work center where they will be used; perhaps storage space is available under the griddle or in other places within the work area such as on a shelf in back of the griddle.
2. *Allow for economy of motion*. This means that one should store items according to their frequency of use. Much-used sauté pans, tools, utensils, and other equipment should be stored as close as possible to the place where they are used. A heavy item may have to be stored at a nearby location where it can be lifted out easily.
3. *Try to reduce storage*. Deliveries can sometimes be planned so that no storage is needed. This would mean timing deliveries from purveyors so that, when they arrive, they go directly into use instead of into storage. Deliveries from the storerooms can be timed in the same way. Handling may be minimized by wheeling items in on mobile units where they may be left (without restorage) for use.
4. *Systematize by organizing*. Items should be placed in the same storage location each time, so the worker almost automatically knows where to get them. One can often observe a good worker who knows where things are stored make a movement to get something without even looking, certain that the item is there. The more compact one can make storage areas, the better the system, because this feature limits the distance one needs to reach or travel to get required items.

Get Ready, Do, and Put Away and Clean Up

Every job can be divided into three parts: get ready; do; and put away and clean up. Since the "do" part of the job produces the item the more "do" one gets for each "get ready" and each "put away and clean up," the higher the operation's productivity. For example, sometimes the first thing a short order cook may do after getting to work is to take out a steel and sharpen a knife. The steel and knife are then put away, and during the day the task is repeated several times for other individual knives. Instead, it might be more efficient for the cook to sharpen all the knives at one time so that one "do" gets the whole job done. Another example might involve partially frying a large batch of bacon and then completing parts of this batch to fill individual orders during the breakfast shift, instead of preparing each individual order from scratch.

Making Motions Economically

Motions can be made more quickly and easily if one knows certain general rules about motions. One rule says, "In doing work, it is easier to make circular motions than back-and-forth ones." This is because circular motions are continuous, whereas back-and-forth motions involve starting and stopping and hence extra energy. The same is true of a car: starting and stopping it in city traffic takes more gas (energy) than driving it continuously on the open highway. Starting and stopping also takes more time. Thus, in cleaning a griddle with a pumice stone, it is easier and quicker to make circular motions than to make back-and-forth ones. It is also easier and quicker to make arched motions than to make straight-line ones. Thus, when reaching for something, a cook should use an arched reach rather than a straight thrust.

Rhythm and Pace

Many short order cooks who work with ease and a high degree of efficiency set a rhythm to their work. Again, it's the old story of the tortoise and hare. A steady, plodding pace gets more done than a series of fitful starts and stops. A good rhyme warns, "Life by the yard is apt to be hard; but life by the inch is more of a cinch!" A rhythmic pace not only makes work easier, it seems to reduce the time required to do it.

Fatigue

People get the energy to do work from a blood sugar in their bodies. When their blood sugar level gets low, they get tired, so conserving energy is a good way to reduce tiredness. A short order cook should feel tired only during the last fifth of a shift. (Tiredness is also influenced by other factors such as mental fatigue or strain, humidity, temperature, light, ventilation, and noise.)

People have only so much energy to burn, and trying to work too many hours in a day or week may cause them to run out of it. The length and amount of breaks taken during a day and the times when they are taken can be a factor. Several short breaks taken at equally spaced intervals are better than a single longer one taken when one begins to feel tired. Rest allows people to renew their energy.

After a certain length of time at work, a person begins to run low on blood sugar. Taking a short break enables the body to increase its blood-sugar level. Figure 1-7a shows the production curve of a cook who is working at a normal rate, with two 10-minute breaks plus a lunch hour during the day's work. This graph does not show signs of hard work on the cook's part. Figure 1-7b indicates hard work but not at a fast pace. Note the drop in production as the cook tires. Figure 1-7c shows the production curve of a bored worker. When the worker sees the end of the shift coming, there is a rise in productivity because the worker is glad to see the shift end. Figure 1-7d shows the production curve of a cook who is doing heavy work at a rapid pace. Note how much more sharply the curve drops than in Figure 1-7b.

The Inverted **T**

People's bodies rest on an inverted *T*, with the spine resting on the hips (see Fig. 1-8). The farther a body is held away from this upright position, the more energy the person must use to maintain it. Working at a

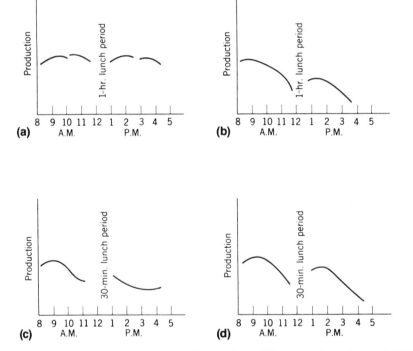

FIGURE 1-7. Production curves indicating how different workers tire on the job.

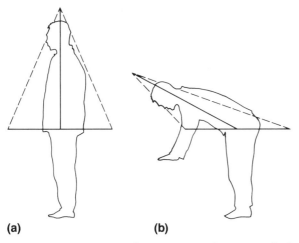

(a)   (b)

FIGURE 1-8. Posture and energy expenditure: (a) The body uses the least energy when the vertical *T* is straight up. (b) More energy is used when it is tipped over at an angle.

worktable that is too low can force the body to bend over more than would normally be necessary and thus can require the worker to use an excessive amount of energy to perform the task. In such a situation, height should be added to the work area in the form of a thick cutting board, some sort of platform to raise the work level, or an adjustment of the length of the legs on the equipment. Planning work so as to keep the body as erect as possible is another way to keep energy output low.

□ Ordering Food

Once a short order cook is lined up for a meal, little else can be done prior to the mealtime rush except busy work such as cleaning or preparing items for the next shift. The order coming from the dining area is what triggers the next action. Once an order is placed, the cook should start processing it at once, unless it must be held up in order to be ready when other orders that take longer to prepare are ready. Allowing orders to pile up can throw a cook behind and cause quality and operational problems.

Orders can be given verbally or in written form. Whichever way is used, the order must come in a complete, readily understood form. This is the job of the ordering person. The transferring medium should transfer the message correctly and in an easily interpretable manner. The short order cook is the receiver and must know how to interpret orders properly. Sometimes there is feedback in the form of the receiver (short order cook) repeating the order so that it is clear the order has been received and properly understood.

If orders are placed verbally, it is a good idea for the receiver to repeat the order to the giver so that both are sure there is no misunderstanding. The great chef Escoffier, who was an excellent organizer and is responsible for the continental kitchen organization in its present staffing pattern, did not like a noisy kitchen, so he did not let waiters call out orders in the kitchen. Instead, they gave their orders in written form to an announcer (*aboyeur*) who stood at the head of the kitchen and in a clear, even voice called out the orders. The voice was penetrating but never raised. The cooks in the various sections heard the orders and knew which ones or which parts of ones they were responsible for. The system worked well and saved much confusion, and it is still widely used in kitchens today.

It is not unusual today for orders to be placed over some sort of speaking device so that the waitstaff does not even have to come into the kitchen to deliver them. A loudspeaker in the kitchen can deliver the message from the dining room. It is also possible to put individual speakers in each section of the kitchen so that orders can be placed at a much lower volume and thus yield a quieter kitchen. In some cases, intercommunication on a speaker system between the order giver and the receiver is possible, but because voices coming over a loudspeaker in the dining area to discuss orders is not desirable, this system is infrequently used.

Orders can be transmitted electronically in a number of ways. One approach is to type orders at a terminal in the dining area; a printout machine in the kitchen at the proper work area prints out the order, notifying the proper cook or cooks of the need. The terminal can also be connected to a cash register that automatically prints out the sales slip, pricing the individual menu items and totaling them. Another device can be carried by a waiter or waitress to a table where guests are seated and ready to order. As each patron orders, the waiter or waitress at the table enters the order into the ordering unit, which activates a printout machine in the kitchen, placing the order.

The most common way of placing an order is by written order carried to the short order section and left there. The order can be stuck on a spindle file, left on the counter, or placed on an order wheel. The order wheel method is the one most commonly used. The waitservice person puts the written order on the wheel next to the last order placed there, which keeps orders in their proper sequence. The cook simply whirls the wheel around to read the next order in line and then begins to process it. At this stage, the order is not physically removed from the wheel.

When the order is ready, the cook places the food on the pickup counter and places the written order with it. The waitservice person then picks up the order slip with the order.*

It is common to time-stamp written orders. Time is also given on orders that are electronically transferred. When such times are put on the order, it is possible to trace the time it took to prepare the order and so to fix responsibility for any delays.

Sometimes signaling devices are used to notify waitstaff that orders are ready. This can be accomplished by means of signal lights that give a number or some other code indicating to the waitservice person holding that number or code that the order is ready. Other notification devices can be used.

Where order checkers are used, orders may have to be cleared through them before being placed. As orders leave the kitchen, the checker also checks to see that the order is correct and of proper quality to serve. In some cases, checkers act as *aboyeurs*.

Often orders are filled so that they can be referred to for information such as the number of orders handled by a waitservice person or a kitchen section, or the number of orders of a specific item served in a given period.

Timing is an important part of a short order cook's job. Processing of individual items must be started at the right time in order for all orders on one waitstaff person's form to come out together. It is undesirable to have an order ready and sitting while other items are being finished. In addition, short order cooks sometimes have to coordinate their processing with other sections that may also be preparing something for the same table. Timing is also essential if orders are to be ready just as guests finish the previous course. This is the responsibility of the waitservice person, who should keep watch on the table, note how fast people are eating, and then give the signal at the proper time for the short order cook to start processing the next part of the order. It takes a knowledgeable waitservice person to do this, since the person must understand how long it takes to prepare steaks, chickens, or other items so that the foods are at their quality peak when picked up.

---

*The Chinese have an interesting way of keeping track of and placing orders. The waitservice person takes the order and writes it out. This is taken to the kitchen entrance, where on a board on the wall are hung numerous clothespins, each numbered. Each clothespin has a special place on the board, and its number is the number of the table it represents. The written order is placed in the clothespin and taken to the kitchen, where it is given to the cooks. When the order is filled, the clothespin and order are picked up by the waitservice person, who returns the clothespin to its proper place and takes the order to the table and serves it.

□ Summary

Short order cooking is not a simple job. It requires knowledge, the ability to use *mise en place*, skill, stamina, stability, experience, versatility, and other attributes.

The short order workplace usually contains a griddle, an open or sealed hot top, and perhaps a broiler, deep-fat fryer, microwave, refrigerator, and waffle iron. It is desirable that equipment placement facilitate work; misplaced equipment makes work harder.

Good work patterns make for easier work and faster production. Confining work to a work center can increase productivity and make work easier. The maximum reach is 26 inches for a man and 23½ inches for a woman; the normal reach is 14 inches for a man and 12½ inches for a woman. The horizontal limits of a work center are 69 inches left to right and 46 inches forward for a man and 62 inches and 41½ inches for a woman. The vertical limits are 88 inches upward and 30 inches above the floor downward for a man and 79 and 27 inches for a woman.

Goals in doing work should include keeping the body as erect as possible and observing good workflow. It is usually easier for a right-handed worker to work from left to right than from right to left. Certain rules should be followed for storage:

1. Store at the point of first use.
2. Allow for economy of motion in storing items.
3. Try to reduce storage.
4. Systematize by organizing.

The more "do" that can be obtained for each "get ready" and each "put away and clean up," the greater the productivity. It is easier to make circular motions than back-and-forth ones, since the starting and stopping of the latter motions require extra time and energy. It is easier to make arched motions than straight ones. Short order cooks should set a rhythm to their work and achieve an even, steady pace; this will enable them to achieve faster and better production and will make the work easier. Fatigue comes when the cook's blood sugar level runs low. A short rest can help the body raise the blood sugar level again. Strain or mental fatigue can cause one to feel tired, as can adverse conditions of temperature, humidity, light, ventilation, or noise.

After lining up, the short order cook waits for orders, which may be given verbally or in writing. Written orders are usually hand-delivered but orders can also be transmitted electronically. Orders should be given clearly, with all the information needed to ensure that the short order cook gets the right message. Sometimes good communication requires feedback, with the cook repeating orders to see if the proper message has been received.

Orders can be left at the short order section on a counter top, on a spindle file, or on an order wheel. When orders are ready, the short order cook puts the order on the pickup counter with the written order. Time stamping of orders is common.

Timing is an important factor in short order work. The cook must know how long it takes to process different orders so as to bring them all up at the same time. Waitstaff can be of great help in indicating to cooks when to start a particular order and when to dish up orders.

☐ CHAPTER REVIEW ☐

1. Just what is short order cooking?
2. What is lining up?
3. What do the words *mise en place* translate into in English? What does the phrase mean?
4. Name the attributes that a person should have in order to do good short order work; then check to see of you named all of them correctly.
5. How is short order cooking practiced in present-day kitchens? Is short order work always done alone, or is the job sometimes combined with other work? In what kind of operation would one expect to do nothing but short order work?
6. Would working in the kitchen of a McDonald's be short order work?
7. What major pieces of equipment are found in a short order section?
8. Is a fry cook or a breakfast cook a short order cook?
9. What is a work center? Give the horizontal and vertical dimensions of a work center for a man and for a woman.
10. If you were preparing breakfast orders, how would you arrange your foods, tools, and dishes so that you would be working in the most efficient manner around a griddle?
11. Your text gives four rules for storing things in the short order section. List them.
12. What do "get ready," "do," and "clean up and put away" mean, and what should one try to do in a job to get the most work for the effort using these concepts?

13. When you scour a griddle with a soapstone brick, how should most of the motions be done—forward and backward or circular?
14. If you were planning to make fifty grilled cheese sandwiches, how would you organize the job of preparing these sandwiches for cooking on the griddle?
15. What does blood sugar do for people? When it runs low, how do people feel?
16. What factors besides physical effort can make a person feel tired?
17. What is meant by the sentence, "Our body frames rest on an inverted *T* and the more we move our bodies out of this *T* position, the more time and energy are required."?
18. How may orders be placed and filled in the short order section?
19. What is an *aboyeur*? What is a checker?
20. Is knowledge of the time it takes items to cook something a short order cook should have? If so, why?
21. To reduce the likelihood of errors in order giving and to make sure that messages are understood, what four factors are needed?

CHAPTER TWO

Equipment, Utensils, and Tools

Knowing how to use and care for equipment, utensils, and tools properly is an important aspect of good short order work. Unless these items are maintained and used correctly, quality products cannot be produced, work cannot be done easily, and good sanitation cannot be achieved. The appearance and upkeep of the equipment are good indications of the ability of the short order cook and of the standards that person has. The way items are used is another good indicator of the cook's ability.

□ Equipment

Most cooks—especially short order cooks—prefer gas equipment to electrical equipment, because gas is more responsive to heat control. With a twist of the fingers one can get high heat, medium heat, or low heat. Electricity is slower to adjust, although some high-speed units produced today have helped to lessen the difference. On the other hand, gas is less clean, and the combustion fumes have to be exhausted. If there is a hood over the gas equipment, however, the fumes are no problem, since they are exhausted up the hood.

Because some heat is lost when gas combustion fumes are exhausted, about 1.6 Btu (British thermal units)* of gas heat must be expended to equal 1 Btu of electrical heat. Nonetheless, there is little difference in the final cost of operation between gas and electricity. Thus, if 100 Btu of electricity cost 12¢, the cost of 160 Btu of gas will most likely be 12¢, too. Gas equipment, because it operates less cleanly, may be a bit more difficult to maintain, but not much so. Both types have about the same durability.

*Btu is the amount of heat needed to raise 1 pound of water 1 Fahrenheit degree.

Different metals are used in different makes and types of equipment, and cooks should understand something about their conductivity, their tendency to react with foods, and their other characteristics. Some metals have good durability because they are very hard and resist wear. In spite of this, they may not be suitable for cooking, either because they react with foods or because they lack good heat conductivity.

Stainless steel, a metal frequently used in food equipment, is an alloy containing steel, chromium, and nickel; it is often called 18-8 because of its 18 percent chromium content and its 8 percent nickel content. It has a good appearance, is easy to clean, and has a high resistance to corrosion and reaction to foods. It is chemically inert, stainproof, nonmagnetic, ductile, strong, and durable.

Unfortunately, stainless steel has poor heat conduction qualities. Heat goes straight through it instead of spreading out, and when the metal is used in cooking equipment, it may develop hot spots where food burns. However, if stainless steel is surrounded by an even heat such as dry air, steam, or hot water, heat penetration is even; consequently, it is used for steam table containers and the like. Stainless steel cooking equipment is marketed, but these items are made of what is called "clad" metal—a triple-layered metal with two outer layers of stainless steel and a copper, iron, or aluminum inner layer. This inner layer picks up the heat and spreads it out so that hot spots do not develop. Sometimes stainless steel sauté pans have an outer covering of copper on the bottom. This outer layer of copper picks up the heat and spreads it out so that it passes evenly through the stainless steel.

Aluminum is a low-cost metal, but it reacts with alkaline or acidic substances and is quite soft. Because of its cost, appearance, and excellent heat conductivity, however, it is used in food equipment, particularly pots and pans but also griddles and gas burners.

Copper is an excellent heat conductor. It also has great beauty but is expensive, is difficult to maintain, and reacts with acidic food. Often copper cooking utensils and other copper units are covered with tin in places where the metal would come into contact with the foods.

Black iron is a good heat conductor and is widely used for baking sheets and roasting pans. It may be treated to be rust resistant. It has the advantage of being black, which enhances its ability to absorb heat. A cake baked in an aluminum pan may take longer to bake and may not bake as well, because its shiny surface reflects heat away from it.

Cast iron is made by pouring molten iron into molds. It is more porous and breaks more easily than rolled iron. At one time it was widely used for cast-iron skillets, Dutch ovens, griddles, and various cooking or baking utensils, but more recently it has met strong competition from aluminum.

Cast iron is a good heat conductor but less so than aluminum. Today its greatest use is in heavy-duty range tops, griddles, and gas burners.

It is important that all equipment used in the short order section satisfy appropriate industry standards. All equipment that must meet sanitary standards should bear the mark of National Sanitation Foundation (NSF) approval. Gas equipment should meet American Gas Association (AGA) standards. Electrical equipment should bear the UL (Underwriters' Laboratories) stamp, which means that it meets electrical standards for wiring and so on. Other equipment should meet established standards of the appropriate associations (see Fig. 2-1).

Because the work done in a short order section varies considerably from operation to operation, it is difficult to precisely say what large pieces of equipment will be there. However, some or all of the following pieces will be seen in short order units: griddle, hot plate, deep-fat fryer, broiler, refrigerator, and microwave. Besides these, a hood is needed to remove fumes and heat; and work surfaces and perhaps a sink should be present.

In the material that follows, the types of equipment discussed are those typical of the ordinary short order section. Some very sophisticated equipment is now on the market but will not be covered in detail here. For example, many cooking units are now run by computer. All the operator does is punch in the desired information (cooking temperature, cooking time, and so on) and then the computer takes over and ensures that the instructions are followed. For the present, however, short order cooks are likely to encounter more traditional equipment on the job.

Griddle

Few if any short order sections are without a griddle or grill. This is a 1-inch-thick, heated, highly polished, special warp-proof steel surface on which hotcakes, eggs, meats, and other items can be cooked. It is usually the workhorse piece of equipment in the short order section. Griddles can be obtained as small as 24 inches wide but 36-inch or larger units are more commonly seen. The distance front to back is usually 24 inches, but some griddles measure 26½ inches front to back. Tabletop (counter) or floor models are available. Counter models have about 17½-inch-high

FIGURE 2-1. Two association standard stamps. The appearance of such a stamp on equipment signifies that the equipment meets the standards of that association.

adjustable chrome legs, while floor models have legs that are adjustable to heights of 34½ to 36 inches. Shelves may be specified under floor models. Tubular (usually aluminum or cast iron) gas burners under the cooking surface may be rated at 20,000 to 40,000 Btuh (Btu per hour) and are distributed one per each 12 inches of width on the frying surface. Each burner has automatic ignition and each should be equipped with its own AGA-approved thermostat or controller so that variable temperatures may be obtained over the griddle. Signal lights should indicate when burners are on. Stainless steel splashbacks about 4 to 5 inches high should be situated on the sides and back to reduce splattering. Griddles should be NSF-approved. A grease trough for catching grease and a grease drawer into which grease can drain and particles can be scraped from the griddle should be located on the front. The juncture where splashbacks are joined to the griddle in the back and sides should be coved to permit easy cleaning, but few manufacturers offer this feature. Figures 2-2, 2-3, and 2-4 show different griddles.

Electrical griddles can do as good a job in short order work as gas units. Temperature control is perhaps a bit better and Btuh requirements are lower because electrical heat is more efficient than gas heat. In electrical griddles, the elements are buried in the cooking surface. Splashguards, grease troughs, grease drawers, and other features of gas units are similarly needed for electrical ones. Care of the surface and use of the griddle are also the same as for gas units.

Before a griddle is used, it should be seasoned—that is, prepared so that foods do not stick on it when cooking. Seasoning a griddle involves the following steps:

FIGURE 2-2. A griddle used in the short order section. (*Courtesy Franklin Products Corporation*)

1. Preheat the entire griddle to 375° to 400°F (190° to 205°C).
2. When the signal light goes out, indicating that the proper surface temperature has been reached, apply a light film of oil or fat over the entire surface.
3. Allow this film to set for about 2 minutes or until it begins to smoke.
4. Wipe the surface free of grease with a clean, dry cloth.
5. Repeat steps 2, 3, and 4.

FIGURE 2-3. Another griddle suitable for short order use. (*Courtesy Anetsberger Brothers, Inc.*)

FIGURE 2-4. A griddle suitable for heavy-duty use in the short order section. (*Courtesy Wolf Range Company*)

The griddle should now be ready for use. Usually a griddle does not have to be reseasoned unless it is cleaned with water, which removes the thin grease film on the surface that prevents foods from sticking. In such a situation, the grease layer must be restored by new seasoning.

A more thorough job of seasoning can be done by spreading a liberal supply of table salt over the griddle along with the thin film of oil in step 2. Then the surface is scoured with a thick cloth pad (to prevent heat from reaching the hand). This gives a deeper penetration of the oil film into the metal and a better, nonstick working surface. The salt and oil film are removed as in step 4.

Water should never be put onto the griddle surface unless it is needed to soften burned-on grease or food particles so that they can be more easily scraped off. For this task, the griddle should be set at 120° to 130°F (49° to 54°C). Otherwise, the griddle should be kept clean with a scraper or spatula and wiped clean with a clean, dry cloth. NEVER use steel wool, since it can leave steel wool particles on the griddle that find their way into patrons' food. A waxy, solid material often collects on the griddle, usually around the sides and in corners. This is polymerized fat or fat particles that have broken down and then joined together to make a solid, waxy material. Scrape this substance from the griddle with a scraper or spatula before scouring, and put it into the grease drawer. Because foods can get an undesirable flavor from it, polymerized fat should not be allowed to build up on the griddle.

Each day at the end of the shift (or more often if necessary), the griddle should be given a good cleaning and scouring. This is done by having the griddle *just warm*. First, burned-on grease and food particles are removed. Then the surface is rubbed with a pumice stone, commercial grill stone, emery cloth, or other polisher, in the direction of the grain of the metal until the surface shines. Often in such cleaning, a bit of oil is left on the griddle, so in polishing this is ground into the surface, giving good seasoning. After this is done, the surface is wiped with a clean, dry cloth. If water or any cleaning liquid is used, the griddle may have to be reseasoned afterward. Figure 2-5 shows a griddle being polished.

During use of the griddle during the day, the cook should continually use a scraper or spatula to clear collected oil and food particles from it. This waste is moved to the grease trough and pushed down into the grease drawer. The trough can be wiped clean with a dry cloth. During the shift, the grease drawer may have to be removed and emptied. It should be thoroughly washed after it is emptied.

It is also desirable from time to time to wipe down the splashguards and the body of the griddle with a cloth moistened in clean detergent water. On some units, the grease trough and splashguards are removable, so they can be taken to the sink and cleaned.

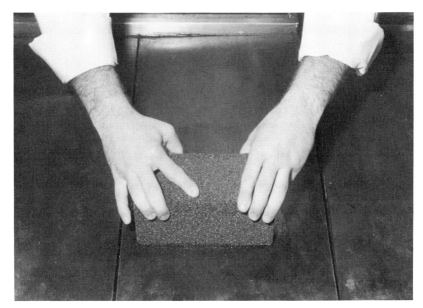

FIGURE 2-5. Polishing a griddle. (*Photo by Michael Upright*)

Between orders during the day, cooks may wipe the heating surface of the griddle with an oil-saturated cloth, thereby giving it a light coating of oil. Only enough should be added to make the griddle shine; too much oil is indicated by pools of collected oil. An oil mop may be used to add this oil. It can be kept in a can of oil nearby for handy access.

To operate a griddle, begin by turning the burner or burners on to preheat the surface. Set the dials at their proper temperature setting. When the signal light goes out, that portion of the griddle has reached its proper temperature. Different foods require different cooking temperatures. Eggs should be cooked at 300°F (149°C); bacon and similar meats at 350°F (177°C); hotcakes at 375°F (190°C); hamburgers, steaks, and the like at 350°F (177°C); and some other items as high as 400°F (205°C). On a four-burner griddle, the first (leftmost) dial would be set at 300°F (149°C), the second one at 325°F (163°C), the third at 350°F (177°C), and the fourth (rightmost) one at 400°F (205°C). On a three-burner system, using the area of the griddle midway between the 300°F (149°C) and the 350°F (177°C) settings yields about a 325°F (163°C) surface temperature, while using the area between the middle section and far right at 400°F (205°C) yields about a 375°F (190°C) temperature; thus it is possible to get the full range of temperatures needed while using only three settings. Some griddles have a front-and-back arrangement for temperature control instead of a left-to-right arrangement. In this case only two temperatures are possible, and the settings chosen may be 325°F (163°C) and 375°F (190°C).

Once the short order cook becomes familiar with the griddle and knows its personality, capabilities, and limits, work is facilitated. The griddle becomes an old and reliable friend that helps make the work of the day manageable. Because it is something of significant value, it should be maintained in the best possible condition. If this is done, the cook's job will be easier, and the food produced will be of the highest quality possible.

Hot Plate

The hot plate may be an open burner or it may be a closed, smooth-surfaced plate with burners underneath. In the simplest setup, two burners (front and back) are located in a 12-inch-wide space, often on the right side of the griddle. These burners may be used to process single, fast orders and items that require (or are better produced) in a sauté pan. Where there is no deep-fat fryer, the pan containing fat may be heated over these burners. Hot plate burners can also be used for things that have to be simmered and cooked for a long time.

Open units should have rugged, cast-iron grates with spillover bowls for long life and easy maintenance (see Fig. 2-6). The burners should be nonclogging, and their flame ports should be protected from spillovers. Burners from 20,000 to 80,000 Btuh are used. Burners should have automatic lighting and simmer-set valves, on both open and closed units. Closed units should have a rugged, cast-iron top with multiple heat-retaining fins on the bottom to increase heat absorption, and they should have a cast-iron or aluminum tubular burner that can give from 40,000 to 80,000 Btuh. Often closed units contain a signal light that indicates when the burner is on.

Short order cooks should know how to adjust the flame on gas burners. Natural gas—largely methane (CH_4)—and propane (C_3H_8) are commonly used. Both methane and propane need to receive oxygen from the air in order to burn and create heat. It is important that the proper amount of air be introduced to get full benefit of the gas and also to get proper heat. All burners come with air-mixing devices that pull in the air and mix it with the gas before this gets out of the burner. Cooks should learn how to use the particular kind of burner that comes with their units. A flame is correct when the center is blue and the tip is white (see Fig. 2-7). A yellowish tip indicates incomplete burning and perhaps some sooting.

FIGURE 2-6. An example of open gas burners. (*Photo by Michael Upright*)

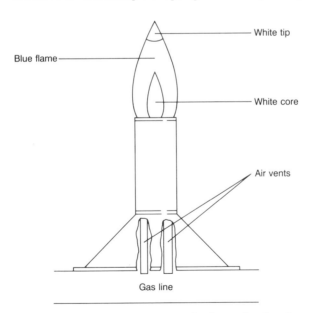

FIGURE 2-7. Proper appearance of a flame that is using all the gas flowing out of the burner and developing maximum heat from it.

Figure 2-8 shows how an open-flame hot plate can be converted into either a griddle or a broiler. Such flexibility may be desirable in very small units where griddle or broiler cooking is only needed part of the time and where open-top cooking is needed at other times.

It is desirable that open grates on hot plates be removable so that they can be taken to the sink and scrubbed. The drip tray underneath should be removable as well, so crumbs and liquid spills can be removed at the sink. If burners are not clog-proof and are not protected by flanges from spillage, cooks must be vigilant to avoid plugging burner holes.

Electrical hot tops may be open or solid. Open units may be somewhat fragile, considering the wear and tear they must withstand, but some today are very ruggedly made and will take almost any kind of punishment. Round or rectangular solid plates have the elements buried in them and so are very durable. Open units should have a drip pan underneath that is removable for thorough cleaning. It is desirable, of course, for electrical units to be equipped with high-speed elements that allow the cook the ability to adjust heat as needed. Solid hot plates tend to hold their heat once they have been brought up to temperature, and as a result they are not as flexible in heat control as open electrical units.

Deep-Fat Fryer

Even though many people wish to reduce their fat intake, deep-fried foods are still a very popular menu item. The number one selling seafood is deep-fried shrimp, and the number one selling side dish is French fried potatoes. Proper deep-frying need not give foods an excessively high quantity of fat. Improper frying, however, can yield greasy and unappetizing foods. The key is knowing how to use the deep-fat fryer.

There are various kinds of deep-fryers. Small counter models are available that are only 12 to 14 inches wide and hold two small baskets. Much larger ones are also on the market (see Fig. 2-9). Most take 220 volts of electricity or a high gas Btu input. Small ones can be picked up and moved, while the big ones have parts that can be removed and taken to the sink for cleaning. Quick temperature control is not as vital here as it is with griddles and hot tops, and for this reason electrical units are popular. They are also cleaner. Some deep-fryers are equipped with lids so that foods build up steam pressure as they fry, which helps cook and tenderize them. It is important that the deep-fryer be easy to clean and that the fat be filtered regularly to remove crumbs, food particles, and other foreign items. Keeping the fat at the proper level is one of the secrets of good deep-frying.

The short order cook should understand what oil or fat is and how to use it properly. At certain temperatures, both fat and oil are liquids; and at that point they are much the same thing. Chemically there is little

(a)

(b)

FIGURE 2-8. Units that can be placed over a hot plate equipped with open burners: (a) A griddle surface unit. (b) A broiler surface unit. (*Courtesy Add-A-Broiler/Griddle manufactured by CCI Industries, Rancho Cucamonga, California*)

(a) **(b)**

FIGURE 2-9. Deep-fat fryers: (a) A gas-fired fryer. (*Courtesy Hobart Corporation*). (b) An electric fryer. (*Courtesy Lang, Inc.*)

difference, and both will fry foods. They are not like water in that, when they reach a certain temperature, they will not boil off. Instead, they break down chemically, which they signal by starting to smoke. The content of this smoke is a substance called *acrolein*, which irritates the nasal passages and throat and may cause the eyes to smart. The breakdown products left in the fryer give foods fried in it an off flavor. Moreover the fat will no longer fry foods to a crisp texture nor give them the proper deep-fried, lightly browned color. Different fats break down at different temperatures. Butter and some other fats breaks down at fairly low temperatures—even at 375°F (190°C). However, frying fats and oils produced especially for the purpose of deep-frying will remain intact at a temperature of 425°F (219°C) or more.

Fats and oils burst into flame when they reach about 600°F (316°C). A fat or oil fire can be extremely dangerous, so short order cooks should watch carefully the temperatures at which they fry foods and keep their fryers set. With the high-speed electrical and gas units now on the market, there is no longer a need to let the deep-fat fryer stand at a high cooking temperature simply because the equipment takes so long to heat up. The temperature can now be dropped between uses and then turned up as needed.

Certain foods can also cause fats to break down. When fats are overheated, one of the products formed is a free fatty acid—a product that is related to fats and oils but that causes the fat or oil to act differently in frying. If bacon, ham, or even some fresh meats are fried in deep fat, some of their free fatty acids enter the frying medium and weaken its frying ability. A fresh fat or oil fries with a crackling sound and the bubbles are white (see Fig. 2-10). As a fat or oil breaks down, however, it becomes less clear and begins to take on a yellowish cast. The sizzle or crackle is also less evident, and instead the fat merely murmurs. When fat or oil really cannot perform its function any longer, the foam has become yellow. There is no crackle, and the foam begins to crawl out of the deep-fat fryer during frying. Foods fried in such fat taste awful.

Metals such as copper or zinc can also cause frying fat to break down. Even iron and aluminum can do so, but not as effectively as copper and zinc. Other things (including common table salt) can cause the breakdown of fat in frying, too. Therefore, foods should not be salted over the fryer or before frying. Since curing salts can cause fat to break down, cured meats should never be fried in the fryer. Generally, foods should be fairly dry when added to the fat. This prevents splattering and reduces breakdown. Putting very wet potatoes into frying fat encourages fat breakdown. Drying them a bit before frying helps maintain the frying quality of the fat. It is important in cleaning a fryer not to use steel wool or other abrasives to scour, because they can wear away the chrome plate covering copper elements—for example, on the thermostat—and expose copper or other metal that will cause fat breakdown.

FIGURE 2-10. Potatoes in a properly filled basket, frying in good-quality fat. Notice the sharp white bubbles. *(Courtesy Procter & Gamble)*

Turnover is an important element in maintaining high fat quality. Frying fat or oil is absorbed in the food as it fries. In fact, McDonald's has found that French fries that hold about 17 percent fat are most palatable to patrons. If a large quantity of food is fried in the deep-fat fryer, the use of fat is greater; if less food is fried, the use is less. If from 15 to 20 percent of the fat or oil in the fryer is used up each day and if this loss is continually replaced with fresh oil or fat, no frying fat or oil will ever have to be discarded. Only filtering is needed. Experience shows that 10 pounds of potatoes absorb 1 pound of fat in deep-frying. Similarly, 10 pounds of batter-covered or breaded foods absorb 1 pound 2 ounces of fat. Therefore, in a small fryer holding 15 pounds of fat or oil, frying about 30 pounds of foods would achieve the desired turnover of 20 percent.

The proper ratio of food to fat should not be exceeded. Adding too much food at one time for the volume of fat drops the temperature too low, and a greasy, unappealing product results. Normally, food totaling about 1½ to 2 times the weight of the fat can be fried each hour. The ratio of food to fat cooked in a fryer should be about 1:5 to 1:8 in a fryer; in a kettle over a burner, the ratio should be about 1:10. Whatever the equipment, frying temperatures must be correct.

If frying oil is used, simply fill the cold fryer with oil up to the full level. If solid fat is used, pack the fat around the elements and then turn the fryer on to very low heat. This process is time-consuming, and it is often quicker to melt the fat in a separate container and then pour it in as a liquid. This method also ensures that the elements or wiring will not overheat while the fat is melting.

Once the oil or fat is in the fryer, turn the temperature dial on. On electrical and automatic gas ignition models, this starts the heating. A signal light will go off when the proper temperature is reached. On some gas models, however, it may be necessary to light a pilot light and then turn on the gas to start heating. If a gas burner does not light immediately, turn it off at once and wait a few minutes for the gas to clear out; then try again.

In operations where a lot of frying occurs each day, it may be necessary to filter or strain the fat several times to remove foreign particles. Ordinarily, filtering is done only once a day, at the end of the shift.

Some electrical kettles have elements that lift up so that the frying kettle can be removed. The fry kettle usually has handles on either side for lifting. Using gloves, the cook grasps handles and carries the kettle to a place where it can be tipped up and the fat poured into a strainer lined with several layers of cheesecloth. The liquid fat then drains down into a large container beneath the strainer.

Other kettles (usually gas-fired ones) have a drain plug on the bottom of the fry kettle to which a filter bag can be attached. Then a container for holding the cleaned fat is placed under the filter bag, the valve to the drain plug is opened and the fat is allowed to filter down.

Siphoning is another filtering technique. To do this, attach the siphon to the fryer frame with either a hook or a clamp, making sure that the siphon hose in the fryer is touching or nearly touching the fryer bottom. Then attach the primer cup, and fill it with cooled liquid fat. Open the cup's valve, and let about half the fat drain down the hose; then quickly reverse the valve so that the top part of the hose is open and the draining fat creates a vacuum, drawing fat up from the kettle and down through a strainer or filtering bag hanging over a container. During siphoning, keep the primer cup filled so that air cannot enter the hose and stop the siphoning. If air does get in, the siphoning will stop and priming must be repeated.

TWO PRECAUTIONS ARE ESSENTIAL BEFORE ANY ATTEMPT IS MADE TO FILTER OR STRAIN THE FAT:

1. Be sure the fat has cooled down before removing the fry kettle, turning the drain plug, or trying to siphon. Oil burns can be extremely painful and dangerous.
2. Be sure the fryer is turned off before attempting to lift up the elements, to drain, or to siphon.

After removing the fat from a fryer kettle, remove the residual crumbs and charred material along with the oil left at the bottom of the kettle. Wipe the fryer out with a clean, dry cloth, add some warm water containing a good detergent, and thoroughly clean the inside of the kettle. If a thin ring of waxy material is evident around the top of the kettle, scrape this off carefully and discard it. This is polymerized fat, the result of some fat breakdown. Scrub the fryer baskets and the fry kettle (if removable) in good detergent water.

Once a week the fryer should be given a more thorough cleaning. Otherwise, heating elements may become coated with food particles and not heat as well as they should. In addition, charred food stuck on them may impart off-flavors to the food being fried.

The first step in the more thorough cleaning is to strain out the fat and remove all waste and oil. Next, using a stiff brush and water containing a strong detergent, scrub the elements thoroughly; then rinse the elements thoroughly, and dry them with a clean cloth. Lift some of the fryer elements out of the fryer, turn the heat to 400°F (205°C) and burn the residue off. After they cool, brush the remaining elements with a stiff brush and wipe them with a clean, damp cloth. This should only be done with elements that are designed to be handled in this way. Check the manufacturer's manual to find out if this approach can be used. Stationary heating elements must be cleaned in place with a stiff brush and strong detergent, then rinsed thoroughly and wiped dry.

Some operations like to add a special cleaner or a strong detergent to water and fill the fryer with it; then the liquid is brought to a boil for 20 to 30 minutes. This wash water is drained or poured off, and fresh water is added to rinse the fryer. This water may then be brought to a boil. After it is removed, fresh rinse water containing a bit of vinegar is added and then drained or poured out. Finally, the inside is dried with a clean cloth, and the fryer is ready to be refilled with fat or oil.

Fryers can be dangerous pieces of equipment. Hot fat can cause severe burns and can catch fire. Cooks should wear long sleeves and, when handling anything hot, should use heavy gloves. The best policy, in fact, is to let the oil and fryer cool down before handling them. Most fryer oils or fats smoke at temperatures above 425°F (219°C) and burst into flame at around 600°F (316°C). Fat fires are extremely dangerous and difficult to put out. Once one has started, the whole facility can burn down, especially if the fire spreads into grease-soaked ventilating flues. During periods of nonuse, the fryer should be kept at below 300°F (149°C). The cook should be sure to wipe up any spilled fat and should be especially careful when lifting food out of fryer baskets. Food to be fried should be slid into the hot fat or lowered slowly in the basket. Some fryers are equipped with timers that automatically lift the baskets out of the fat when a certain frying time has been completed. Remember that water and hot frying fat do not mix; a fourth to a half cup of water dropped into hot fat can cause an explosion in which the water expands suddenly into steam and throws hot fat out of the fryer. Sometimes foods can also explode, throwing out fat. Fat on the floor poses a hazard for slipping and falling and should be wiped up immediately. If this is impossible, some salt should be thrown onto it to give traction, and it should be wiped up as soon as possible.

Broilers and Salamanders

Where the volume of broiled food produced is large—and with patrons concerned about foods fried in fat, broiling is increasing in popularity—a broiler is used; otherwise a salamander (a sort of overhead broiler) is used (see Fig. 2-11). Both cook by radiant heat, whereas griddles, hot tops, and fryers cook by conducted heat. Radiant heat is heat transferred by electromagnetic waves, just as light is. It is produced when a heating element glows with a white heat, which occurs at from 1,500° to 2,000°F (816° to 1,093°C). Some broilers have ceramic or metal alloy units that reach this temperature quickly, thus giving off considerable quantities of

FIGURE 2-11. A salamander is an overhead broiler that cooks by radiant heat. Note how a water spray is put in front at the top so, should a fire occur, the spray can put it out. (*Photo by Michael Upright*)

radiant heat entry. Other broilers utilize infrared electromagnetic waves that increase overall cooking time but nevertheless are quite effective. Infrared temperatures range from 1,000° to 1,500°F (538° to 816°C). Gas or electric broilers are usually used; charcoal broilers are seldom seen in the short order section.

A salamander (often called a back-shelf broiler) is a small overhead broiler usually situated on an elevated shelf over a range or fry top. In the cooking section salamanders are used to brown au gratin dishes or to do other light broiling work.

Broiling equipment should be easy to clean. Grease can build up and be burned onto grids, guides, and surfaces. These parts should be removable so that they can be taken to the sink and scrubbed in a solution of strong detergent and hot water. Parts that are not removable should be accessible for cleaning. Moving mechanisms should be protected from spillage and from accumulation of food particles. Drip trays should be removable for cleaning.

Units should come to a broiling temperature in 3 to 5 minutes; some of the new high-speed type come to a broiling heat in 1½ minutes. Conventional broilers direct the heat over a grid on which food is placed. The food is broiled on the upper side and then turned and broiled on the other side. Some broilers have the heat source located underneath the food; some others apply heat from both sides, with the food hung between the two heat sources. It is desirable to arrange for the fat and drippings from broiled items to drip down onto a tray that carries this material down into a collecting drawer. Both the tray and the drawer should be removable for cleaning. A new type of broiler broils from underneath on a 1-inch wavy grid; it is equipped with a quartz broiler hood that can be lowered over food items to broil them from the top. Another new broiler is small and has a moving grid. The food is placed on the grid, which slowly moves through the broiler where it is exposed to extremely hot jet-air cooking from underneath; cooking also occurs from the top. In some of these broilers, broiling time is reduced because of the higher and more efficient heat input.

Large broilers, which may be single or stacked, are available with 475 to 850 square inches of grid. Salamanders have grid surfaces of 230 to 530 square inches. Counter broilers have grids of 20 × 20 inches to 30 × 30 inches (400 to 900 square inches). The latter size grid would hold about 45 4-ounce (3½ inches diameter) hamburgers.

The grids should be made of good-quality, nonwarp cast iron. Since the heat generated can be intense, all of the equipment subject to such heat should be made from nonwarp materials. Some broilers have a heating cabinet located above the broiler. This is used to finish the cooking process begun in the broiler. For example, a thick steak ordered well done would dry out too much if completely cooked by radiant heat, so it is partially cooked in the broiler and then put onto a pan and finished in the oven.

Microwave

A microwave oven does not cook by conventional types of heat (see Fig. 2-12). Instead, an energy generator sends high voltage through a magnetron (an electronic vacuum tube that emits high-intensity energy waves). These waves are directed by a waveguide and stirred by a rotating paddle that disperses them evenly throughout the oven cavity. The waves are then absorbed by food or water contained in the oven, stimulating a fast motion of electrons within the item. This friction, known as *kinetic energy*, creates heat. Microwaves can penetrate to depths of from 1½ to 3 inches. They pass through china, paper, glass, and plastics without heating these up. However, never put a metal object or container in the microwave, because metal can reflect the waves and burn out the magnetron tube. Even china decorated with gold or silver leaf cannot be used. It is a good idea to use cookware especially made for microwave use.

Even though the microwave door has small holes in it so that the cook can see through, almost no energy can get out. The federal

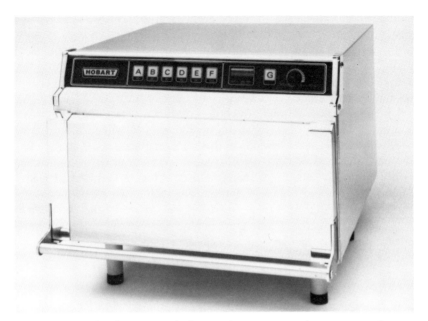

FIGURE 2-12. A microwave unit that can input a tremendous amount of energy into a small amount of food in a short time. As more and more food is placed into the unit, the time of cooking is extended. (*Courtesy Hobart Corporation*)

government has established a regulation that fixes the maximum allowable emission rate at one microwave per square centimeter, measured 2 inches from the microwave oven. It is important that microwave ovens be kept very clean. Any food buildup that might prevent the door from closing completely could lead to the release of dangerous energy into the working area. It is also advisable for the operator not to peer into the window too closely while the machine is on. The operator should stand about 2½ feet away. The federal government also requires that there be two safety interlocks or switches on the microwave, each of which independently prevents open-door operation. One of the interlocks is hidden so that it cannot be deactivated intentionally. Some units have an infrared lamp inside them for browning food, since microwave energy does not brown food.

At one time it was rare to find a microwave in a short order section, but today, with so many processed foods available that need only be rewarmed to be ready for service, it can be a very useful piece of equipment. Thus, an order of eggs Benedict can be readied in only the time it takes to fry the ham and poach the eggs; the amount of canned or frozen hollandaise sauce needed can be measured out and zapped in a microwave in just a few minutes. Similarly, there is little need to have any soup prepared, since today frozen soups packaged in portion units can be brought to serving temperature in a microwave in minutes. A portion of frozen macaroni and cheese can be zapped in a few minutes, as well. Microwaves are also excellent for thawing some items. Frozen vegetables (and some other kinds, too) cook beautifully in them.

Some microwave units are equipped with a device that allows the heating of the food to occur at full, medium, or low heat. Intermittent or pulsing heat is also available; in this system, the energy is on for a few seconds and then off and then on again and off again in a constant series. Pulsing is good for thawing items and for cooking some thick or deep-dish items (such as a casserole) that may take longer to heat up. Some experimental microwave units release steam in the chamber to help cook the food. Microwaves are not suitable for all kinds of cooking, but for the short order section they can be extremely useful. Production should be built around them.

Refrigerators

It is desirable to have some refrigeration in the short order section for holding perishable foods. Without a refrigerator, it is difficult to keep close at hand all of the items needed. Few sections need freezers, but sometimes these are seen because of the substantial use of frozen foods today.

The most commonly used refrigerator is a small under-counter reach-in model that provides from 20 to 30 cubic feet of storage space. On some models, slide windows or slide doors are used instead of swinging doors.

It is important in short order work to set aside spaces in the refrigerator for specific foods. If this is done, much hunt and search time—time that a cook does not have—is avoided. The cook knows exactly where to look and in a few seconds can reach in and grasp any item desired. Storage may change as the menu changes.

Refrigerators should be the heavy-duty type with good refrigerating units, heavy hardware, and a durable finish. They should be easy to clean and should be kept scrupulously clean by being washed down inside and out with good, warm, detergent-treated water. Accumulated food should be removed in two steps: first, softening with water; and then either brushing it away or removing it carefully with a blunt object such as a spatula. It is wise to check refrigerator temperatures regularly. Cooks should also try to avoid opening and closing the refrigerator too frequently, but this is difficult to accomplish in the short order section because it is difficult to anticipate orders and to remove enough of all of the items needed at one time.

Warmers

Food warmers are needed to hold prepared food items hot for service. Usually a warmer is also needed to warm plates and dishes. This is often handled by running steam pipes or electrical units through dish cabinets. Heat used for food warmers may come from steam, gas, or electricity. They may be dry bed (no water) or they may contain heated water. Steam units are usually surrounded by water. All types have proved to be satisfactory. It is important that warmers have good temperature control; food warmers can overcook foods if the holding temperature is too high.

Food warmers may be as small as 12 inches wide by 26 inches deep. Usually these contain small round pots that hold about a quart of food such as gravy or sauce. Items such as stews and roasts are not usually held in the short order section, since these foods ordinarily come from the cooking section. However, in operations where the short order section does combined work, a larger steam table may hold such foods for service from there.

Dry warmers have the advantage of not giving off steam, which can be a bothersome form of heat. On the other hand, they can be more difficult to clean inside, since food spilled or dropped into them tends to dry out and encrust on the surface. Water units should be flushed out daily. Food warmer tops are typically made of stainless steel; they should be cleaned frequently with a solution of detergent and warm water and then dried with a soft cloth. Food containers, too, are usually made of stainless steel, which is durable, cleans easily, and does not react with foods.

Hoods

Hoods perform the important function of drawing heat, grease, moisture, steam, and odors out of the kitchen or work area (see Fig. 2-13). Some today contain pollution-removing equipment so that undesirable fumes are not exhausted into the atmosphere. Fire control devices can be installed, as can heat retention units that catch the heat and redirect it for use (as in heating water). The closer the hood is to the products it is to pick up, the better; but enough clearance must be provided beneath the hood to enable the cook to work under it.

It is important that hoods be properly maintained. The outside should be wiped down frequently with warm water containing a good grease-dissolving detergent. Inside, the treatment may have to be more elaborate. First, hoods usually contain filters that collect grease and dirt. These should be removed and washed thoroughly to remove all dirt and grease. Sometimes they are sent through the dishwasher for this purpose. Collected grease on the inside should be wiped away, and any drip

FIGURE 2-13. A hood is placed over cooking equipment to catch and carry away hot air, fumes, and steam. Note filters in upper top, under the hood; these are to catch dirt and grease. They can be removed to be washed. (*Photo by Michael Upright*)

catchers or gutters should be cleaned out. After such cleaning, the inside should be washed down with warm water containing a good grease-dissolving detergent.

Unclean canopies can be a significant fire hazard. Grease collected on them, in the filters, and in the passageway to the outside can catch fire and burn with surprising ferocity. Such fires have often resulted in the burning down of entire establishments. Thus, any fire around equipment should be watched. Sprayed or splattered grease can catch fire and rise up into the hood, and in a minute the entire hood can be aflame. The best way to put such a fire out is to smother it. Water is less effective than some kinds of foam that do not let air get to the grease. Some hoods have such foamers installed in them; when the temperature rises above a certain level, the foamers automatically go on. Other hoods have automatic closers that shut to stop the draft up the passageway. The short order section should have a good fire extinguisher of the proper type close at hand, and workers should know how to use it.

Sinks

Often the sink used in a short order section is a single-tank, counter type, placed in a worktable space. Such a sink is usually stainless steel and should have coved corners. A sink 24 × 28 × 14 inches deep is large enough to hold most pots and pans used in the section. Although very little ware washing may take place there, water is sometimes needed and thus a sink serves a need. There is little problem in maintaining a sink.

Worktables

Work surfaces should be carefully planned in relation to work center needs, including height, needed space, and needed storage. Since they are usually made of stainless steel; they clean fairly easily. Storage spaces and drawers must be cleaned frequently. Wood cutting boards or tabletops should meet NSF standards—such as being made of suitable hardwood with strips not over 1¾ inches wide, strongly bonded together. They should be smoothly machined or sanded, straight-grained, and free of knots, decay, warp, larvae channels, open checks, or splits. The unit should be easy to scrub and sanitize. It is more desirable to have separate cutting boards than to have them set into the table; and plastic cutting boards are preferable to wood ones. It is important that tables not be overloaded so that they begin to sag.

Minor Equipment

A lot of minor equipment is needed in the short order section. Some pieces may not be stored in the short order section, but the short order cooks may use them from time to time, and they should know how to operate, maintain, and clean them.

Toasters Toast may be made by waitstaff personnel instead of in the short order section. If so, the cook must ask the waitress or waiter to supply the toast that is to go with an order such as a BLT sandwich. Where the toast is an accompaniment to an order such as bacon and eggs, the waitstaff person will automatically prepare the toast and place it with the order before serving. Normally, a pop-up or slot type toaster is used in the section; if quite a bit of toast is made, the toasters can be grouped in a battery of two or more. Four-slot types are common. Toast can also be made on a griddle, in a broiler, or in a hot oven. A heavy-duty broiler can toast 1,200 slices of bread or half buns per hour.

Waffle Irons Waffle bakers usually are produced in single units. They may be placed in a battery, if demand is heavy. Waffle irons need conditioning before use, but once conditioned they need little subsequent seasoning, since the fat in the batter (usually in a ratio of 4 ounces of shortening, butter, or other fat or oil per pound of flour) should continue to furnish enough grease to keep them oiled. If the waffle baker is kept at a proper baking temperature, the waffles will not stick. However, if it is too cold or too hot when the batter is added, they may stick. Cleaning should be done with a stiff fiber or wire brush. Then the iron should be reseasoned. If too much batter is placed in the iron at one time, it will overflow out of the iron. The resulting mess can easily be cleaned up by wiping the outside of the waffle iron with a clean rag dipped in warm water containing a detergent.

Egg Cookers In some operations, egg cookers are used. The eggs are submerged in boiling water for cooking, and a timer-controlled release allows them to rise out of the water at the end of the cooking period. Often these devices are operated by waitstaff personnel.

Mixers Normally a short order section does not have a mixer, but occasionally some food may need treatment in one. Sometimes the system calls for preliminary preparation of the product in another section by a worker other than a short order cook, after which the food item is delivered to the short order section. At other times the short order people must go outside the section to use the mixer. Most preparations require a small mixer. Capacities of table or bench models run from 5 to 20 quarts, and these may be mounted on a mobile cart, so that they could be moved to the short order section. For small-volume mixing, such as a pint, a blender or food processor may suffice.

Mixers have a motor that simultaneously turns and rotates a whip in a mixing bowl underneath. Workers should watch to make sure that lubricants and other foreign substances do not fall into the food being mixed. Low, medium, or high mixing speeds are possible, which gives the machine the flexibility to mix or whip. It is important in using a mixer not to let some utensil or tool fall into the bowl while the mixer is in operation, since this might cause a bad accident or other mishap. Mixers should be wiped clean with a cloth that has been dipped in warm water containing a detergent and then wrung out. Whips and bowls should be taken to the pot and pan sink for treatment.

Choppers and Cutters Food choppers and cutters may also be stored and operated outside the unit (see Fig. 2-14). A food cutter comes with a rotating bowl and a plow formation on the lid to guide the food under two power-driven knives. This handy unit can chop a fairly large

FIGURE 2-14. A new type of food chopper. (*Courtesy Hobart Corporation*)

quantity of food in a short time. However, cooks must use great care in operating this machine. *Never* use the hands to push food into the chopper; instead use a plastic or wooden mallet designed for the purpose. Raising the lid of the bowl stops the motor. A red light usually goes on to signal that the cutter is in operation. Food choppers or grinders may operate as attachments on another motor-driven piece of equipment, but for heavy work, separate equipment is appropriate. With these devices, the operator uses a mallet to push the food down into a feed device at the top; again, *never* use the hands to push food down. The food is caught by a rotating screw that pushes it along and through the cutting mechanism, which is usually a plate and knife combination. Plates have holes ⅛ to ½ inch in size. When the cook has finished using the chopper, the chopping device should be separated from the motor, disassembled, and thoroughly washed and sanitized.

Slicers Slicers may be hand-operated, semiautomatic, or completely automatic. If the volume of work to be done is small, a hand-operated unit may be sufficient. The cutting knife of a slicer is round and is rotated by a motor or by hand while another part of the mechanism pushes the food to be cut down into the blade so that a slice can be cut. This pushing mechanism can be set to give very thin, medium, or thick slices. The variation in thickness possible is usually from $\frac{1}{10}$ inch to $\frac{3}{4}$ inch. Some older slicers may not have a mechanical pushing device but may instead cause the food to go down into the slicing blade by relying on gravity and weight. After using a slicer, the operator should unscrew the nut holding the blade and carefully remove the blade. The rest of the mechanism should also be disassembled so that the blade and other parts touching the food can be washed and sanitized. Wipe the slicer down, cleaning it well.

Extruders Some short order sections may use an extruder—a machine somewhat like a grinder that mixes and then extrudes a food product. Most commonly these are used to prepare mixed french-fried potato dough for frying. Some extruders on the market today work almost automatically, measuring the necessary ingredients and then mixing and extruding the product for further processing. In some cases, it is possible to set the machine to extrude either a single portion or a large batch.

Disposals A disposal is a motor-driven unit, often installed in a sink, that grinds and flushes food waste down into the sewage system. Small disposals may be installed in different sections, but often a central disposal for the entire kitchen is located in a central position, and waste must be taken there to be disposed of. Usually the operation is simple. Waste is dumped into the unit, and the push of a button starts the machine and also starts a flow of water to flush the ground waste down into the sewage system.

Can Openers Can openers may be motor- or hand-driven. They consist of a clamping device that holds the can in place, a cutting blade that pierces the can, and a rotating device that moves the can around to remove the top. After they are used, they should be wiped clean.

Infrared Food Warmers Infrared food warmers are equipped with lights that hang above food and direct infrared waves downward to keep the food warm. They are not designed to cook food, but since the rays keep the food hot, some cooking may take place. Therefore, food should not be left under them too long. They are handy devices for holding food, making it possible for the short order cook and waitstaff personnel to coordinate preparation and pickup of orders.

□ Utensils

Pots and pans should be of heavy gauge (thickness of metal) in order to have good durability and not dent, and yet they should be light enough to handle easily. They need to conduct heat rapidly and well, across the entire contacting surface. Bottoms should be flat and should rest well on the cooking surface, to capture as much heat as possible. Covers should fit; spouts should have non-drip edges. The utensil should have no sharp edges, corners, or joints that make cleaning difficult. Handles should be firmly attached and give extra strength. The metal used should be noncorrosive.

Good care and maintenance are essential. Banging pots and pans around (especially those made of the lighter metals) can destroy their cooking qualities. With proper care, it is possible for a pot or pan that has been used for 20 years to look like new.

Pans

Sauté pans should be seasoned or conditioned before being used. This is accomplished in the same manner as for griddle tops. Often the salt treatment is used, and some semi-hard material such as cork or cloth is used to scrub the salt into the oiled metal. Once conditioned, the pan should not be washed; after use, it should simply be wiped clean with a dry, clean cloth. Egg pans are especially critical. It is impossible to go through a fast breakfast routine with egg pans that stick, and often egg pans are kept separate from others because their condition is so crucial to good egg frying.

Heavy-duty Silverstone-coated pans are often used, which helps considerably in avoiding sticking and makes cleaning the pan much easier. This coating is baked onto the metal, so it is bonded to it. Such pans can take a lot of wear but not abuse. Sharp instruments should not be allowed to touch the cooking surface.

Frying pans should have sloped sides so that a spatula or other instrument can be inserted underneath products for turning. Pans for braising require a tight cover and should have straight sides. The pan must be suited to its use, and numerous items are especially suited to doing specific jobs.

A sauce pan is a straight-sided pan with a handle. It is important in using pans with handles to ensure that the handle never sticks out where someone might run into it and throw the pot off the stove. Bad accidents can happen in such a situation. In some cases a double boiler will be needed. This is a set of two pans, one of which fits into the other. Water is placed into the lower unit, which is then heated so as to bring the material in the upper container to a proper cooking temperature.

Pots

Pots vary in capacity from 1 pint to many gallons. Most of the pots in the short order section are small; 1 or 2 gallon pots are often the largest ones on hand. They are used to simmer, boil, or otherwise cook items in liquid. It is unlikely that any stockpots will be used. The larger pots should have strong grip handles on either side so that they can be lifted with two hands.

Sauce pots are open pots with grip handles on the sides. A brazier is a deep pot in which items such as braised short ribs are cooked. It should be equipped with a tight-fitting cover. Table 2-1 describes some of the more commonly used pots and pans and their uses.

Strainers

Several kinds of strainers are used in the short order section. Some are made of wire and have rounded shapes. They rest in the container and the cooked material is poured in and allowed to drain. Others may be made of thin metal that has had tiny holes punched in it for draining. A commonly used strainer is the China cap. It is long and tapered to a point; perhaps it was so named because it resembled a kind of cap the Chinese once wore. It has very small holes and is often used to purée or strain fine items. A rounded ladle is placed in the cap, the material is poured in, and the ladle is moved in an up-and-down motion beneath the surface of the material, creating a suction that forces the material through the tiny holes, finely dividing it. Often a cook will process cooked beans in liquid in this way to obtain a bean purée for bean soup.

It is wise to wash a strainer immediately after use because, if left to stand, the material caught between the meshes can dry and harden, making cleaning difficult. Material between the meshes that stubbornly resists cleaning often can be removed with a good stiff brush. A sharp rap may also clear such material. Some strainers are fragile, however, especially the wire kind, so they must be handled with care.

Bowls

Some bowls will be used to hold foods for storage or mixing. They usually are made of metal (often stainless steel), and they have rounded bottoms so that stirring, beating, or mixing is facilitated. Nonetheless, enough of the bottom surface must be flat to ensure that the bowl remains stable at rest. Bowls should be made of sufficiently high-gauge metal to be strong and durable.

Cutting Boards

At least one cutting board will be located in the unit, and it will receive much use. Cutting boards made of wood should preferably be made of maple and should be joined in a manner similar to that described for wooden tabletops. Often a board 15 × 20 × 1¾ inches thick is desired, but thicker ones may be used to raise the work height to an optimum level.

TABLE 2-1. Common Pots and Pans and Their Uses

Pot or Pan	*Description and Use*
baking pan	A pan made of aluminum, stainless steel, or the like; rectangular and about 2 to 2½ inches deep; used for general baking purposes, such as for casserole dishes.
brazier	A heavy-gauge round pot with a tight-fitting cover; used to sear meat and then to braise it with some moisture at low temperature; equipped with loop handles for lifting off the stove.
China cap	A heavy-gauge, strong metal strainer with a long handle and a hook to hang the cap inside a pot; used for straining sauces and semisolids, using a roller or ladle to force food through the perforations.
chinois	A strainer shaped much like a China cap but made of fine mesh; used to produce foods finer than those that go through a China cap.
colander	A stainless steel, aluminum, or plastic perforated bowl; used to drain foods.
double boiler	Two pans, one fitting inside the other; the lower holds hot or boiling water that cooks or heats the food in the upper pan.
frying pan	A pan similar to a sauté pan; used for frying eggs and potatoes, making omelets, or doing other light frying work.
hotel or steam table pan	Also called a *service* or *counter pan*; made of aluminum or stainless steel; standard size is 12 × 20 × 2½ inches, but there are half-size pans (12 × 10 inches) and quarter size pans, too; covers are available; used for steaming, steam tables, storage, and baking—a general utility pan.
roasting pan	A large rectangular pan about 6 inches deep, often made of black rolled steel and strapped for extra strength; used for roasting ham, turkey, ribs, leg of lamb, and the like.
sauce pan	A pan equipped with a long, strong handle for lifting; usually has a tight-fitting cover; used for making sauces and cooking foods in some liquid.
sauce pot	A pot usually equipped with loop handles for lifting; must have a tight-fitting heavy cover; used for same purposes as a sauce pan, but a larger utensil.
sauté pan	A shallow pan with sloping sides for sautéing food; may have a cover so that foods can be braised; has a long handle for lifting; may be called a *sauteuse*. A straight-sided sauté pan is often used for braising after sautéing a food.
sautoir	A round, straight-sided pan with a long handle; used for sautéing food or cooking it in shallow fat; may have lid for braising.

(continued)

TABLE 2-1. (continued)

Pot or Pan	Description and Use
sheet pan	Sometimes called a *bun pan*; standard size is 18 × 36 × 1 inch, but there are also half pans (18 × 13 × 1 inch); used as a general utility pan, but often meats are placed on them in single layers for ovenizing or placing under a broiler; can be used for storage of multiple items such as made-up sandwiches if these are covered with a plastic wrap.
skillet	A cast-iron frying pan for frying food; may have cover for braising; if deep, it may be called a Dutch oven.
steam table or bain-marie units	Containers usually made of stainless steel; steam table pots have a cover; placed in hot water in a bain-marie or steam table to keep foods warm.
stockpot	A deep, round pot for simmering or boiling food; equipped with large loop handles for lifting, and may have a faucet with strainer; may have tight-fitting cover; only smaller sizes have use in the short order section.
strainer	A metal bowl with perforations for draining food; equipped with a long handle and a hook that fastens to the inside of a pot.

Plastic cutting boards are common. They should be made of a plastic approved by the National Sanitation Foundation (NSF). In particular, they should be warp-proof and should be able to withstand considerable heat without melting or warping. The size and thickness should be about the same as for wooden cutting boards.

Miscellaneous Utensils

Miscellaneous utensils such as measures and trays are used, depending on the kind of work. Figure 2-15 illustrates some of the utensils that have been discussed heretofore.

Chinaware

Porcelainware was first made in China, hence the name. Porcelain differs from other ceramic materials such as earthenware, pottery, and stoneware, all of which are also used for dishware. The difference is in the clay used and in the heat treatment applied to each piece.

Vitrification is a process in which different substances are first blended together and then, through heat, fused together to make one homogeneous material rather than a mixture of materials. The material becomes very hard. Earthenware is a baked clay material that is unvitrified; it is soft and porous and may or may not have a glaze. A common

FIGURE 2-15. Some utensils used in the short order section: (a) Bake or roast pans, which can also function as steam table pans. (b) Silverstone-coated frying pans. (c) Baking or roasting pan with cover. (d) Sauce pot. (e) Steam table pans. (f) Pan strainer. (g) Sauce pan. (h) Double boiler.

FIGURE 2-15. (continued) (i) Bain-marie pots. (j) Plain frying pan.
(k) Colander. (l) Shellfish steamer that can be inserted into a pot.
(m) Stockpot with spigot. (n) Strainer. (o) Sauté pan. (Items (a)–(g) courtesy
Vollrath Company, Inc., Sheboygan, WI; items (h)–(o) courtesy Epicure Cookware,
Commercial Aluminum Company)

example is the standard clay pot for plants. Pottery is similar to earthenware but is often made of better clay and is glazed. Examples are some kinds of vases. Both earthenware and pottery are unsuitable for use by foodservices, because they shatter too easily. Stoneware is vitrified and has a glazed surface. It is most suitable for use in serving dishes such as casseroles and cassolettes that must withstand sudden changes in temperature without shattering. Because it is breakable, stoneware should not receive heavy shocks.

China or porcelain is made from a very good grade of clay and may be mixed with other substances to give it desired characteristics. It is highly vitrified, glazed, and very hard. It is used for plates, saucers, cups, and so on. Porcelain is breakable, and ordinarily the type foodservices use is heavy and reinforced to take substantial wear and some rough handling. If a plate or other porcelain dish receives a sharp rap from the bottom but does not break, it may at first seem unharmed; but soon a series of cracks may appear with jagged lines running outward. This is called a *star crack* (see Fig. 2-16). It is also desirable not to scrape one dish over another, since this can wear down the glaze.

Some glass materials are used. The types of clear glass used for drinking glasses and some other ware are called *lead glass, lime glass*, and *rock crystal*. Lead glass is less brittle than lime glass and can be blown into a shaping mold during formation of glass items. Molten lime glass must be deposited (not blown) into a mold to make the item. Crystal is an extremely high-quality glass and is rarely used in a foodservice, except in operations of the expensive, white-tablecloth type. It requires special handling.

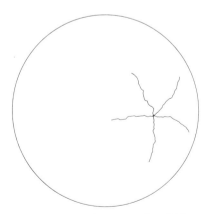

FIGURE 2-16. A star crack, which usually results from a blow to the central portion of a dish.

Today some plastic materials are used in foodservices, but they do not have good durability in utensils and so their use remains limited.

Knives

Small working implements operated by hand are tools. Since hand and tool come in contact, the tool's handle is important. Good grasps are essential on the tool so that the hand grasps the tool securely. The grasp angle should be suitable for the angle of use so the hand works comfortably (see Fig. 2-17). The grasp should also be designed with indentations to fit the fingers so the fingers fit more closely around the handle. Table 2-2 summarizes information about some tools used in the short order section.

Knives are by far the most used kitchen tool, in fact so frequently that they are a symbol of the cook's profession. Many cooks prize their knives so much that they purchase their own set, mark them plainly, and take care of them themselves. No one else is allowed to use them. At the end of a shift the knives are cleaned carefully, wrapped in a clean, soft cloth, and stored in a locker where they are secure.

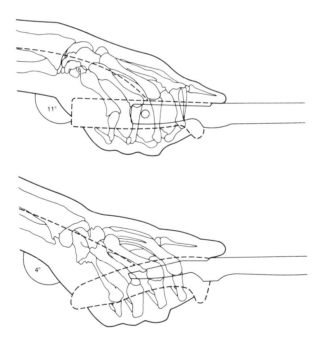

FIGURE 2-17. A proper grasp on a tool in relation to the hand and its muscles and bones. When the hand gets out of alignment, the resulting action causes not only tiredness but inaccurate and messy work.

TABLE 2-2. Small Tools Used in Short Order Work

Tool	Description and Use
cleaver	A heavy, carbon steel broad-bladed unit; used for cutting through bones and cartilage in cutting meat.
forks	A cook's fork is a long-handled, strongly made fork used to turn heavy roasts and general heavy-duty work; a broiler fork has a shorter handle and heavier prongs and is used to turn meats, fish, and poultry as they broil; a carver's fork is a relatively light tool with slender prongs used to hold meat in carving; a pot fork is sometimes used to turn meats and other foods being boiled or simmered or to manipulate foods in sauce pans.
ladle	A long-handled cup, most commonly made of stainless steel, used for measuring or portioning foods; different sizes are used, and the ounce size is identified on the handle.
pizza cutter	A round, sharp wheel blade with a wooden handle, used to cut pizza or other foods; bakers use a similar tool for cutting doughs.
sandwich spreader	A small spatula with a broad, short blade; used to pick up a portion of filling and spread it on a sandwich or other item.
scoop	A round, cup-like tool with a mechanical release; used for portioning ice cream and other foods; scoops vary in size, and the numbers refer to the number of portions the scoop makes per quart of food. Some manufacturers color code the handles to identify which size they are:

Blue	No. 30	Orange	No. 10
Yellow	No. 24	Dark red	No. 12
Light red	No. 20	Orchid	No. 8
Green	No. 16		

Tool	Description and Use
skimmer	A flat, concave, perforated stainless steel or wire mesh long-handled tool; used to skim off scum and other products, to search for and pick up items in stock or other liquids, to hold solid foods back while pouring out the liquid.
spoons	A cook's spoon is a long-handled, rounded spoon that holds about 3 ounces of food when rounded full; a solid basting spoon is useful for holding food or as a general-duty large spoon; a perforated spoon is used to pick up small items from a liquid; a slotted spoon is used to pick up larger items from a liquid.
whips	Piano wire or balloon whips have flexible wires that can be used in thinner liquids and can reach into corners during stirring; heavy whips are made of straight, heavy, stiff wires and are used to mix heavy sauces or other foods.

A good knife should have the following characteristics: a good-quality carbon steel blade capable of taking a sharp edge and holding it; good weight and balance; proper length for the intended use; and a well-made, sanitary handle that is easy to grasp. If the knife does not have a choil (see Fig. 2-18), it should have a good finger guard so that the hand cannot slip onto the blade. Figure 2-19 shows some of the more common knives and spatulas used in the short order section.

Knife Sharpening A steel is used to true the edge of a knife, bringing it to its peak of sharpness. A stone is used to sharpen a knife. Some steels today are not made of steel but consist of molded ground flint or diamonds in a steel shape. Figure 2-20 shows how to steel a knife.

Using a French Knife The French knife (also called a *cook's* or *chef's knife*) is the most frequently used instrument in the kitchen. Handled correctly, it can do a vast number of jobs cleanly and accurately. Messy work with a knife is the mark of an amateur. Figure 2-21 demonstrates how to hold a knife to achieve best control, cutting speed, and accuracy, lessening chances for an accident. Grips may vary from this one, depending on the kind and size of the knife and the kind of work being done. It takes practice to get used to this grip, but once learned it enables the cook to do a lot of skilled work. Figure 2-22 shows how to use a French knife in slicing. Notice how the fingers of the holding hand are curled under to protect them.

Figure 2-23 illustrates one of the most commonly used procedures for cubing with a French knife. The way to chop is shown in Figure 2-24, and Figure 2-25 shows some of the most common shapes and sizes of cuts made when using a French knife.

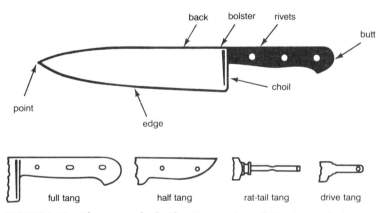

FIGURE 2-18.   The parts of a knife. (*Courtesy Russell Harrington Cutlery, Inc.*)

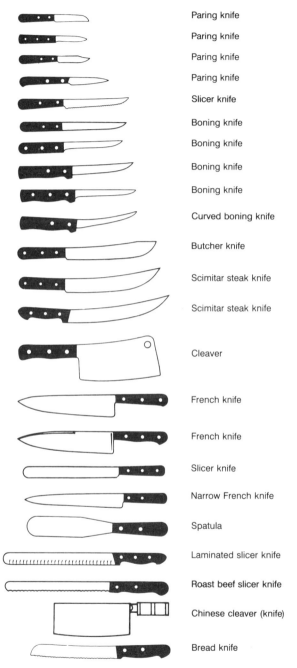

Paring knife

Paring knife

Paring knife

Paring knife

Slicer knife

Boning knife

Boning knife

Boning knife

Boning knife

Curved boning knife

Butcher knife

Scimitar steak knife

Scimitar steak knife

Cleaver

French knife

French knife

Slicer knife

Narrow French knife

Spatula

Laminated slicer knife

Roast beef slicer knife

Chinese cleaver (knife)

Bread knife

FIGURE 2-19.   Knives and spatulas used in the short order section. (*Courtesy Russell Harrington Cutlery, Inc.*)

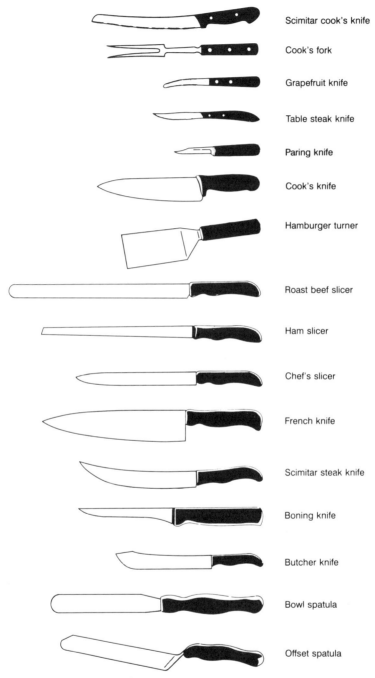

Scimitar cook's knife

Cook's fork

Grapefruit knife

Table steak knife

Paring knife

Cook's knife

Hamburger turner

Roast beef slicer

Ham slicer

Chef's slicer

French knife

Scimitar steak knife

Boning knife

Butcher knife

Bowl spatula

Offset spatula

FIGURE 2-19. (continued)

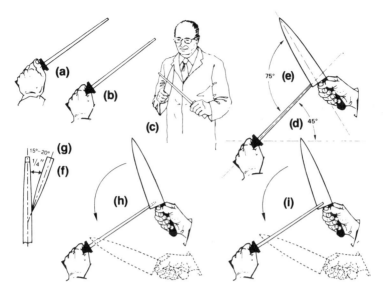

FIGURE 2-20.   In order to use a sharpening steel properly for the best results, a relatively simple technique should be mastered: 1. Grasp the sharpening steel firmly in your left hand (if you're right-handed that is), placing the thumb securely behind the guard as shown in either drawing (a) or (b), whichever position suits you most comfortably for safety. 2. Hold the sharpening steel away from your body at a comfortable distance (something short of full extension with elbow slightly bent) about waist height. See drawing (c). 3. Sharpening steel may be held at an angle of approximately 45° as in drawing (d); however, any angle from 0° to 45° may be used as an accommodation to individual preference. 4. Hold the knife securely by the handle in your right hand as if you were going to use it for cutting. Place the heel of the blade against the steel at a 75° angle as shown in drawing (e). 5. While keeping the cutting edge of the knife against the steel's surface, raise the back of the blade approximately ¼″ off the steel as illustrated in drawing (f). The purpose of this action is to position the knife blade against the steel at an angle of 15° to 20° as shown in drawing (g). 6. Try to maintain this angle and apply constant, moderate pressure as you draw the blade smoothly across and down the full length of the steel in one continuous motion until the tip of the blade completes the stroke by passing off the steel near the handle guard. See drawing (h). Go as slowly as you wish to be sure of accuracy. 7. Return knife blade to original position but now with the opposite side of the blade placed on the underside of the steel (see drawing (i)) and repeat steps 5 through 6. (*Courtesy Russell Harrington Cutlery, Inc.*)

FIGURE 2-21. How to hold a knife for best control, cutting speed, and accuracy. Grips may vary, depending on the kind of knife, its size, and the work being done. (*Photo by Michael Upright*)

FIGURE 2-22. Using a French knife. Grasp the knife so that it will not slip, and place it on the item. With the other hand, firmly grip the item to be cut. Notice how the fingers are curled under to protect them. Holding the knife at about a 45° angle, bring the knife down on the item, with the tip on the cutting board. Place the curled fingers against the blade. With the knife sliding against the curled fingers, slice forward and down, cutting through the item. Repeat the motion after moving the curled fingers back so that another cut of desired thickness can be made. Move the heel of the knife up, and pull backward, keeping the tip of the knife on the board. Shove the item forward with the curled fingers. Continue, working quickly until all items have been sliced. (*Photo by Michael Upright*)

FIGURE 2-23. Making cubes from slices. (*Photo by Michael Upright*)

FIGURE 2-24. Chopping with a French knife. Center the item or items to be chopped on the board. Some preliminary slicing may be done to get the item ready. Then place the tip of the knife down on the cutting board over the item to be chopped. From time to time, sweep the food back into the center, and continue chopping until the desired degree of fineness is achieved. (*Photo by Michael Upright*)

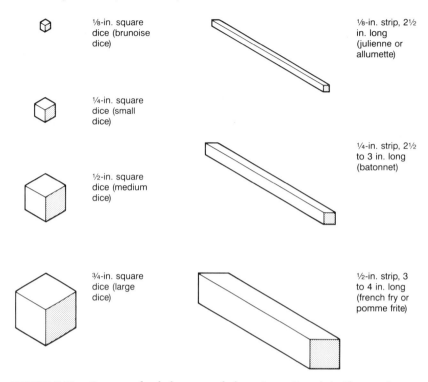

<table>
<tr><td>⬡</td><td>⅛-in. square dice (brunoise dice)</td><td></td><td>⅛-in. strip, 2½ in. long (julienne or allumette)</td></tr>
<tr><td>⬡</td><td>¼-in. square dice (small dice)</td><td></td><td></td></tr>
<tr><td>⬜</td><td>½-in. square dice (medium dice)</td><td></td><td>¼-in. strip, 2½ to 3 in. long (batonnet)</td></tr>
<tr><td>⬜</td><td>¾-in. square dice (large dice)</td><td></td><td>½-in. strip, 3 to 4 in. long (french fry or pomme frite)</td></tr>
</table>

FIGURE 2-25. Common food shapes made by using a French knife, together with their sizes.

☐ Summary

A knowledge of how to use and care for equipment, utensils, and tools is important for successful short order work. Most cooks prefer gas cooking equipment because of its flexibility in changing temperatures, but electricity is cleaner and in many cases works just as well or even better.

Cooks also need to know something about the metals used in utensils, tools, and equipment. Many utensils are made of different metals, each of which has its own particular characteristics. Thus, a plain stainless steel unit is not good to cook in, because stainless steel does not spread heat out well and consequently develops hot spots that can result in burned food. Copper is an excellent heat conductor, but it should not be used where food acids can react with it. Aluminum is a soft metal that can be corroded (eaten away) by alkalies and abrades easily.

Griddles should be conditioned before being used. This involves placing a coating of oil on the griddle and heating it to about 375° to 400°F (190° to 205°C); often the oil is scoured into the surface with salt.

If water or other liquids touch a seasoned griddle, the seasoning may be lost, in which case the process must be repeated. Frying pans and other utensils in which foods are fried must also be seasoned in this way. Knowing how to care for and operate a griddle is essential for the short order cook.

Hot plates may be open or closed and are used to provide quick direct heat for boiling, sautéing, or doing other work that requires high heat. Burners must have proper flames and must be kept clean and free of material that might clog burner holes. The drip tray under the burners should be cleaned frequently.

Deep-fat fryers also need special care. Everything must be kept scrupulously clean, and the frying fat must be filtered frequently. If enough food is fried, it is seldom necessary to throw away any fat, because the older fat is used up at a brisk rate in the frying and fresh oil is added to replace it. Fresh fat has whitish bubbles that break sharply in frying; old fat has yellowish bubbles that foam rather than crackle.

Excessive heat breaks down fat, and the fat then gives food a poor flavor. Some metals, curing salts, table salt, and even water tend to break down fat. If a fryer is filled with too much food, the temperature drops too low to give good frying action, and a poorly fried product results. It is important for the short order cook to know how to filter the fat and keep it up.

Broilers and salamanders cook with radiant heat. A salamander is an overhead broiler, usually smaller in size than a full-size broiler. Both should be kept clean, inside and outside. Grids should be scoured frequently, and the drip trays should be removed and emptied.

A microwave can be a very useful piece of equipment in a short order section, since it enables the cook to process many small orders of food quickly. Metal objects must not be put into a microwave, because they can destroy the magnetron tube that generates the microwave energy. Microwaves do not produce conventional heat. Instead, they produce rays that strike the food and cause its molecular structure to vibrate, which develops heat. It is important that microwave units be kept very clean. If soil causes a door to remain open at all, potentially harmful microwaves can slip out.

The proper use and care of refrigerators is also essential. Good storage procedures, such as storing the same food in the same place at all times, can reduce search time when going after foods stored there. Cooks should check frequently to ensure that temperatures are proper for keeping food.

Food warmers, hoods, sinks, and worktables are also usually a part of the short order section, and cooks should be familiar with the care and use of these items.

Pots and pans should be durable and heavy enough not to dent in handling. At the same time, however, they should be light enough to provide ease in handling. They should not be treated roughly. Pans used for sautéing and frying often are sloped so that a spatula or other tool can easily be inserted under cooking food in order to turn it. Pans in which liquid is used as the cooking medium usually have straight or slightly sloping sides. Lids should be tight fitting. Pots are used to simmer, boil, or otherwise cook items in liquid. Large ones should have grip handles on either side to make two-handed lifting possible. The bottom should be flat so as to capture as much heat as possible. Handles of pans should not project over the stove's edge, because otherwise someone might brush against it and knock the pan off the stove.

Some short order sections use a double boiler—a unit in which one pot fits down into the other. The lower pot holds hot or boiling water, and heat is transferred from it to foods in the upper container.

Strainers, collanders, measures, trays, and other utensils are also used. They should be heavy-duty to withstand wear. Ceramic or clay materials are also used, but earthenware and pottery are not satisfactory for foodservice use. Stoneware is a vitrified clay often made into items in which foods are cooked and served. China is porcelain, a high-grade clay that has been vitrified. It is used primarily for dishes. Ceramic or clay items should receive careful handling.

Tools are small pieces of equipment used by hand to do work. When used properly and cared for well, they become valuable assistants to the short order cook in doing good work. Good grasps that suit the hand position and the fingers are essential. Knives are perhaps the most important tools the cook uses. Each type of knife has its own special use. Knives should be kept sharp by stoning and steeling. Both of these operations are performed by holding the knife at a 20° angle and maintaining an even, smooth stroke. French knives have considerable use. Holding the knife and the material being cut properly is important to performing rapid and good work. Proper handling of the knife also prevents accidents.

═══════════════ ☐ CHAPTER REVIEW ☐ ═══════════════

1. Why do cooks prefer gas? Cite disadvantages and advantages of gas and electricity in short order cooking.
2. What are the major pieces of equipment used in the short order section?

3. Cite the qualities of stainless steel, aluminum, copper, iron (black and cast) that make them suitable for specific uses in equipment.
4. What is the proper care of a griddle?
5. How are variable temperatures obtained when a griddle with three separate burners is used?
6. What kinds of hot plates are available? What is their purpose?
7. Describe a proper gas flame.
8. Indicate what happens to fat when it is overheated. What is acrolein?
9. How can one reduce the breakdown of fat and thus retain its good frying qualities?
10. What happens when hot fat is exposed to certain metals, salt, curing salts, water, and other substances?
11. How does one achieve proper turnover in using frying fats?
12. What methods are used to filter frying fat? How should one clean a fryer and its auxiliary equipment?
13. What is a broiler? a salamander? What kind of heat do they produce to broil foods?
14. What precautions should a short order cook take in using a microwave?
15. How are microwaves produced, and how do they heat foods?
16. Describe the care that should be given to a waffle baker.
17. How do mixers work, and what is their use?
18. What kinds of food choppers or cutters are used? What precautions should be observed in using them?
19. Indicate what each of the following utensils is, and specify its use:

stockpot	sautoir
sauce pot	sauteuse (sauté pan)
brazier	skillet
sauce pan	double boiler
China cap	

20. What volume does a No. 20 scoop hold when level full?
21. What is porcelain? stoneware? What is the major use of each in foodservice utensils?
22. What two qualities must a good grasp have?
23. How does one stone a knife? steel it?
24. Explain how a French knife is properly used to slice an item. Describe the use of the other hand during slicing.
25. Describe the proper way to chop with a French knife.

26. Indicate what each of the following tools is, and specify its use:

scimitar or steak knife   skimmer
butcher knife   offset spatula
sandwich spreader   whip
perforated serving spoon   cook's fork

CHAPTER THREE

Procedures and Techniques

A good short order cook must have considerable skill and knowledge about how to prepare various items. It takes skill and dexterity to flip a hotcake so that it remains nice and circular, to flip eggs over easy, or to properly broil a steak. An amateur can ruin a product, while a skilled craftsman or craftswoman can make the product a triumph. As previously noted, skills are developed by learning and practice, and a lot of manipulations are required in a day's work in the short order section. In addition, a cook has to know what techniques to apply to get the desired results. Sautéing a breaded veal cutlet is not the same as frying bacon. The cutlet requires some frying fat to sauté properly; the bacon needs none, since it contains fat enough for frying. A cook also has to know how long to boil a soft-cooked egg versus a hard-cooked one. To produce appetizing fish and seafoods, the cook should know how to avoid overcooking them. Some red meats need moderate cooking times, while others need long cooking times. Good results come from knowing.

□ Procedures

There are many ways to cook foods, and short order cooks should know most of them—even though some are used only rarely. Basically, cooking or the application of heat to foods can be divided into moist-heat cooking and dry-heat cooking methods. In moist-heat cooking, the food is cooked in some liquid that contributes moisture to the cooking process. In dry-heat cooking, no liquid is applied, although in some instances moisture does collect from the food itself so that some cooking occurs through moist heat. In some moist-heat cooking, only the natural juice in the food is utilized (as in braising meat), while in other moist-heat cooking methods, liquids are added (as in poaching eggs).

71

□ Moist-Heat Methods

Water is the most common liquid used in moist-heat cooking, but other liquids such as wine, tomato juice, vinegar, and stock can be used. The water usually acts as a medium for conducting heat to the food, but it can also act to keep food moist and to produce certain desired results such as utilizing moisture to change connective tissue collagen into water and gelatine, thus tenderizing the meat. Moist heat methods include boiling, simmering, stewing, parboiling, poaching, blanching, steaming, and braising. Sometimes reducing and deglazing are classified as moist-heat methods.

Boiling

When heat is applied to water, the water holds the heat and thus increases in temperature. However, when water reaches a certain temperature, it boils; this is another way of saying that it begins changing into steam. The steam rises as it forms, causing the water to move or roll. Water at sea level normally boils at 212°F (100°C), but at higher elevations, the boiling point occurs at a lower temperature. Cooks should know this, since, once boiling starts, the water cannot get any hotter; raising the heat only causes the water to boil harder. When water boils at a lower temperature, the cooking time is extended. And if the elevation is high enough—say as high as Pike's Peak in Colorado (14,110 feet)—water boils at such a low temperature that the food may boil all day and still not be completely cooked. In such a case, the food should be put into a pressure steamer and cooked under pressure, where a higher heat is possible.

It is desirable in boiling food to have the water *just* boiling, since this usually gives a better product. Hard boiling can break up food such as pared potatoes and does not make things cook any faster.

Simmering

Water held at about 212°F (100°C) is hot enough to cook foods fairly rapidly without boiling. Tiny bubbles may rise, and there may be some slight movement of the water, but it will not be as vigorous as in boiling. This is called *simmering*, and some foods such as meats may be more tender, flavorful, and juicy if cooked at a simmer rather than at a boil. A common saying in the kitchen is "Don't let the water laugh out loud [boil]; let it only smile [simmer]."

Stewing

Stewing involves simmering or lightly boiling a food item for a fairly long time in only enough water to cover or nearly cover the food.

Stewing meats for an extended period is often done to make the meats more tender. Stewing is unlikely to be a common procedure for the short order cook.

Parboiling

Gently boiling food in a small quantity of water to partially cook it is called parboiling. This is done to get some foods in proper condition for further treatment—for example, parboiling sweetbreads to make their membranes easier to remove. Parcooking is a method of partially cooking food by any cooking method.

Blanching

If a food is dipped into hot liquid for a brief period or if boiling liquid is poured over it, the treatment is called *blanching*. This also is done to prepare food for further treatment or to achieve some other desired result. Usually the blanching process is enough to fix color in vegetables and to deactivate enzymes that might otherwise cause undesirable changes in the food during later processing.

Steaming

Vapor (gas) made from boiling water is called *steam*. It is hotter than water even though it too is at 212°F (100°C), because additional heat is required to convert water into steam. Thus, steam cooks faster than does boiling water. It is possible to boil water in an enclosed chamber and have the steam create a pressure that puts more and more heat into the steam as the pressure rises. This is what happens in pressure cooking. The temperature of steam under various pressures used to cook food are as shown in Table 3-1.

TABLE 3-1. Steam Temperatures at Various Pressures

Steam Pressure (psi)*	Temperature	
	°F	°C
0	212.0	100.0
2	218.3	103.5
4	224.6	107.0
6	229.8	109.9
8	235.0	112.8
10	239.4	115.2
12	249.6	120.9

*pounds per square inch

It should be remembered that steam under pressure is much hotter than steam under normal conditions and therefore can burn a person much worse. Steam under pressure also has considerable force and, if the pressure gets too great, can blow up the chamber in which it is contained, causing a very bad accident.

Short order cooking usually requires very little steam cooking, but there are times when it may be needed. There are two kinds of steam cookers. In one type, called a *free-vent steamer*, the steam is not under pressure but is directed forcefully at the food, destroying any vapor barrier surrounding the food and heating it rather quickly. In the other type of steamer, called a *pressure steamer*, steam is allowed to contact the food under pressure. Some high-pressure steamers—steamers that cook above 15 psi—are used for cooking vegetables in small batches. Cooks should thoroughly understand how to use steam equipment properly before using it and should also observe all safety precautions required to make it safe to use.

Braising

Braising and stewing are much alike except that braising often consists of cooking in a small quantity of moisture that comes from the food product itself. Braising is often used to cook meat to a tender state. Braised foods may be what is called *blond* (nonbrowned by heat) or *brun* (browned by being seared with heat).

Reducing

Often a recipe will call for the reduction of a liquid. This is done by applying high heat to the liquid to drive much of it off as steam. The small quantity left is then called a *reduced* item. The procedure is often performed to concentrate flavors for sauces and other items.

Deglazing

It is sometimes desirable to extract encrusted materials and flavors from the bottom of a pan in which food has been cooked. Liquid is added and then (with the aid of scraping and stirring as heat is applied) the boiling liquid is allowed to pick up these materials and bring them into solution. This process, called *deglazing*, is often used in preparing sauces.

☐ Dry-Heat Methods

In dry-heat cooking, heat is carried to the food by radiation, conduction, or convection. Heat from glowing elements or fire can be radiated via infrared waves to reach the food, heating and cooking it. Such heat at times can be intense and may occur in broiling or grilling. Conducted heat is used to deep-fry items, with the fat acting as a conductor, or to sauté food in a pan set over heat, which travels up through the pan and then to the food. An example of convected heat is the hot air in an oven used to cook a roast.

The short order cook should understand the nature of the heat used and what it is supposed to do. Methods of dry-heat cooking include broiling, grilling, griddling, pan broiling, barbecuing, roasting, baking, sautéing (frying), pan frying, deep-fat frying, and sweating.

Broiling

When some metals or ceramics reach a temperature of 6,000°F (3,316°C), they glow with white heat and emit energy as infrared waves that are absorbed by the food, cooking it. Usually the degree of heat can be controlled by adjusting the grid. Thus, thin pieces of meat may be broiled at a distance of 2 to 3 inches from the heat, while thick items such as steaks are cooked at distances of 8 inches or more. Having the steak farther away lowers the heat, giving the infrared waves time to penetrate into the interior of the meat without charring the outside. Foods with some fat in them broil better than foods that lack fat. Thus, salmon and trout broil well, because they contain a considerable amount of fat, while sole does not broil well, because it lacks fat. Similarly, lean veal broils poorly, while beef steaks larded with fat broil very well.

Sometimes leaner cuts of meat are basted during cooking to give them moisture and help them broil better. Sometimes even meat that has some fat, such as tenderloin steaks, may be dipped into seasoned oil before being placed on a broiler grid. This prevents the steaks from sticking to the hot grid and also helps start the broiling sooner, since the fat added to the surface of the meat conducts the heat into the meat faster.

In some cases, a thermometer may be inserted into thick pieces of meat to indicate their degree of doneness. It is important when broiling an excessively thick piece of meat to partially broil it and then finish the meat in a 350°F (177°C) oven. This avoids overcharring the outside of the meat while properly cooking the interior. Cooks need to understand what additional preparation a piece of meat needs in broiling. This depends on the cut of meat, the thickness, and the desired degree of doneness.

In some cases a broiled piece of meat is planked, meaning that the meat is prebroiled and then placed in the middle of a plank, where it is surrounded by a garnish of colorful cooked vegetables and ringed with a border of duchess potatoes. Melted butter is drizzled over the top, and the plank is placed under a broiler or into a 350°F (177°C) oven to be finished.

Very tender items, such as fish, may break up when broiled. Consequently, these are often placed in a double grid so they can be turned easily (see Fig. 3-1).

When an item is placed on a hot grid, the grid rods are usually very hot and they sear the item, making slightly charred lines on it. One can usually tell how often an item has been turned by noting the grid marks. An item that was turned only once will have parallel grid marks, while one turned twice will have crisscrossed grid marks (see Fig. 3-2). It is the mark of a good craftsperson to make these grid marks symmetrical, crisscrossing at a 45° angle. This is done by making a 90° turn on successive turns, pressing the meat gently onto the grid after the turn.

Meats should not be turned by being pierced with a fork. Rather, they should be flipped over with a fork or turned with a spatula or tongs. If there is a rind of fat, the fat can be pierced by a fork and the meat turned.

Studies have shown that when fat from meat drips onto hot coals or anything quite hot, the fat breaks down and may even catch fire, sending up a sooty smoke. When fat breaks down in this manner, some carcinogens (cancer-producing agents) are formed that can get onto the meat. It is therefore advisable to avoid producing flames from burning fat during broiling.

Grilling

There is some confusion about the use of the word *grill*. To some cooks it means to cook food over a broiler device that has a heat source on the bottom; to other cooks, it means to cook on a griddle. In this text we use the term to mean the former. Cooking on a griddle will be called *griddling*.

Since there is little difference between the techniques used in broiling and those used in grilling, the earlier discussion of broiling

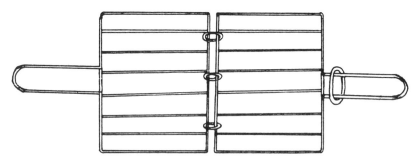

FIGURE 3-1. A double grid used to hold fish and other items under a broiler. This device enables the short order cook to turn fragile items on the broiler without breaking them.

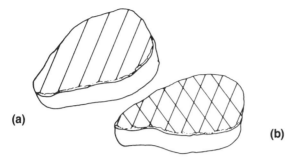

FIGURE 3-2. Grid markings on steaks: (a) Markings on a steak that has been broiled in only one position on the grid. (b) Markings on a steak that has been placed first at a 60° angle and then at a 120° angle so that the grid markings crisscross.

applies to this procedure also. Perhaps more care should be taken to see that flames are not developed from burning fat, but that is about all.

Pan Broiling

If meat exudes some fat from its tissues during cooking, the item may be pan broiled. This is done by preheating a heavy, seasoned skillet until it is very hot, and then placing the item into the pan and allowing it to cook. As it cooks, fat exudes, giving more of an effect of sautéing than of broiling. (Excess fat should be poured off.)

Roasting

Roasting is done in an oven, and the pieces of meat or other items to be roasted are usually quite large. Usually a meat thermometer is inserted to gauge doneness. The item is roasted by being surrounded by hot, dry air. No water is used, and the meat is left uncovered so that moisture can escape. In a few cases, such as with veal, a cover may be used to keep the item moist. (Veal has very little fat that might contribute moistness.)

To roast, set the oven dial at the correct temperature; low temperatures produce a tenderer, juicier, and more flavorful product. Most authorities recommend no salting. Salt only penetrates meat to about ¼ inch, and it retards browning by drawing moisture to the surface. Moreover, many patrons today also prefer to have little or no salt on their foods.

Some cooks recommend a method of searing the meat first at high temperature to brown it and give it a browned flavor. They then drop the temperature and continue the roasting process at this temperature. The old theory that searing the meat sealed in the juices has not been proved. In fact, when meat is seared, the evenness of the cooking is not as great, there is more shrink and thus a loss of portions, and carving can be more difficult because the high temperature may yield a somewhat misshapen piece of meat. If a convection oven is used, the roasting temperature should be about 50 Fahrenheit degrees (10 Celsius degrees) lower than one would use in a normal oven.

Often a trivet (perforated underliner or rack) is put into the roasting pan before the roast is placed there. The pan should fit the quantity of meat to be roasted, being neither too full of meat nor too big for the amount of meat. Turn the meat fat side up so that the fat can run down over the meat and baste it as it melts. Leaner poultry such as chickens and turkeys should be roasted with the back side (where the heaviest layer of fat is) up, then toward the end of roasting, they should be turned and allowed to finish breast up. If it is desirable to roll the meat in its juices as it roasts, simply omit the trivet. In some cases meat is basted while it roasts, to keep it as moist as possible. Sometimes meat is larded with strips of fat so that this fat can contribute moisture. Larding is a method of laying fat meat such as bacon strips or strips of salt pork over the roast so that the fat will melt and baste the meat as it roasts.

A *mirepoix* is a group of chopped vegetables such as carrots, turnips, celery, and onions that is added to a roast to give it added flavor. The *mirepoix* flavors the juices more than it does the meat.

The cook needs to judge the end temperature at which the roast should be withdrawn from the oven. Large pieces of meat have enough heat in them to make the internal temperature rise an additional 15 to 25 Fahrenheit degrees (8.25 to 13.75 Celsius degrees) after removal from the oven. Thus, if a rib roast is desired at a rare stage (140°F or 60°C), it should be removed from the oven at about 120°F (49°C). After being removed, the roast should be allowed to sit for 15 to 30 minutes before carving. This firms up the meat, making it easier to carve and causing less juice to be lost during carving.

Delayed service cookery is a method of roasting meat at a very low temperature and then holding it at a temperature of 140°F (60°C) plus or minus 5 Fahrenheit degrees (2.75 Celsius degrees), until needed for service. This method allows meat to be held for 48 hours or more at a desired stage of doneness. Shrinkage is minimized and flavor, tenderness, juiciness, and evenness of cooking are increased. Ground meats should not be cooked in this way.

Baking

Baking is the same as roasting. It is often reserved for describing the oven cooking of bakery goods, while the term *roasting* is applied to meat cooked in an oven.

Barbecuing

Items can be barbecued in an oven, in a rotisserie, on a broiling spit (where the meat turns in front of a device giving off radiant heat), or in a pit. Usually the meat is basted with a tangy sauce while cooking. When items are barbecued in a pit, the method is different. The pit is filled with combustible material, and a fire is lit. Medium-size stones are then thrown in to get extremely hot, at which point the meat wrapped in foil is thrown down over the rocks and the pit is sealed tightly. The meat roasts in this enclosed chamber. After the pit is opened up and the meat is removed and carved, the tangy sauce can be added.

Sautéing

While roasting, baking, and barbecuing are usually not performed by the short order cook, sautéing is. Often sautéing is just called *frying* or *pan frying*. Sautéing involves frying a food item in a small quantity of oil or fat, with the amount of oil or fat to be used depending on the item. A rounded portion such as a chicken leg requires more fat to reach it and conduct the heat into it than does a flat piece of meat such as a cube steak. Sautéing can be done on a griddle as well as in a sauté pan (*sauteuse*). Such a pan has slanting sides so that the cook can easily get implements under the item for manipulating it.

The fat is first added to the pan, and the pan is heated to the desired temperature. The item is then slid (not dropped) into the pan, and the item is browned on both sides in the hot fat. The level of heat and the length of time of cooking depend on the nature of the item, its thickness, and the degree of doneness desired. Very thin items cook fast, so the heat must be fairly high in order to brown the outside while the interior is just getting done. The heat may be lower when items are thicker. With quite thick pieces, the item is sometimes browned on both sides and then cooked to partial doneness before being finished in the oven. Covering the pan and cooking very slowly produces a well-cooked thick product. If this is done on a griddle, the item may be covered with a pie pan or a sauce pan lid and finished in this way.

Often after a sautéed item has been removed from the pan, the pan is deglazed using water, stock, wine, or some other liquid to pick up the encrusted material on the bottom. This liquid is then served as a juice (*jus*) poured over or under the item upon service, or it may be served on the side. The liquid can also be used to make a sauce to go with the sautéed item.

Pan Frying

Pan frying is the same as sautéing, however, some authorities differentiate between the two methods when a skillet is used instead of a *sauteuse* or when the item to be cooked is rather large. The same results achieved in pan frying, sautéing, and frying can be achieved on a griddle.

Frying
The term *frying* is often used synonymously with the terms *sautéing, pan frying*, and *griddling*. It refers to cooking an item in a small quantity of fat.

Deep-Fat Frying
Cooking food submerged in or on top of fat or oil is called *deep-fat frying*. The action is one in which a food that has some moisture is put into fat, which extracts some of this moisture during frying, giving a crispness to the outside while cooking the inside. Browning occurs because the fat is hot enough to produce a slight charring.

The degree of crispness obtained depends on a number of factors, including the following:

1. *Temperature.* Too cold a fat gives a soggy, greasy outside and an uncolored product. Too hot a fat gives too much crispness, over-browning, and perhaps an uncooked inside.
2. *Fat:food ratio.* Too much food added to the fryer drops the tempera-ture of the fat, and the results noted in factor 1 occur.
3. *Kind of fat.* Fats such as butter cannot be brought to a high enough temperature in deep-frying to produce good crisping.
4. *Type of food.* Some foods, such as breaded or battered items, develop a crisp crust more easily than do uncovered items such as a potato; moistness can also be a factor.
5. *Length of cooking time.* In some cases the amount of browning desired can be a factor in the length of frying time. The size of the food pieces, the frying temperature, type of covering on the food, kind of food, and other factors influence frying time.
6. *Size of food item.* Large items may have to be cooked at a slightly lower temperature to get thorough cooking. Small ones need a quick cooking time so that they do not dry out too much.
7. *Type of outer surface.* If there is a bit of sugar in the outer coating, browning is increased. Absence of a substance that browns easily on the outside reduces browning.

Batter-dipped foods and some other products that can stick to the frying basket should not be placed in it and then lowered into the fat. Instead, they should be slid carefully into the fat so that no spattering occurs. If dropped, they should be dropped very carefully. Other foods can be put into the frying basket up to a proper level, and the basket can then be lowered carefully into the fat. Lower the basket gently and slowly to prevent the fat from boiling up as moisture touches it. After this original surge occurs, the bubbles level off and there is less danger of a boilover. When the food has reached the proper stage of doneness— sometimes indicated by its rising to the top of the fat—lift the basket out of the fat (some fryers have automatic raisers that work on timers), and allow the food to drain for a moment. Then carefully spill the basket contents into a pan, or place them on absorbent paper. Serve the food hot. If it must be held before service, keep it in a dry, warm place or under an infrared lamp. Salt just prior to serving, since salt destroys crispness.

Most frying fats have minimal flavor carryover from one food fried in the fryer to the next. However, some foods such as fish can impart a strong flavor to the fat, and french-fried potatoes made afterward may take on a somewhat fishy flavor. Some operations have two or more fryers because of this. Others may deep-fry the strong-flavored item in a pan over the hot plate and not risk contaminating the fat in the main deep-fat fryer with a fishy flavor. Figure 3-3 shows debris from a fryer whose fat needs to be filtered.

Some operations use a pressure fryer, which is equipped with a lid that is closed after the food has been added. Steam develops, creating steam pressure in the chamber and cooking the food item more rapidly. Thus, chicken can be cooked in a shorter time and be more tender and flavorful. It is necessary in using a pressure fryer to observe cooking times accurately to avoid overcooking. Frying temperatures may be somewhat lower, too.

FIGURE 3-3. Sediment and materials that have collected in a deep-fat fryer. Such impurities cause fat to break down faster and produce off-flavored food.

Sweating

At times food may be put into fat that is cooler than that used for frying and allowed to stew. This process is known as *sweating*.

☐ Seasoning Food

A good cook has to know how to taste and season food so that it tastes right and is flavored correctly. Therefore, the short order cook must understand something about the basic factors underlying taste and flavor and about how foods should taste. The cook should be a discriminating taster and should know when a flavor is correct and when it is not.

We have only four kinds of taste buds, and most of these are located on the tongue, but some are also located in the mouth and throat. These four tastes are sweet, sour, bitter, and salty. The Chinese add a fifth, which they call *hot*—the sensation one gets when eating something liberally seasoned with cayenne pepper. Most of our sweet and some of our salt tasting buds are on the tip of the tongue; salt and acid (sour) buds are found around the edges of the tongue; while our bitter taste buds are in the back of the tongue (see Fig. 3-4).

Besides having one or more of these tastes, a food possesses aromas. These are usually volatile essential oils that carry an odor. Often, identical substances are put in perfumes. Aromas are sensed in the

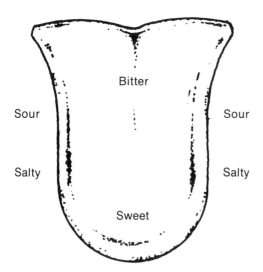

FIGURE 3-4. Regions of the tongue where the four major taste sensations occur.

olfactory nerves. There are hundreds of odors and perhaps thousands of aromas associated with foods, but they are extremely difficult to classify and almost as difficult to describe. People often identify a food by its aroma and not by its taste. Thus, one can hold the nose firmly so that no smell is possible, take a small sip of vanilla, and be unable to identify it by the taste; but if the nose is released, one immediately identifies it as vanilla.

When the taste of a food is combined with its aroma, the result is called *flavor*. For example, the bitterness and other tastes evident in vanilla plus its distinctive aroma constitute its flavor. Flavor is also associated with the texture, consistency, and temperature of the product. The factors contributing to flavor vary with different foods and different conditions.

Cooks can do very little about food aroma, except perhaps by scorching food, but they can do something about taste, because all four tastes can be added. It is also possible to modify one taste by adding another. Thus, if salt is evident in a food, a slight bit of sugar may mask it; and a bit of acid (sourness) might help further.

Most people are more sensitive to sour and bitter tastes than to sweet or salty ones. However, with their reduction in salt intake, many patrons today have become more sensitive to it.

The person who grabs for the salt shaker even before tasting the food has fatigued the salt taste buds to the point where an excess of salt has to be used to make an impression on those buds. Many operations today no longer salt foods during cooking but send them to patrons to do their own salting. A menu note may tell patrons about this and may even explain that a salt substitute is available on the table, should the patron desire to use it in lieu of regular salt. It is all part of trying to satisfy patrons.

Usually foods should be seasoned at the end of a cooking period, just before service. In some cases seasonings may be added at the start of or during the cooking period. At times, it is desirable to introduce flavors from external sources during the cooking period, such as by adding a *bouquet garni* (small bundle of spices and herbs in a small cloth) to a stew or sauce. As was noted earlier, salting meat before cooking it is rarely done because it interferes with browning and only penetrates a short distance into the meat. The cook should add very little seasoning to the food, because the seasoning may become stronger as the liquid cooks down. It may take time for a flavor to develop. For example, if whole spices are used, the flavor takes longer to come into the food than if ground spices are used.

Too much cooking can cause a loss of flavor because many flavors are volatile (that is, they can boil off easily). At times a flavor may be added by a process called *flaming*. Thus, a wine or brandy may be added to the pan and the product heated until the alcohol vaporizes; it does this at 173°F (78.5°C). By tipping the pan as it is held over the fire, the cook can make this vapor catch fire, burning off the escaping alcohol. What remains of the added ingredient is the flavor of the item.

At times, cooks can build flavor into food by soaking a food in a seasoned liquid; an additional result of this treatment may be to tenderize the product, as happens with soaking beef for a period in an acidic liquid to produce a sauerbraten. The soaking liquid is called a *marinade*, and often it is made a part of the cooking liquid of the product in moist-heat cooking. Some vegetable marinades called *vinaigrettes* are used for cold dishes such as salads and hors d'oeuvres.

Marinades are ordinarily made of three substances: oil, an acidic liquid, and seasonings. The oil may be used to preserve moistness; usually a flavorless oil is selected, but sometimes special oils such as olive oil or sesame oil are used to impart a particular flavor. The acid may be vinegar, lemon juice, wine, or some other fruit or vegetable juice. It helps give flavor and may act as a tenderizing medium. Sometimes a flavored acid such as tarragon vinegar may be used to impart a special flavor. Seasonings include items such as spices, herbs, vegetables, or other flavoring products—orange rind, for instance. Some marinades are cooked, which causes a quicker blend of flavors, but uncooked marinades are often seen.

Usually a product is soaked in a marinade for at least an hour and sometimes for days under refrigeration. The bigger the item to be marinated, the longer the process will take. The item should be covered completely by the marinade, and an acid-resistant container should be used to hold both the item and the marinade. Normally the item is turned in the marinade during the soaking period.

□ Preparation Terms

Many terms are used in the kitchen to indicate proper procedures. Some relate to food preparation, while others are used during cooking or other processing methods. It is often important in preparing foods that they be cut into various shapes. These should be uniform in size and neatly done to ensure evenness of cooking and to enhance appearance. Table 3-2 lists some of the more common terms used in food preparation; in addition, many others have been covered previously.

TABLE 3-2. Common Terms in Food Preparation

Term	Meaning
bake	To cook food in dry, hot air, usually in an oven.
beat	To mix vigorously to incorporate air.
blend	To mix two or more ingredients thoroughly.
brush	To clean with a stiff brush; to brush on ingredients such as butter.
burn	To burn sugar on top of a food with a hot poker, as for an omelet; to overbrown butter; to overcaramelize sugar.
butter	To cover with melted or soft solid butter.
chop	To cut into irregularly shaped pieces.
crimp	To make deep gashes on a fish or other food.
crisp	To moisten and refrigerate until crisp; to cook in hot fat until the outer surface is crisp.
emincer	To cut into very thin slices; pronounced "e´-man-say."
en papillote	To bake a food that is wrapped in paper.
flour	To coat with flour; to dredge in flour. (Usually salt, pepper, and other seasonings are added to the flour, and paprika may be added to give color.)
fold	To combine by using two motions; cutting vertically through the mixture, and turning over and over by sliding the implement across the bottom of the mixing bowl with each turn. (Usually the implement is a spatula or whip in a mixer, but with very delicate products, such as butter sponge, the hands should be used.)
glaze	To give food a glossy coating.
grind	To reduce to small particles by grinding.
knead	To work a thick product with a pressing motion by folding and stretching; to work with a mechanical mixer, using a dough hook.
lard	To pull strips of salt pork, bacon or other fat meat through meat prior to cooking it. (A larding needle (*lardoon*) is used to pull the fat through the meat.)
mash	To smash into fine particles.
mask	To cover completely. (Usually applied to a cover of mayonnaise, gravy, or thick sauce, but may refer to a cover of forcemeat or jelly.)
melt	To liquefy, such as by turning a solid fat into an oil by heating.
mince	To chop into fine pieces.
ovenize	To place in an oven to fry; to oven roast.
pare	To trim or cut off the outside covering; compare *peel*.
peel	To remove the outside skin or rind by mechanical means or by heat.
pipe	To place a border around an item.
plank	To broil fish or meat on a plank and then surround it with vegetables and a border of duchess potatoes.
pulp	See *mash*.
render	To free of fat by means of heat.
rice	To force a food through a press that has tiny holes in it, producing a sort of rice.
scallop	To bake food, usually cut in pieces, in a sauce or other liquid, with a top usually composed of buttered crumbs; *au gratin* may be synonymous.

(continued)

TABLE 3-2. (*continued*)

Term	Meaning
score	To cut lightly across an item; to mark lightly, as in scoring an omelet by burning.
sear	To brown the surface by a short application of heavy heat, often to develop color and flavor in meats, fish, or poultry.
shake	To toss vigorously up and down.
shape	To form into a desired pattern either with the hands or with molds.
shirr	To bake, as with eggs.
shred	To cut into thin strips or tear into small pieces.
slice	To cut with a knife or mechanical slicer into thin pieces; not to cut or chop, but to carve.
soak	To immerse for an extended period of time in a liquid in order to rehydrate it; to prevent a food from drying out by immersing it in a liquid; to keep from tarnishing in the air. (It can be a preliminary step in cleaning.)
steep	To allow a substance to stand in liquid below the boiling point for the purpose of extracting flavor, color, or other factors.
stir	To mix ingredients with a circular motion in order to blend them or to obtain a uniform consistency.
toss	To mix by shaking up and down lightly.
turn	To carve or trim in some manner, as with a *turned mushroom* that is carved on top; to turn over a food.

□ Manipulations

The short order cook must be able to perform a number of skilled manipulations. Knowing how to do these is perhaps even more important than understanding the terms that describe them—although not much more. Some of the more important and common manipulations are discussed next.

Finishing

Soups, sauces, and other liquid preparations are sometimes given a final preparation treatment called *finishing*. Little or nothing is done to the food after such treatment. Thus a sauce may be finished with the final addition of a bit of cream, butter, a liaison (a mixture of egg yolks and cream), or some wine. After adding a finishing mixture, the cook does not boil the item but only brings it to a serving temperature. If the product is boiled, the smoothness in flavor obtained is lost; and if boiling occurs after the addition of a liaison, the egg yolks may curdle and ruin the product. Often in using a liaison, the cook will slowly add some of the hot mixture to the egg yolks and cream while stirring well, and then add this combination to the hot mixture while stirring vigorously to incorporate the liaison mixture before it cooks. Figure 3-5 shows how this is done.

Flipping

Flipping is a common manipulation in short order cooking. It is done during sautéing or pan frying. The pan must have slanted sides so that the food in the pan can be guided up and then given the impetus to move up and turn over, falling back into the pan. The manipulation takes considerable skill and dexterity.

To flip an item, lift the handle of the pan and give it a slight shake or jerk to move the item to the front edge of the pan. Now, with a sudden movement, direct this edge upward, causing the item to slide up the edge and turn over. This movement is done more with the wrist than with the arm. The cook must be sure to move the pan back far enough to catch the item as it comes down. If eggs are flipped this way in making them "over easy," care must be taken to do the flipping gently so as not to break the yolks. Figure 3-6 shows this manipulation.

Roux

Knowing how to use a roux is an important bit of knowledge for a short order cook. A roux is a mixture of fat and flour in equal parts by weight

(a)   **(b)**

FIGURE 3-5. Adding a liaison to a hot sauce in two steps: (a) Some of the hot mixture is put into the liaison and then thoroughly mixed in. (b) This mixture is added to the hot mixture and blended in thoroughly with a wire whip.

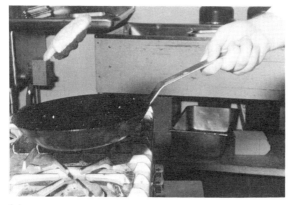

(a)

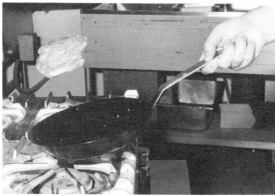

(b)

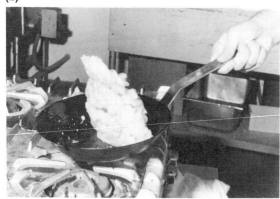

(c)

FIGURE 3-6. Flipping foods in a pan. (a) The solid breaded cutlet is sent upward and turning by a deft, quick up-and-pull-back motion. (b) The pan is moved back and under the cutlet to catch it. (c) Loose objects are not lifted as high with the same movements—note them here as they land in the pan turning over. (*Photos by Michael Upright*)

used to thicken liquid items such as soups and sauces. The fats used are clarified butter, clarified margarine, animal fats such as chicken, beef, or lard, vegetable oil, and shortening. The liquid in melted butter or margarine must be separated from any suspended material by pouring off the melted fat. If this is not done, the liquid can thicken the flour in making a roux and cause problems. The separating process is called *clarification*. Butter makes a roux that has a pleasant flavor; margarine, a roux that is slightly less so. Animal fats can made a good roux but have a flavor that may or may not be good for the product. The roux should be suited to the basic flavor of the liquid to be thickened. Vegetable oil and shortening contribute little flavor.

The flour used should have a high starch content. Bread flour has less starch than pastry flour, and all-purpose flour is in between these two in starch content. Sometimes the flour is prebrowned in an oven before being used. There are two degrees of browning: light and heavy. While it takes only 10 ounces of pastry flour to give 1 gallon of liquid a medium thickening, it takes 18 ounces of lightly browned flour and 32 ounces of a heavily browned flour, since the browning destroys some of the starch's thickening power. Acids also reduce starch's thickening power, by destroying some of the starch, so more flour must be used with acidic liquids. Meat sauces are slightly acidic, so they must have a bit more flour than, say, milk sauces. Often if vinegar or lemon juice that must be added to a sauce can be withheld until late in the process, it is added after thickening has occurred. Acid in a sauce that is held at a hot temperature continues to break down starch as the sauce sits. Disproportionately more flour must be used when making a large batch of an item than a smaller one. It seems that larger batches may not rise as high in temperature as a smaller one and so more flour must be used to obtain the same degree of thickening.

To make a roux, the cook melts fat in a sauce pan, adds the correct amount of flour to it, and thoroughly mixes the two. Gentle heat is applied while the roux is stirred. To make a white roux, the roux is cooked for about 10 minutes or until it is frothy, chalky, and slightly gritty. A blond roux is cooked a bit longer and has a cream color. A brown roux is cooked until the roux is light brown and has a nutty aroma. Care must be taken to not char the roux at this point. Often heavily browned flour is used to make this roux, in order to reduce the amount of time the roux must be over the fire.

Some operations make roux in large batches to last a week or so. When this is done, the process usually is transferred to an oven, and a large roasting pan is used. The roux is stirred frequently while the oven is kept at about 375°F (190°C).

Unless a roux is properly added to a liquid, problems such as lumping can occur. Normally, a cold roux is added to a hot liquid or a hot roux is added to a cold liquid. Adding a hot roux to a hot liquid may cause lumping unless the roux is very vigorously stirred in. Combining a cold liquid and a cold roux leaves the roux in pieces, and lumping may occur if the heat comes up quickly. After adding a roux, good stirring must be maintained until thickening occurs. It is desirable to cook the liquid for about 10 minutes so as to complete the thickening and develop a desirable flavor.

The reason the fat is incorporated with the flour is to separate the flour particles so that they cannot cling together and cause lumping. Making the roux surrounds every flour particle with fat so clumping is not possible. Figure 3-7 shows how to add a cold roux to a hot liquid and how to add a hot liquid to a cold roux. Chapter 4 discusses the use of other thickening agents.

(a)

(b)

FIGURE 3-7. Methods for combining roux and liquids: (a) Adding a cold roux to a hot liquid. (b) Adding a hot liquid to a cold roux.

Turning

A short order cook does a lot of work involving the manipulation called *turning*. A spatula or turner is the tool normally used to do this. In griddle work and in sautéing or frying items such as hash browns, eggs, steaks, and hamburgers, turning is required. The manipulation is made by first giving a gentle thrust under the item so that enough of the item lies on top of the spatula or turner to ensure that everything will come with the turn. Then, with a slight twist of the wrist, the cook turns the material over. In the case of eggs "over easy," the turn must be very gentle so as not to break the yolks. Other turns must be made carefully to avoid scattering the items, as could happen with hash browns. At times, turning may be performed by the cook using a fork or tongs.

□ Mise en Place

Mise en place was mentioned in Chapter 1 as consisting of getting ready for the meal hour and keeping one's work area organized and clean during food production. *Mise en place* is so important in short order work that it is included here in a discussion of cooking techniques.

Upon coming on shift, one has a good idea of what has to be done during the shift. However, details must be filled in. The menu should be consulted to confirm what items have to be prepared and what readying of these items has to take place in order for preparation to be fast and for quality to be retained. In some operations, it may be advisable to check in with the chef or the sous-chef. Some operations set up a work schedule for the various kitchen sections, indicating what items must be produced and often what their quantity should be (perhaps based on a forecast).

Certain reports may also have to be completed during the shift, such as a *red meat report* indicating the usage of expensive items such as steaks and lobsters. If such a form must be completed at the end of the shift, specifying the number of each expensive item prepared, an original inventory is needed. This may consist of "on hand" and "issued to" categories, yielding a total for use during the shift. Subtracting the number prepared of each item from the total inventory yields the number of items remaining on inventory at the end of the shift.

Once the meal service period begins, there is little time to do basic preparations; consequently, the short order cook should have everything possible done before the rush time starts so that items can be processed rapidly. Preliminary preparations may include breading, parboiling, pre-cooking, and preparing some recipes such as for hotcakes, hollandaise sauce, boiled rice, or corn fritters to go with Maryland fried chicken. One quality control measure that should be in place in the operation is that foods should not be preprepared unless such prepreparation results in a product that, when finally finished, has the desired quality. Some cooks like to "sandbag"—that is, to prepare a lot ahead of time "just to be sure." This practice should not be permitted unless such preparation is needed to carry over during a big rush or orders and unless the quality of the finished product is adequate to satisfy patrons.

To know how to proceed in organizing work, the cook must look at each menu item to be prepared and break it down into its stages of production. For example, if one expects to have a sizable amount of french-fried potatoes, it might be well to preblanch some potatoes—if not to use frozen preprocessed potatoes—so as to have a fairly good supply of precooked potatoes on hand for processing potato orders rapidly. Second, the cook must know what can and cannot be done beforehand without loss of quality. Remember that nothing should be preprepared that will not satisfy the patron. Final cooking of items should occur as close as possible to service, to retain maximum freshness.

The cook should know which elements of food preparation or of a recipe can be done ahead of time, leaving only the last-minute manipulations to be done when the order comes in. The quality of many items, such as baked potatoes, hamburgers, and sautéed fish, depends on their last-minute preparation. A potato baked too far ahead of service sits steaming and losing its lightness of texture; when finally served, it is far inferior to a potato that has come hot from the oven and when opened gives a burst of lightness from the sudden release of steam developed during roasting.

Some things can be started even as the overall processing continues and other preparations are proceeding. Good short order cooks are able to organize and have all of these *mise en place* things going on simultaneously. A key point is to know what foods can be prepared for service and held without deterioration of quality and which ones cannot. Many soups and sauces can be preprepared and held without any loss of quality, but mashed potatoes prepared 30 minutes ahead of service time may congeal into a product that no one could be proud of. Again, the cook must know how long it takes to prepare various items so that they all come out at the time of desired service.

Finally, remember to keep the workplace organized and cleaned up. Too many novices in the short order position fail to observe this rule and instead allow disorganization and confusion to defeat their ability to produce good foods. A good cook automatically clears away things that may interfere with future work efforts.

□ Summary

Foods may be cooked by either moist- or dry-heat processes. Moist-heat methods include boiling, simmering, stewing, parboiling, poaching, blanching, steaming, and braising. Reducing and deglazing also use moisture to achieve their purpose. Boiling consists of cooking liquids with boiling water. Simmering involves letting the cooking liquid reach a boiling point but not allowing bubbles of steam to break the top; thus it is a very gentle boil. Stewing is boiling or simmering in a moderate amount of water. Parboiling is partially cooking food in water. Blanching is an even slighter partial cooking in water. Steaming is cooking by steam, which is hotter than water and therefore cooks faster. Regular normal-pressure steamers may be used for this purpose, or pressure steamers (which speed up the cooking time even more) can be used. Sometimes food may be braised *blond* style, in which the food item is not browned. *Brun* refers to browning the item before braising. Reducing is a method in which the liquid in a pan is boiled to get rid of some of it. Deglazing is a method of adding a liquid to food materials that have collected on the bottom of a container, in order to extract them.

Dry heat methods include broiling, grilling, pan broiling, barbecuing, roasting, baking, sautéing (frying or pan frying), deep-fat frying, and sweating. Some of these methods use radiant heat primarily, while others use conductive or convective heat.

Broiling involves subjecting foods to radiant heat. The cook must know how to manage the equipment to meet the cooking needs of the product. Some items that are broiled may be planked afterward, and the cook should know how to perform this technique properly. Grilling is a broiling method in which the food item is placed over the heat source. Pan broiling consists of cooking items in a dry pan over fairly high heat. Roasting is cooking foods in an oven using convective heat to cook the product. Investigations have shown that searing (cooking the outside of a meat at high heat) does not reduce the meat's shrinkage or moisture loss. It may increase the flavor by creating a caramelization of the surface materials. Trivets are used to raise a roast above its juices. A *mirepoix* is a group of chopped vegetables often used to season a roast. Delayed-service cookery of meat products is a method in which the meat product is cooked at very low temperature to a desired degree of doneness and then held at a low temperature for service. Barbecuing is roasting in which a tangy sauce is basted over the product so as to give it a special flavor. Sometimes barbecuing is combined with broiling, while at other times it may involve pit roasting, with the tangy sauce added afterward.

Sautéing, pan frying, and frying are much the same. Each describes cooking in a small quantity of fat. The product may be covered and braised afterward. Deep-fat frying is frying in a large quantity of fat with the product immersed in the fat or floating at the surface. It is necessary to follow proper procedures in order to get a good deep-fried product. These procedures vary, depending on the fat temperature, the ratio of food to fat, the type of food, the length of cooking time, the size of the item, and the type of outer coating it has. Foods that stick to the basket should be slid into the hot fat carefully. It is best not to salt deep-fried foods until just before service. Some fish products can flavor a fat, so if these are cooked in the fat, it may only be usable afterward to fry similar products. Some fryers cook under pressure, which serves to tenderize the food as it fries. Sweating is a method of allowing a food to stew in relatively cool fat. It is not a commonly used process.

Understanding the basic factors underlying the flavor of food is helpful in understanding how to season foods properly. Foods must be properly seasoned to be good, and the short order cook has to be knowledgeable about seasoning as well as about cooking. People can taste only four things—sweet, sour, salty, and bitter—but they can detect a wide array of aromas. When taste is combined with aroma, the result is flavor; good seasoning depends on a proper combination of these. It is possible to modify the taste of a food by combining it with another taste, but little can be done about aromas, other than adding spices or other ingredients that add aroma to foods. Usually foods are seasoned at the end of a cooking period. It is also possible to add flavor by means of techniques such as flaming or marinading. Because many patrons today wish to reduce their salt intake, many operations do not salt foods during preparation but allow patrons to do it themselves.

A short order cook must know the meaning of many cooking items in order to perform the work required. Knowing what the terms mean and how to proceed in performing them correctly is essential.

Short order cooks also need to be able to perform various manipulations that involve considerable skill. Finishing is a process in which a liquid such as cream, butter, liaison, or wine is added to a sauce, soup, or other item at the end of its preparation. This gives the product smoothness and improved flavor. Turning is a method of slipping a thin, blunt tool such as a spatula underneath a product and, with a deft twist of the wrist, turning the item over. Flipping involves maneuvering the pan so as to toss the item up in the air while at the same time giving it momentum so that it turns over.

Knowing how to prepare and use a roux is an important part of a short order cook's knowledge. A roux is a mixture of equal parts fat and flour. It acts as a thickener when added to soups, sauces, or other liquids to thicken them. Various fats may be used to prepare roux, and each has advantages and disadvantages that the cook should know. The kind of flour used is also important. A high-starch flour provides the most effective thickening. A roux should be prepared by melting the fat, adding the flour, and cooking for 10 minutes to get rid of any raw taste in the product.

Sometimes flour is lightly or heavily prebrowned for roux. This process adds flavor and color but destroys some of the thickening power of the flour; acidic foods also have this antithickening effect. A common or regular roux is very white but chalky and frothy in appearance when done. It has a slightly gritty texture. A blond roux is cooked until the roux is a cream color. A brown roux is cooked until the color is light brown; care must be taken not to burn brown roux.

Mise en place is a work process in which the worker organizes in advance the work to be done and makes sure that the work area is kept clean and organized during the work period. It is necessary to plan ahead. Upon coming on shift, the cook should set up the entire day's work plan, reading the work to be done. Things that can be done to prepare items ahead of time without loss of quality on service should be done. It takes experience and good planning to do a good job of *mise en place.*

□ CHAPTER REVIEW □

1. What is cooking by moist heat, and why is it done?
2. Name at least five moist-heat cooking methods.
3. What is the difference between boiling and simmering?
4. What is the difference between blanching and parboiling?
5. Why does steam under pressure cook faster than unpressurized steam coming off boiling water?
6. What is cooking by dry heat, and what kind of meats are cooked by this method?
7. When the temperature reaches 6,000°F (3,316°C), what kind of heat is produced? What do we call this heat?
8. What three kinds of heat are used in cooking foods?
9. If a steak has broiler marks on it that look like #, how many turns has this side had?
10. Describe how to pan broil a well-marbled steak.
11. What is the difference between roasting and barbecuing?

12. Match the description in the column on the right with the proper word in the left column:

sear — To broil a steak and put it on a board, surrounding it with vegetables and a border of duchess potatoes.

mirepoix — A utensil that holds fish in broiling.

trivet — To cook the outside surface of a meat at high heat.

plank — A mixture of vegetables.

double grid — To brown.

brun — An underliner placed beneath a roast to keep the roast out of its own juices.

13. Mark each of the following statements True or False:
   a. A thick piece of meat can be partially broiled and then placed into an oven to be finished.
   b. Braising is a dry-heat method.
   c. A *sauteuse* is a pan in which a meat item can be fried.
   d. Grilling is cooking on a griddle.
   e. Deglazing is a method of putting encrusted materials at the bottom of a pan into solution, using a liquid.

14. Name seven factors that a cook should know when deep-frying foods.

15. How many tastes do we have, what are they, and where are they located?

16. What is flavor?

17. When are many cooked foods seasoned?

18. Describe the process of flaming.

19. Define the following cooking terms: *burn, fold, lard, ovenize, scallop, score, shake, steep, toss*.

20. What is the difference between flipping and turning?

21. How is a roux made? What is a common roux? a blond roux? a brown roux?

22. Why must one use more brown roux than regular roux to get the same thickness?

23. What is *mise en place*?

CHAPTER FOUR

Principles of Short Order Cooking

□ Recipes

Few builders would attempt to build a house without having a set of plans to guide them. Likewise, few cooks should try to make a food item without having a recipe to guide them—not unless the preparation is relatively simple (such as frying two eggs) or unless they have memorized the recipe.

Recipes are guides that enable the cook to produce items of desirable quality and quantity at a desirable cost. Recipes are a strong base on which the cook can stand and be assured of doing a satisfactory job. They also increase the chance that, each time a specific food is produced, it is the same.

However, a recipe cannot stand alone. The person using it must know the basic principles and techniques required to bring about the results desired. Upon picking up a recipe, the cook should know how to proceed in order to complete it. The cook must also recognize that ingredients can vary and must be able to make changes in a recipe. Experience and knowledge are essential in using the recipe. The cook must be able to look at the food being prepared and know that the product is going to come out satisfactorily. For example, a hotcake recipe may call for a standard proportion of flour to liquid, but sometimes the flour used may have greater or less absorptive power on the liquid than usual, and as a result the batter may come out a bit too thick or too thin. The cook should realize this and adjust the batter by adding more flour if it is too thin or more liquid if it is too stiff.

A good standardized recipe (one that produces a known product of known quality and quantity at a known cost) should contain the following information:

1. The name of the recipe and its code number.

2. The total yield, the number of portions, and the size of each portion.
3. The ingredients, in order of use, in weight and measure.
4. Equipment needed, such as measuring equipment, pans (by size), and portioning equipment.
5. Instructions for using the ingredients, grouped as they are used.
6. Cooking times and other directions for getting proper results.
7. Directions for portioning, plating, and garnishing the item.
8. Substitutions or other changes that might be made to produce a slightly different product.

Following is an example of a standardized recipe for making cornbread.

□ Southern Cornbread, Pioneer Style

Yield: Twenty-five 2-oz portions   **Portion:** One 2 × 2 in. piece

Ingredients	Weight	Measure	Procedure
Cornmeal	1 lb	1 qt	1. Blend dry ingredients
Salt		2 t	together.
Soda		2 t	
Eggs	4 eggs	¾ c	2. Beat eggs until well blended.
Buttermilk or sour milk	2 lb	1 qt	Add milk and blend well.
			3. Add liquid to dry ingredients and blend together.
			4. Heat oven to 450°F (232°C). Pour batter into generously buttered pans, muffin cups, or corn stick pans. Bake panned batter for 20 to 25 minutes or muffins or corn sticks for 10 to 15 minutes or until just set.

In using a recipe, unless it is known, read it over carefully, noting how the ingredients are to be used and what amounts are needed. Check to see that all the ingredients needed are on hand and that the equipment, utensils, and tools needed are there. Do all of the preparations and assemblies before you begin processing the recipe.

A cook should know several things about weighing and measuring ingredients. First, a pint is not "a pound the world around." A pint of flour weighs ½ pound; a pint of molasses weighs more than 1 pound. Weighing is the most accurate measurement, but some recipes do not provide the necessary data on this, instead giving only the volume measure. Some things such as brown sugar must be packed into the measure, while flour should be lightly sifted beforehand or only lightly mixed. Before measuring baking powder, baking soda, or other items for which a small difference in measuring might make a big difference in the final product, stir it to make it light. All measurements should be level full.

Second, if measurements such as 3½ cups of shortening are called for, be sure to pack the shortening into the measure so that no big air expanses are there, causing it to fall short of the desired amount.

Third, know the number of teaspoons in a tablespoon (3), tablespoons in a cup (16), cups in a pint (2), cups in a quart (4), cups in a gallon (16), pints in a quart (2), quarts in a gallon (4), and so on.

Fourth, know what makes a portion. An 8-ounce steak is not a big one to some patrons; a 16-ounce steak is, but bone can make a difference. A good-sized portion of vegetables is about 3 ounces, which amounts to one rounded baking spoon of vegetables. A good portion of potatoes is about 5 ounces. An adequate portion of fish without bone, skin, or other waste is about 5 ounces. A rasher of bacon may consist of from three to six strips, according to management's definition. A three-egg omelet is enough for a healthy eater, but a one- or two-egg omelet may be adequate for a lighter eater. There's a lot to knowing how much most people want and what it takes to satisfy it. In a facility that serves young truck drivers or others who have demanding appetites, the order must be large; whereas in a different type of operation, the order may be different. Recipes may thus have to be modified according to the nature of the operation.

Fifth, recipes are standardized according to standard types of ingredients used in foodservices. Thus, *large* eggs are the standard size when a recipe specifies using a certain number of eggs. Bread flour is needed for rolls and yeast breads, but pastry or cake flour may be needed in other instances, depending on the recipe and product.

Recipe Conversion
Cooks are often required to make conversions on recipes and this at times can be challenging. Suppose that a recipe for 25 portions is to be translated into 100 portions. The calculation is not difficult because every ingredient is multiplied by a factor of 4 (100/25 = 4). (The multiplying factor of 4 was obtained by dividing the present amount into the required amount.) A more difficult calculation would be to translate a recipe for 25 portions into one for 35 portions. The result is 35/25 = 1.4. To decrease a recipe, the rule is the same: *divide the present amount into the required amount.* Thus, if one were to reduce a 100-portion recipe to 25, the multiplying factor would be 0.25 (25/100 = 0.25). Similarly, if one wanted to decrease a recipe for 35 down to 25, the calculation would be 25/35 = 0.7142857, which one might reduce to 0.7 to make the multiplication simpler.

An example of these calculations can be shown for a hotcake recipe for 25 portions of three hotcakes per portion raised to 100 portions. The 25-portion list of ingredients is as follows:

Flour, pastry	2 lb (2 qt)	× 4	= 8 lb (8 qt)
Baking powder, double-acting	1 oz (3 T)	× 4	= 4 oz
Salt	⅓ oz (2 t)	× 4	= 1⅓ oz (8 t)
Sugar, granulated	1¾ oz	× 4	= 7 oz
Eggs	12 oz (1½ c)	× 4	= 3 lb (3 pt)*
Milk, low-fat	1½ qt	× 4	= 6 qt (1½ gal)
Oil, vegetable	½ c	× 4	= 2 c (1 pt)

The resulting amounts for 100 portions are not difficult to measure, except that perhaps the salt should be made 1¼ ounces instead of 1⅓ ounces, since the scale possibly has only ¼-ounce gradations. The difference is minor.

An example of reducing a recipe can be shown for decreasing a recipe of 35 portions of beef gravy to 25 portions:

Beef fat	5 oz × 0.7	= 3.5 (3½) oz
Flour, pastry	5 oz × 0.7	= 3.5 (3½) oz
Beef stock and pan drippings	2 qt × 0.7	= 1.4 qt (1 qt + 1⅔ c)

The resulting quantities are not difficult to measure, except that one might have difficulty in arriving at 0.4 quart of beef stock and drippings. The solution would be to break this quantity down into cups. Since 1 quart contains 4 cups, 4 c × 0.4 = 1.6 c, which could be made into 1⅔ cups, so the quantity of stock and drippings would be 1 qt + 1⅔ c. Table 4-1 lists some of the common measures used in food preparation.

The Metric System

Sometimes recipes list ingredients in metric amounts rather than in U.S. units. Usually this poses no problem, since it is just as easy to work completely in the metric system as to work completely in the U.S. system, once one becomes used to it. As a matter of fact, it is easier to work with the metric system than with U.S. units because everything in it is based on decimals. Thus, recipe conversion is much easier. One does not have to worry about converting ounces into pounds, tablespoons into cups, cups into pints, pints into quarts, and quarts into gallons. It is also very easy to make a transition from weight to liquid measure or vice versa, since 1 gram (g) equals 1 milliliter (ml) or liquid and 1 liter (l)

---

*Note that 4 × 12 oz = 48 oz, which, when divided by 16 ounces in a pound, equals 3 pounds.

equals 1 kilogram (kg) or 1,000 grams. Tables 4-2, 4-3, and 4-4 list information relevant to the metric system.

The metric system uses the Celsius system for temperatures. This is also a decimal system, with 0°C at the freezing point of water and 100°C at the boiling point of water. Sometimes it is necessary to convert Celsius degrees to Fahrenheit degrees or vice versa. Table 4-5 lists many Celsius/

TABLE 4-1. Abbreviations and Amounts of Common Measures

Abbreviations							
t	= teaspoon	pt	= pint	pk	= peck	lb	= pound
T	= tablespoon	qt	= quart	bu	= bushel		
c	= cup	gal	= gallon	oz	= ounce		

Amounts		
Measure	Equivalent	Liquid Weight
3 t	= 1 T	= ½ oz
16 T	= 1 c	= 8 oz
2 c	= 1 pt	= 1 lb or 16 oz
4 c	= 1 qt	= 2 lb or 32 oz
2 pt	= 1 qt	= 2 lb or 32 oz
4 qt	= 1 gal	= 8 lb or 128 oz
8 pt	= 1 gal	= 8 lb or 128 oz
16 c	= 1 gal	= 8 lb or 128 oz
2 gal	= 1 pk	= 16 lb
4 pk	= 1 bu	= 64 lb

TABLE 4-2. The Metric System

Quality	Unit	Abbreviation
weight	gram	g
volume	liter	l
length	meter	m
temperature	degree Celsius	°C

TABLE 4-3. Metric Divisions and Multiples

Prefix	Value	Example
milli-	one thousandth	1 millimeter = 0.001 meter
centi-	one hundredth	1 centimeter = 0.01 meter
deci-	one tenth	1 decimeter = 0.1 meter
kilo-	1,000 times	1 kilometer = 1,000 meters

TABLE 4-4. Conversion Scales for Weights and Liquid Measures

Weights					
½ oz	=	14 grams	9 oz	=	254 grams
¾ oz	=	21 g	10 oz	=	283 g
1 oz	=	28 g	11 oz	=	311 g
1½ oz	=	43 g	12 oz	=	340 g
1¾ oz	=	50 g	13 oz	=	368 g
2 oz	=	57 g	14 oz	=	396 g
2½ oz	=	71 g	15 oz	=	425 g
2¾ oz	=	78 g			
3 oz	=	85 g	1 lb	=	453g
3½ oz	=	99 g	1¼ lb	=	566 g
4 oz	=	114 g	1½ lb	=	679 g
5 oz	=	142 g	1¾ lb	=	792 g
6 oz	=	170 g	2 lb	=	905 g
7 oz	=	199 g	2¼ lb	=	1018 g
8 oz	=	226 g			

Liquid Measures			
1 teaspoon	= 0.005 liters	1½ cups	= 0.36 liters
1 tablespoon	= 0.015 l	1¾ cups	= 0.42 l
2 tablespoons	= 0.03 l		
¼ cup	= 0.06 l	1 US pint	= 0.47 l
½ cup	= 0.12 l	1¼ US pt	= 0.60 l
¾ cup	= 0.18 l	1½ US pt	= 0.72 l
1 cup	= 0.24 l	1¾ US pt	= 0.83 l
1¼ cups	= 0.30 l	1 US quart	= 0.94 l

Fahrenheit equivalents, so they do not have to be calculated. The actual method for converting Celsius to Fahrenheit is as follows:

multiply the °C by 9/5 or 1.8, and add 32°F.

Conversely, to convert Fahrenheit into Celsius, one does the following:

subtract 32° from the °F, and multiply the result by 5/9 or 0.555.

Thus, to convert 60°C to Fahrenheit:

$$60°C \times 1.8 = 108° + 32° = 140°F.$$

And to convert 182°F to Celsius:

$$182° - 32° = 150° \times 0.555 = 83.25°C$$

□ Food Facts

Different foods react differently in cooking. A starch in the presence of moisture swells. The protein in an egg becomes firm. A fat melts and when the temperature gets too high breaks down. Cooks need to know these reactions so that they can achieve desired results. Some reactions are delicate and complex, and unless the cook knows how to handle them and how to take proper precautions, trouble can develop.

TABLE 4-5. Fahrenheit/Celsius Temperature Equivalents

−40°F = −40°C	120°F = 49°C	320°F = 160°C
−30°F = −34°C	125°F = 52°C	330°F = 166°C
−20°F = −29°C	130°F = 54°C	340°F = 171°C
−10°F = −23°C	135°F = 57°C	350°F = 177°C
−5°F = −21°C	140°F = 60°C	360°F = 182°C
0°F = −18°C	145°F = 63°C	370°F = 188°C
5°F = −15°C	150°F = 66°C	380°F = 193°C
10°F = −12°C	155°F = 68°C	390°F = 199°C
15°F = −9°C	160°F = 71°C	400°F = 204°C
20°F = −6°C	165°F = 74°C	410°F = 210°C
25°F = −4°C	170°F = 77°C	420°F = 216°C
30°F = −1°C	175°F = 79°C	430°F = 221°C
32°F = 0°C	180°F = 82°C	440°F = 227°C
35°F = 2°C	185°F = 85°C	450°F = 232°C
40°F = 4°C	190°F = 88°C	460°F = 238°C
45°F = 7°C	195°F = 91°C	470°F = 243°C
50°F = 10°C	200°F = 93°C	480°F = 249°C
55°F = 13°C	205°F = 96°C	490°F = 254°C
60°F = 16°C	210°F = 99°C	500°F = 260°C
65°F = 18°C	212°F = 100°C	510°F = 266°C
70°F = 21°C	220°F = 104°C	520°F = 271°C
75°F = 24°C	230°F = 110°C	530°F = 277°C
80°F = 27°C	240°F = 116°C	540°F = 282°C
85°F = 29°C	250°F = 121°C	550°F = 288°C
90°F = 32°C	260°F = 127°C	560°F = 293°C
95°F = 35°C	270°F = 132°C	570°F = 299°C
100°F = 38°C	280°F = 137°C	580°F = 304°C
105°F = 41°C	290°F = 143°C	590°F = 310°C
110°F = 43°C	300°F = 149°C	600°F = 316°C
115°F = 46°C	310°F = 154°C	

Starches

Starch has the property of swelling in the presence of moisture and heat. In cooking this tends to thicken (or gelatinize) the liquid in which the starch is placed. Starches start to thicken at around 144° to 162°F (62° to 72°C) and finish at around 203°F (95°C). Waxy maize starch starts to thicken at around 155° to 167°F (68° to 75°C), and no second thickening occurs; if this starch is heated above 195°F (91°C), a slight thinning occurs. Failure to cook starches sufficiently may impart graininess and a raw starch flavor to the final product.

The starch in foods varies. Flour consists of from 63 to 73 percent starch, and this starch is the same as that found in corn, arrowroot, and tapioca. However, other substances in these flours cause different reactions. Flour also contains proteins that produce a sort of cloudy paste. The greater the proportion of starch and the lower the proportion of protein in the flour, the clearer the resulting paste. Arrowroot gives a very firm and fairly clear paste. Tapioca starch has a sort of stringiness to it, but the paste is fairly clear. Cornstarch forms a moderately firm paste that is fairly clear. All of these starches are thinner when warm than when cool.

Another kind of starch is waxy maize or converted starch. It is very clear and does not set up into a firm paste when cooled. Instead, it remains about as thick when cold as when hot. Because of its soft qualities and its bright clearness, this starch is used for berry pies and other preparations where it is desirable to show the foods in the paste. Waxy maize starch is not good for cream pies, starch-thickened puddings, and the like; but flour, cornstarch, arrowroot and others work well in these preparations, because they set up a firm paste that holds its shape. Waxy-maize starch forms a paste that does not curdle when frozen and thawed and so is often used in foods to be frozen.

Acid breaks down starch. Therefore, if the liquid into which a starch is placed is acidic, more starch must be used. Heat promotes such breakdown, too, so some acids are not put into products until after the thickening has occurred and the product has cooled down somewhat.

There are about 770 billion starch granules in 1 pound of cornstarch. These granules are insoluble in cold water, but in hot water they swell. If enough are in the liquid, this swelling causes them to crowd against each other, thickening the liquid. However, the starch granules must be separated before being added to a hot liquid. This can be accomplished by separating the granules with oil or fat, as in roux. Alternatively, they can be mixed with sugar and added. Sometimes cooks mix starch with a liquid, producing a *slurry* which they then add slowly to a hot liquid while stirring vigorously. The paste that results from a flour-and-liquid slurry does not taste as smooth as a roux-and-liquid mixture. When a slurry is used, some of the hot mixture to be thickened can be added to the slurry and mixed in well, and then this mixture can be stirred vigorously into the larger mass of hot liquid (see Fig. 4-1).

Emulsions

A number of common emulsions are used in foodservice. For example, both mayonnaise and French dressing are emulsions, although the latter is an unstable one. Gravy and many sauces, including hollandaise sauce and some of its derivatives, are emulsions, too. A cake batter is an emulsion. Cooking uses oil-in-water emulsions, which means that the oil is present in small globules surrounded by a water phase. In making mayonnaise or hollandaise sauce, the cook first beats the eggs and then

FIGURE 4-1. Some of the hot mixture in the lower container has been added to the upper slurry and mixed in well. This mixture is now being poured back into the main hot mixture to complete the thickening process.

gradually beats in the oil for the mayonnaise or the melted butter for the hollandaise sauce. Water is the *continuous phase*, while oil is the *broken phase* (divided by the liquid). When the continuous phase holds, the emulsion is termed *stable*, but when the continuous phase breaks down and the oil separates from the water phase, the emulsion is *unstable*; such an emulsion only forms when the mixture is shaken vigorously, as may be done with French dressing. A mayonnaise is an example of a stable emulsion. Sometimes when a sauce or gravy that has a fairly high amount of oil or fat in emulsified form is heated to a high heat, some of the oil or fat separates. In such a case, it may be necessary to beat the product well to reincorporate the escaped fat or oil. Emulsifiers include whole egg, egg yolk, starch pastes, agar, tragacanth, hydrophilic colloids, gelatin, casein, gum arabic, pectins, Irish moss, and condensed milk. The Food and Drug Administration regulates what emulsifiers can be put into foods.

Vegetables

Many reactions produce good-tasting or attractive vegetables, while many others can produce bad-tasting or unattractive vegetables. Vegetables are on the ascendancy as a food, because they can be made into good appetizing products while contributing valuable nutrients and fiber. Color and texture are important factors in winning patron approval for what is served, and cooks can do much to preserve these qualities and ensure that the vegetables reaching patrons meet with their approval.

Color The color of cooked vegetables should be true, bright and fresh. Good fresh vegetables, freshly cooked, make excellent accompaniments to a meal. Today the mode is to undercook vegetables slightly, which helps to preserve their flavor, color, texture, and nutritional value. Vegetables may be classified generally as red, white, green, or yellow/orange. Bright, fresh colors signify better texture, color, flavor, and nutrition.

Red vegetables are usually colored by pigments called *anthocyanins* or *lycopenes*. Beets, plums, and many other foods contain anthocyanins. To produce bright red products with these vegetables after cooking, the reaction should be acidic. Thus, beets are often prepared in an acidic medium because this turns the anthocyanins in the beets a bright red. Anthocyanins are water soluble.

Carotenes are substances that the body uses to make vitamin A. Carrots, yellow squash, peaches, and cantaloupe contain carotenes and owe their particular color to them. Another type of carotene is lycopene, which is red and is found in tomatoes. *Lycopene* does not react as anthocyanins do, so it is stable in both acidic and alkaline surroundings. It is also nonsoluble in water and is difficult to destroy in cooking.

White vegetables such as potatoes and cauliflower contain a pigment called *flavone* that turns white in an acidic medium and yellow in an alkaline one. Placing just a bit of soda into the cooking water of boiling onions produces a yellow color so deep that one can dye Easter eggs in it. Conversely, adding a bit of cream of tartar (tartaric acid) to a mashed potato mixture turns the flavones in the potatoes a very bright white. Sometimes, however, an acid can cause undesirable reactions. Too much acid on cauliflower, for example, results in a reddish or brownish color that is related to broken-down sulfide products, which have an unpleasant taste. Consequently, this type of reaction should be handled carefully. If too much of any acid or alkali is added to a food, the reaction may change. Generally in cooking, the old adage, "If a bit is good, a lot more will be better," is simply not true.

Green vegetables are very delicate because the chlorophyll coloring them green can be destroyed in cooking. Heat changes this pigment to an olive green color, and acid speeds the reaction. To cook green vegetables without losing the fresh green color, cook them fast. The modern way of cooking lightly is good for this. Leave the cover off when boiling vegetables, because most green vegetables contain acid that can escape if the cover is off, especially in the early stages of cooking. An alkaline reaction can help preserve greenness in vegetables, but unfortunately it also destroys some valuable vitamins, so one should avoid using this approach. Moreover, an alkaline reaction can cause a soft, sloughy vegetable with an unappealing flavor.

Texture Vegetables depend for their crispness and their soft texture on their degree of cooking. Other factors such as the presence of an alkaline medium can also make a difference. The substance that gives texture to vegetables is called *cellulose*. This is the fiber in vegetables that give them structural strength. However, cooking can soften cellulose and leave the vegetables less crisp. As noted previously, the modern technique of slightly undercooking vegetables allows them to retain some of their crispness.

The Chinese method of stir-frying is a method of heating a vegetable through, without thoroughly cooking it; the result is that some crispness and the fresh flavor of the vegetable are retained. The cook must understand when a vegetable should be served slightly underdone, with some hard core left inside, and when it should be soft and mellow.

Cooking The way vegetables should be cooked differs according to their physical and color properties. Tender vegetables with a mild flavor but with good moisture (such as fresh peas, string beans, carrots, and summer squash) require quick cooking. If they have been frozen, add them to a small bit of boiling salted water, and cook them as quickly as possible. Steaming is also a good technique to use with this type of vegetable, but the timing must be precise to prevent overcooking. *Overcooking* can ruin these vegetables, since they are tender and need some of their original texture.

Some vegetables of the onion and turnip family have good moisture but need either short- or long-term cooking. Members of the onion family contain allyl sulfides, which have a strong flavor when the vegetable is raw but which can be driven off through long moist-heat cooking. Vegetables of the cabbage family need short-term cooking because they develop strong flavors when kept heated for a long time. Acid speeds these undesirable flavor reactions. Often finely dividing allyl-flavored vegetables helps dissipate any objectionable flavor.

Moist, starchy vegetables such as potatoes and yams steam well. They also can be boiled: drop them into boiling water, cover, and gently boil. When they are tender, drain them well and serve as soon as possible. Holding starchy vegetables under water may result in a soggy product.

Dry, starchy items such as dry beans and other legumes, macaroni products, and rice should be dropped into lots of boiling water and cooked until tender. Legumes may be presoaked to speed their cooking. About 1½ gallons of water is sufficient to cook 5 pounds of legumes. Breaking of the skin indicates proper tenderness. No acid should be added until the legumes are done, since this prolongs cooking time and yields a less tender product. Macaroni products and rice are also cooked in plenty of water. Drop them into boiling water, stir well to separate them, cover, and cook gently until they are tender. When cooking macaroni products (pastas) make sure that they retain some resistance. This the Italian cook calls *al dente*, which means "to the tooth." Drain pasta well, blanch it immediately in cold water, and store it in cold water until needed.

Rice should be tender but not too soft. Rice can be cooked in two parts water to one part rice *by measure*. Cover the pan tightly and bring its contents to a boil. Stir only once after boiling begins. Then put the pan on low heat, covered, for about 20 minutes. During the last 5 to 8 minutes it can be uncovered so that the rice steams, leaving the grains light and separate. If the rice has absorbed all of the water but remains dry and hard, add more water. Too much water produces an overcooked, soft, pasty rice.

For cooked breakfast cereals, add them to the proper amount of boiling water and stir; then cook the cereal gently while covered. Try to stir as little as possible, since stirring creates a pastier product. When the cereal is done, no raw taste of starch should be evident. Fine cereals such as farina and cornmeal may lump if added too quickly to boiling water. For this reason some cooks make a cold-water slurry of them and add this to the boiling water. The cold water used in the slurry should be treated as part of the total water specified for the recipe. Cooked cereals are best when served as soon as possible after cooking. With today's availability of instant cooked cereals, it may be well to use these and prepare them to order. All one needs is the proper amount of boiling water to pour over the cereal. After stirring, the product is ready to serve.

Eggs

A short order cook who prepares breakfast orders becomes well acquainted with eggs. One paramount consideration is that the egg must be of good quality—either Grade AA or Grade A. Poor-quality eggs spread out in the pan when fried; in addition, the yolk is low and breaks easily. It is difficult to poach a poor-quality egg because the white spreads out and is difficult to dish up. It may have a poor appearance and will look puffy. A good-quality egg has a high-standing yolk and a white that clings to the yolk and also stands high (see Fig. 4-2). When a good-quality egg is added to the sauté pan, very little of the white runs out; the egg also holds together well in poaching (see Fig. 4-3). The size of egg used for breakfast is usually Large, and all recipes are standardized for this size. In some cases other sizes may be used, but this is not the normal procedure.

Eggs are temperamental things and can quickly become a poor-tasting and bad-looking product. Egg yolks are high in iron, and the white of an egg has considerable sulfur in it. Heat tends to combine the iron with the sulfur as iron sulfide, a greenish-black substance that has some of the smell of a rotten egg. One can also encounter this smell in a chemistry laboratory or around some hot springs. In an egg, it is not good tasting. Hard-cooking an egg too long causes the sulfur and iron to join together around the yolk, and a dark ring appears. The egg will be relatively tough and will not have a good flavor. A hard-cooked egg is properly cooked when the yolk is a bright yellow with no dark ring around it (see Fig. 4-4). Eggs can also darken and develop the iron sulfide flavor if they are exposed too long to heat, as sometimes happens when a dish of eggs is left in the steam table. The bottom of the eggs in the dish becomes spongy and dark and acquires an iron sulfide flavor.

Eggs hold their quality well at around 32° to 35°F (0° to 1.5°C), but they lose quality rapidly at room temperature. Figure 4-5 shows how long an egg retains quality when held at 36°F (2.2°C) and how rapidly it loses quality at 61°F (16°C) and 77°F (25°C). It is well to take out *only* the eggs needed during a shift. Taking a whole case out of refrigeration and using only a part of it while the remainder stands in a hot kitchen does little for egg quality.

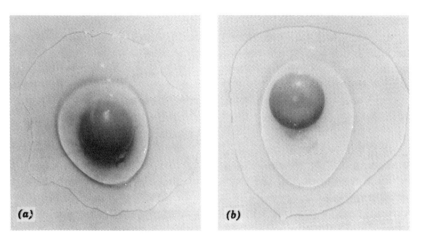

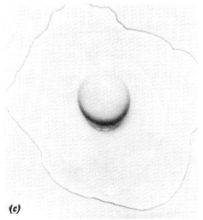

FIGURE 4-2. Eggs of different quality grades: (a) High quality (AA grade). (b) Lesser quality (A grade). (c) Still lower quality (B grade). (*Courtesy USDA*)

When heat strikes an egg, the protein in the egg coagulates—that is, it changes color and firms up, becoming "done." Coagulation is not instantaneous but occurs at around 156°F (68.8°C) for whole eggs; yolks coagulate at 144° to 168°F (62° to 70°C) and whites coagulate at 140° to 149°F (60° to 65°C). An egg custard coagulates at around 175° to 185°F (79° to 85°C), and a stirred custard thickens at about the same temperature. When an egg is mixed with a liquid and with ingredients such as sugar, the coagulation temperature goes up. The egg also becomes somewhat unstable and can curdle; that is, the liquid can separate from the egg, resulting in formation of a curd. In a custard, this becomes a mass containing a lot of small holes out of which liquid seeps; this is then called a *broken custard*. When a stirred custard separates, the small curds of egg in the liquid become visible and the custard is thinner than it should be. This separation process has the technical name *syneresis*. Cheese can also cause an egg-based sauce to break into curds.

Although short order cooks will seldom be required to beat eggs into a foam, they should know how to do it. One can beat whole eggs into a foam, but it is easiest to do whites and yolks separately and then blend them carefully together. An egg white will not beat into a foam if oil or fat is present; even the fat that is in an egg yolk can prevent it from foaming. Therefore, the whip and all utensils must be very clean and free from any grease. Eggs beat to a foam better when they are warm; and a bit of acid helps to give a tenderer and more stable foam. While eggs should be as fresh as possible for breakfast cooking, a very fresh egg does not beat into a foam well, because the protein in the egg is too tight.

Boiled Eggs Cold eggs added to hot boiling water may crack, so it is better to have them slightly warmed if they are to be boiled. Times for cooking eggs (at elevations of 3,000 feet and less) are as listed in Table 4-6; at higher elevations, longer times are needed.

FIGURE 4-3. The three eggs of different quality shown in Figure 4-3, after poaching. Note how the quality shows in the cooking. (*Courtesy USDA*)

FIGURE 4-4. Hard-boiled eggs cooked properly (top) and improperly (bottom). Note dark line around yolk in bottom. (*Photo by Michael Upright*)

To cook eggs in quantity, put them in a perforated insert and set this into tepid water in a steam-jacketed kettle or a pot that can quickly be brought to a boil. Cover the eggs with water plus about 1 inch of depth. Breakfast eggs are best cooked in water at 190° to 195°F (88° to 91°C). After they are done, plunge them immediately into cool water to stop any continued cooking, and send the eggs to service. If eggs are to be sliced, cook them at a hard boil. This firms the egg and makes it better for slicing. If hard-cooked eggs are to be chopped up for use in egg salad, do not boil them in the shell; rather, poach the eggs outside the shell. Some cooks like to drop shelled eggs into warm water and then place the pan in a steamer and hard-cook them.

TABLE 4-6. Cooking Times for Boiled Eggs

Doneness	212°F (100°C)	190° to 195°F (88° to 91°C)	Steam Pressure (7 psi)
soft-cooked	3 min	6 min	1 min 25 sec
medium-cooked	4 min	8 min	
hard-cooked	12 to 15 min	20 to 25 min	3 min 10 sec

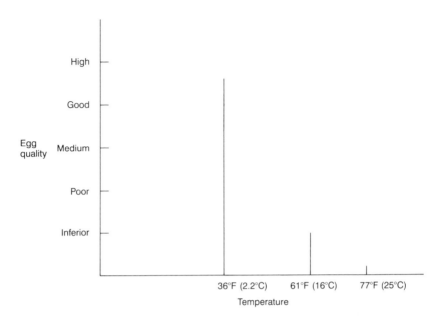

FIGURE 4-5. Egg quality deterioration after 100 days' storage at three different storage temperatures.

Note: After 18 days' storage, the eggs stored at 77°F (25°C) were judged to be of inferior quality and were withdrawn from the study.

FIGURE 4-6. Sliding eggs into a pan of simmering water for poaching.

A coddled egg is an egg that has been brought up to room temperature and then had boiling water poured over it in the ratio of 1 pint of water per egg. Size the pan according to the pints of water and eggs used. Cover the container tightly and allow it to stand without heat until the desired level of doneness is obtained. The resulting egg is much tenderer than an egg cooked in boiling water.

Poached Eggs Eggs should be poached in water that is about 2 to 3 inches deep in a 4-inch-deep flat pan; use 1 T salt and 2 T vinegar per gallon of water, but do not exceed these limits. Salt and vinegar encourage the protein to bunch up and thus stop the egg from spreading, but too much gives no better results and may flavor the egg undesirably. Bring the water to a gentle boil. About 8 to 16 eggs can be poached per gallon of water, and three or four batches can be poached in the same water before it must be changed. Cook the eggs for 3 to 5 minutes. If the temperature is too low, the eggs may be too difficult to handle. When adding eggs to the water, slide rather than drop them in it (see Fig. 4-6). Sliding them in helps hold them together. Dropping them down causes them to flatten somewhat as they hit the water. Remove poached eggs with a perforated ladle or slotted spoon to get good drainage. Eggs can be poached in a steam table; they should be started a few at a time so that service is constant. Special egg poachers with greased cups are used by some facilities.

When eggs are shelled, they are usually broken one at a time into a bowl, to see whether they are of proper quality. To crack an egg, strike it sharply against the side of a dish, griddle, cutting board, or other hard surface. If the strike is too gentle, too small a crack is made and the egg opens with difficulty. If the strike is too hard, some of the egg may come out too soon or the yolk may be broken. To open an egg with one hand, cup the hand over the egg with the bottom exposed. Crack the egg against a hard suface, and with the thumb and first two fingers move the front part of the egg forward while with the remaining two fingers move the back part of the egg backward. The egg can easily be dropped into a bowl for inspection or into any other container desired. This method takes practice, but once learned it is a quick and easy way to get eggs into production. Watch for and remove egg shell. If a yolk breaks dump the egg into a separate container and use it for scrambled eggs, omelets, French toast, or some other purpose for which whole beaten eggs are needed.

Fried Eggs The pans used for frying or scrambling eggs and for making omelets should be well seasoned so that the eggs do not stick. Single-egg pans should be 4 inches in diameter and double- or three-egg pans should be 6 to 8 inches in diameter. Most cooks like to use special pans exclusively for eggs. It is desirable to cook eggs with clarified butter—butter that has been melted and separated from any sediment. This gives a preferred flavor to the egg and also allows the butter to reach a higher temperature without smoking or burning. Have the fat hot before sliding the egg or eggs into the pan. Then drop the heating temperature. The hot fat helps stop the egg from spreading and keeps it more bunched up. Do

FIGURE 4-7. The undersides of a properly fried egg (left), and of a poorly fried egg (right).

not allow the bottom of the egg to crisp or brown (see Fig. 4-7). To make country-style eggs, add about a tablespoon of water just before the eggs are done, and then cover the pan tightly; the resulting steam cooks the top. Alternatively, one can baste the top with hot fat. The term *over easy* means that the egg is flipped and allowed to cook for just a few seconds so that the top is coated with coagulated white.

Eggs fried on a griddle are not as attractive as pan-fried eggs. Use plenty of fat, and have the griddle at 300° to 325°F (149° to 163°C). Place eggs on the griddle in the same sequence in which they are to be removed. A device that holds eggs in cups so that they can all be placed on the griddle at one time is available. For cafeteria service, eggs should be cooked until just set. Then place them in a well-buttered steam table pan, and send them to the service unit.

Scrambled Eggs Ordinarily, the eggs used for scrambled eggs are well blended before being added to the pan. However, for country-style scrambled eggs, the eggs are added to the pan and mixed while scrambling; as a result, some white and yolk will be evident as separate matter. In regular scrambled eggs, the blend of white and yolk is complete. The pan should be well seasoned, and a thin bit of oil or clarified butter should be added first to the pan; the heat of the pan should be lowered as the eggs coagulate. Stir only a bit; the eggs should coagulate in about ½-inch segments. Lift the eggs carefully during cooking to allow the uncooked portion to flow underneath. Remove the eggs while they are still soft and moist. Too much heat or too extended heat toughens them and may cause them to develop off-flavors and off-colors. For quantity work, scrambled eggs can be cooked in a steam table or bain-marie. Sometimes whole eggs are combined with a medium white sauce and cooked until they just set; these hold well at 200°F (93°C) for 30 minutes. About 1 T of water, milk, or cream per egg may be added, producing a slightly softer egg.

Omelets One egg makes a small omelet, two a medium-size one, and three a large one. The eggs should be well blended but not frothy. Use a well-seasoned pan covered with about ⅛-inch of clarified butter, margarine, or oil. Bring the fat to a fairly high temperature. The eggs should bubble as they are poured in. Tilt the pan in all directions to distribute the eggs. Then drop the heat, and cook the eggs at moderate temperature. Lift cooked portions so that uncooked egg can run underneath, but do not break the egg or allow the mass to bunch. While the surface is still moist, increase the heat to brown the bottom. To fold or roll, tip the pan at about a 60° angle, fold, and shape the egg with a spatula. Before folding the omelet, the cook may add a filling such as shredded cheese or crab Newburg. Press the still moist edges lightly to seal them, turn the omelet, and cook it for a short time. Then turn it onto a warm plate, shape it with a clean cloth, and serve. Omelets filled with some sweetened center are frequently "burned"; this involves sprinkling the omelet with powdered sugar and using a hot metal instrument to burn a design onto the omelet top. The caramelized flavor of the burnt sugar adds to the flavor of the omelet. Figure 4-8 reviews these steps.

Foamy omelets are unusual items in foodservice. They are made by whipping yolks and whites separately into a good foam and then blending the two. They are baked in an oven or put into a pan that is covered immediately afterward. Like plain omelets, foamy omelets can be filled, folded, and scored.

Shirred Eggs Shirred eggs are shelled eggs that have been placed in a well-greased cassoulet and heated until some slight coagulation is seen. The eggs are then finished in an oven. When done, the yolks should still be soft. If a bit more coagulation is allowed, the eggs may be finished under a broiler, but care must be taken in this case not to overcook the eggs. High heat toughens the eggs. Cream, milk, cheese, bacon, chicken livers, or other foods may be added before cooking; sauces may be added during the last stage or after cooking is completed.

Dairy Products

Milk is a liquid made up largely of water (about 88 percent) but also containing about 3.5 percent protein, 5 percent sugar (lactose), and 3.5 percent fat (butter). It is a nutritious food, yielding a number of vitamins and minerals in good supply. Milk and its derivatives are delicate

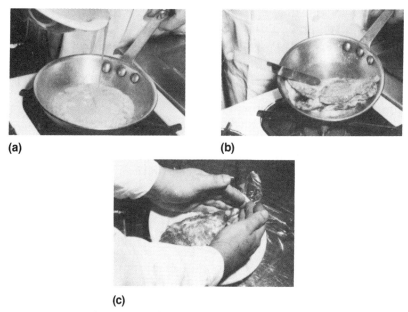

(a)

(b)

(c)

FIGURE 4-8. Making a French omelet: (a) Have the fat fairly hot, and pour the well-blended eggs into the pan. (b) Lift until the entire mass is well coagulated; then fill and fold. (c) Shape, if desired.

substances and need to be handled carefully in cooking. Many dairy products can scorch or curdle very easily.

Evaporated milk is less apt to curdle than fresh milk. Salt encourages curdling, so low salting is advised. Fresh milk has a pH of 6.5 to 6.6 which means that it is only slightly acidic. (A pH of 7.0 means exactly neutral, neither acidic nor alkaline.) At a pH of 4.6, milk curdles. This can be the result of natural souring or the action of an acid such as lemon juice (with a very low pH of 2) which lowers the milk's pH and causes the casein (protein) in the milk to separate from the liquid. Heat makes milk more unstable and more apt to curdle. When making a soup that will contain an acidic substance such as tomato, the milk is slightly thickened first with a roux or other thickener to bind in the casein and prevent it from separating out. The acid component is added to the milk base and not vice versa. The tannins in asparagus, Irish potatoes, and other vegetables act to curdle milk. Likewise, curing salts and natural salts such as calcium chloride encourage curdling. Often a product that is likely to curdle is made just before service, and served at once, since holding increases the likelihood of curdling.

To avoid scorching, milk should be heated over water, in a steam-jacketed kettle or in a steamer. However, prolonged heating below scorching temperatures can darken milk and give it a somewhat caramelized flavor.

Dry milk is less expensive than either fresh or evaporated milk and can be used successfully in batters such as those for waffles and hotcakes. Because it is rather unstable as a liquid, dry milk is seldom used for soups or sauces. Usually 1 pound of dry milk is blended with 1 gallon of water to produce the equivalent of fresh milk.

Cheese should be cooked at low heat. A hard, dry cheese blends into a sauce or other liquid better if it is grated and moistened with a warm liquid a short time before being added to the product. Processed cheese contains an emulsifier that helps blend it into liquids. Ripe cheese blends in better than fairly new cheese. In adding cheese to a thickened starch mixture that also requires eggs, a cook adds the eggs first and then the cheese; this helps make the cheese blend in better.

Cream, sour cream, and other milk products are used as finishing agents for sauces and other items. They are blended into the product just before service, and the product is never boiled after they are added. Such finishing is done to smooth out flavors and increase richness.

Meat, Poultry, and Fish

The flesh of animals, poultry, and fish is sufficiently similar that many general statements can be made about it. Where these types of flesh differ significantly, the differences will be noted.

Flesh is about 75 percent water and 25 percent solids; most of the solids are protein. Flesh contains only a small quantity of sugar, but this is important in browning. Some meat proteins are soluble in cold water but coagulate in hot water.

Flesh contains fat that may be found in juices, as marbling (tiny flecks of fat distributed around the flesh), and as an outside covering or interlayer between pieces of flesh. Young animals have less fat than older ones. Body fat contains from 15 to 50 percent water.

Lean flesh is composed of long fibers bound together by connective tissue. The younger the animal, the finer the fiber; and fine fibers usually indicate tenderer flesh. There are two kinds of connective tissue: *collagen*, or white tissue; and *elastin*, or yellow tissue. Collagen can be dissolved by heat and moisture, and acid helps speed the reaction. This is why cooks braise, boil, steam, or otherwise give tough flesh moist-heat cooking. The tenderest cuts are found in the least exercised muscles—along the back of an animal—and these can be cooked by dry-heat methods, because they contain so little collagen. Elastin is tough and fibrous but cannot be changed by cooking. Cooks tenderize flesh that contains a lot of elastin by grinding it, cubing it, pounding it, or even adding a tenderizer that does dissolve it.

When meat protein is subjected to heat, it coagulates: the liquid protein firms up, turns a different color, and loses moisture. The moisture that is lost is termed *drip*. The meat also shrinks. High heat causes greater moisture loss and shrinkage than occurs when low heat is used. Extending the cooking time has the same effect. Thus, the higher the cooking temperature and the longer the cooking, the greater the loss of moisture and the greater the shrinkage (see Fig. 4-9). It is thus desirable to cook meat at a low temperature, if possible, and to shorten the cooking time. To accomplish the latter, however, the cook must be dealing with meat that is tender enough to be chewable after a short cooking time.

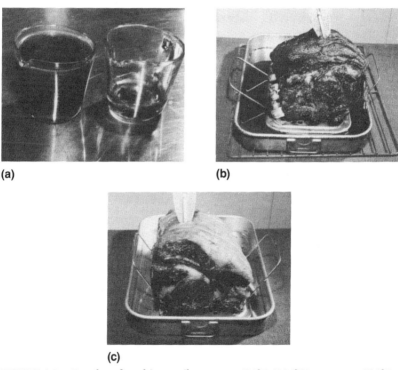

(a)

(b)

(c)

FIGURE 4-9. Results of cooking a rib roast at 400°F (204°C) versus at 325°F (163°C): (a) Drippings from the higher-temperature roast (left) and from the lower-temperature roast (right). (b) The higher-temperature roast has a shrunken appearance. (c) The lower-temperature roast is plumper, provides more portions, and is more flavorful and juicy.

Thus, today authorities say "roast meats at low temperatures and, instead of boiling them, simmer them." An exception to this rule arises when a small piece of meat is to be roasted. Cooking at a low temperature extends the roasting time, and this extended time in the oven tends to dry out small pieces of meat—say, roasted squab—excessively, so cooks raise the heat to roast these fast and avoid drying them out.

Aging tenderizes flesh by allowing natural enzymes to work on it and make it more flavorful and tender. Aged flesh cooks to a done color faster than does unaged flesh. Some cuts of beef, lamb, and mutton are aged. Veal, calf, and pork seldom are. Poultry is rarely aged, but some game birds are "hung" to make them more tender. Fish lacks connective tissue and so is usually tender without aging. In fact, cooks sometimes crimp (slash) along the sides of a fish that has just been killed, in order to prevent it from falling apart when cooked. Very few preparations of fish involve long cooking times. Fish is usually best when just done. Meat cooked while in the state of rigor mortis is much tougher than it would be before or afterward. Such meat is termed *green*.

Some of the flavor in flesh comes from protein and nonprotein factors, but most of the flavor comes from essential oils. Fat is an organic compound similar to these essential oils and so easily absorbs them. The flesh, being largely water, cannot do so, and therefore fat is a very important part of the flavor of flesh. Often the flavors of the feed an animal was given are incorporated in the flesh, which is why corn-fed animals are prized. The hams from Smithfield County, Virginia, are prized because the hogs there are fattened on peanuts, giving a nutty flavor to the flesh.

The flesh and bones of meat, poultry, and fish are used to give flavor to stocks. Large bones are usually cracked so that flavor can be extracted from the marrow. Often in commercial kitchens a stockpot is maintained continuously, and all edible meat scraps, bones, liquid from vegetables, and edible vegetables that would otherwise be thrown away—except plate garbage—are added to the stockpot. The bones of young animals yield the most gelatin and for this reason may be more desirable for making a stock. Too long simmering produces a cloudy stock. Fish bones and flesh can only be cooked for about 1 hour, poultry a little longer, and beef about 5 hours before beginning to cloud. Stocks are used as a base for soups, sauces, and gravies.

Frozen flesh is sometimes used in foodservice. It is usual upon thawing for some drip or *purge* to come from the flesh. Investigations have shown that this purge is high in nutrients and flavor and so should be retained if possible. By cooking the flesh while it is still in the frozen state, purge can be prevented. It is not always possible to do this, however, so at times the loss cannot be avoided. Frozen flesh should be thawed under refrigeration. Enclosing the flesh in a moisture/vapor-proof package and placing it beneath running water speeds thawing over leaving it to thaw at room temperature. Putting the flesh in front of a fan also does. In some cases, microwave defrosting may be feasible.

□ Beverage Facts

Coffee

Coffee, tea, and cocoa are heated beverages that a short order cook may have to prepare. To be able to produce satisfactory beverages, a cook must know quite a lot. To many patrons, beverages are an important part of the meal.

Coffee is the green bean of a cherrylike fruit that grows on tall bushes. We get most of our coffee from South and Central America and from Africa. The green bean is roasted to develop its flavor and color. Coffee beans of different kinds are blended to combine desirable flavors in the brew. The color of roasted coffee may be light (cinnamon color), medium (deep chestnut color), or dark (almost black). Coffee contains caffeine, which is a mild stimulant; the use of caffeine-free coffee is increasing because patrons want to avoid this stimulant. Keep coffee in a cool, dry place in vacuum-packed containers. Keep opened packages or cans of coffee in a freezer to preserve the coffee's freshness; coffee can lose much of its flavor and freshness in a few days at room temperature. However, unopened vacuum-packed coffee retains its flavor for a fairly long time without special treatment.

Good coffee depends first on having a good coffee of the proper grind for the available equipment. Second, it depends on the kind of equipment used and its cleanliness: unclean equipment develops stale and rancid flavors that detract from the coffee's flavor. Third, it depends on the kind and temperature of the water used. Fourth, it depends on the skill with which it is made: the accurate measurement of both the coffee and the water is essential, and the procedure used must be suited to the equipment.

Urn Coffee Urn coffee is made when a fairly large quantity of coffee is needed in a relatively short time. The urn must be kept scrupulously clean. Have a clean coffee bag, and measure the coffee into it accurately. The urn should be hot. Urns can be obtained that automatically measure the right amount of hot water; some even distribute it (see Fig. 4-10).

The following method is for making such coffee the old-fashioned way. After adding the coffee, measure the hot water and pour it over the

FIGURE 4-10. An example of a coffee urn which has a spray arm that sprays water at the proper temperature over the coffee grounds resting inside in a bag. The urn has controls that can be set so that the exact quantity of water to suit the amount of ground coffee is automatically delivered. Note also that the proper steps for making coffee are shown on the equipment. (*Photo by Michael Upright*)

grounds in a circular motion, wetting all the grounds. Continue to draw and pour hot water until the proper amount is obtained. Coffee grounds should be in contact with water for from 4 to 6 minutes. After this, remove the bag to avoid introducing undesirable flavors into the coffee; the bag should already be drained. Good urn coffee depends on a proper temperature of the water. Leaving the bag in allows tannins (bitter substances) to drip into the coffee. Coffee flavor is best extracted when the water is just below the boiling point. Water that is too soft or too hard does not make good coffee; a bit of hardness is all right. After the bag is removed, draw off about 1 gallon of coffee and dump it back into the brew; as coffee is made, it forms strata or layers of different strength and flavor. The dumping of the bottom-most gallon mixes the entire lot together, producing a uniform brew. Place the top on the urn, and hold the coffee at a temperature of from 185° to 190°F (85° to 88°C).

Clean the urn immediately after each use. Add some hot water, and scrub the interior thoroughly with a brush. Then drain and rinse out the urn. Take apart the faucet, or (if it has a cap on it) remove the cap and scrub the pipe leading out of the urn. Wash the faucet, using a good detergent in the water, and rinse it thoroughly. Scrub the spigot. Then rinse the whole urn again, using several rinses. If the urn is not to be used again, add several gallons of hot water and leave the cover partly open. This water should be run off when the urn is to be used next time; then rinse the urn.

Once a week, clean the urn more thoroughly, using an urn cleaner. Follow the manufacturer's instructions. These usually call for the urn to be at least three-quarters full of warm water. Turn the heat off, mix the detergent in thoroughly, and let this stand overnight. In the morning, drain out the water, and once again clean out the faucet and the pipe leading to it. Also, scrub out the glass gauge that shows how much water or coffee is in the urn. Avoid filling the urn with very cold water when the urn is hot, because the ceramic inner container may crack. Urn baskets should be soaked in a good detergent water and thoroughly scrubbed. Do not use steel wool. If the urn has a spray-head, make sure that the holes in it are not clogged. A stiff wire brush or a small piece of wire can be inserted into clogged holes to unplug them.

Coffee Makers Many operations today use coffee brewers that make 8 or 12 cups of coffee per pot. Usually the coffee is purchased in specific premeasured portions suited to the equipment. This is added to a basket which is placed under an instant water heater. A button is pushed, and very hot water comes out of a small spout and flows through the grounds into a bowl beneath. Some units contain a measured amount of water above the grounds; this water is heated to a temperature slightly below the boiling point, at which time the tank is opened and the hot water flows through grounds. Often disposable paper filters are used, and these are discarded with the grounds. Figure 4-11 reviews these steps.

Again, the equipment must be kept scrupulously clean. Use a good detergent, and scrub the equipment well. It may occasionally be necessary to descale the water container above the grounds. Special compounds are used for this. If this is not done, the electrical elements may not be able to heat the water to a desirable temperature, and a weak,

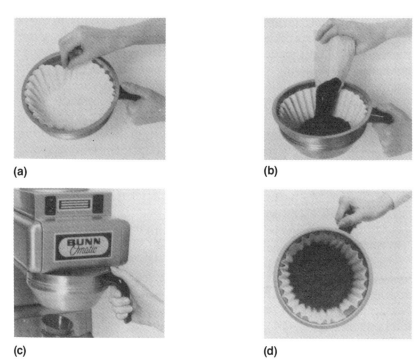

(a) **(b)**

(c) **(d)**

FIGURE 4-11. Using a modern coffee maker: (a) Place a paper filter into the funnel. (b) Pour in prepackaged fresh coffee grounds, and shake lightly to level them in the filter. (c) Slide the funnel into the coffee machine head, place an empty decanter on the warmer plate, and push the brew button. (d) As soon as brewing is complete, remove the funnel and discard the grounds. (*Courtesy Bunn-o-Matic Corp.*)

insipid brew will result. From time to time, the temperature of the water should be checked as it comes out of the spout prior to flowing over the grounds. The temperature of this water should be at least 205°F (96°C).

Vacuum Maker Sometimes coffee is made using a vacuum maker. This is a good system and served as the source of the term *drip coffee*. The device consists of two bowls, upper and lower. The upper bowl is fitted with a long tube that extends down nearly to the bottom of the lower bowl. The two bowls fit closely together so that pressure developed in the lower bowl cannot escape. The lower bowl is filled with the *proper* amount of water, and the upper bowl contains the required coffee; a filter device separates the two bowls. If the lower bowl does not have a fill mark, leave at least 1 inch of space between the water and the upper bowl for expansion. Heat the water in the lower bowl. As the water comes to a boil, steam is developed that forces the hot water up into the upper bowl to mingle with the grounds. Next, take the bowls from the heat. This leads the steam in the lower bowl to condense, creating a vacuum in the lower bowl that pulls the brew back down through the filter. The water should stay in contact with the grounds for about 2 to 3 minutes. Then remove the upper bowl and the filter, and wash each well. Place a pour top on the lower bowl, which is now filled with coffee (see Fig. 4-12).

Percolated Coffee Few operations use percolated coffee today. To make a proper brew by this method, measure both the water and the coffee carefully. Connect the percolator and allow the coffee to percolate for about 10 minutes. The method involves heating the water on the very bottom of the percolator so that steam forces the water up through the centrally located vertical tube and out over the grounds.

Boiled Coffee Cooks even less frequently encounter boiled coffee, but in some rare instances (such as in a summer camp or some other operation lacking adequate facilities) coffee must be boiled. A coarser grind is used for this purpose than for drip or even percolated coffee. Coffee in the proper amount is put into a clean cloth bag and this is put in a pot to which the proper amount of cold water is added. The pot is heated, and the water is allowed to come to a boil. Boil the coffee for 10 minutes, and then remove the bag. The coffee is ready to serve.

Coffee Characteristics A good cup of coffee is judged on the basis of its color (which should be a dark, rich brown), its clarity (a silver spoon should be visible almost to the bottom of the cup), and its body (the

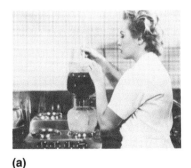 

(a)   **(b)**

FIGURE 4-12. Final stages of making vacuum coffee: (a) The vacuum coffee maker with the top bowl filled, before the vacuum created below pulls the coffee back into the bowl. (b) The upper bowl being removed with the grounds, leaving the servable coffee in the lower bowl.

brew should be denser than water), and good cream added to the brew should feather—spread out in waves rather than mixing in. Finally, a good brew should have a natural sweetness (although not too much), a rich coffee flavor, and a very slight bitterness. The overall effect should be one of pleasant flavor.

Tea

A camellia bush is the parent of tea. The original plant probably came from southern Asia. Records show that tea was in use by about A.D. 600 in China, where it eventually became the national drink. Three kinds of tea are made from the leaves of this plant: green, oolong, and black. Green tea is an unfermented tea; that is, the leaves are not allowed to stand untreated for any length of time but are instead fired (dried) immediately. Oolong tea leaves are allowed to stand only a short time after they have been rolled (slightly crushed); then they are fired. Black tea is rolled and allowed to stand some time before firing. The standing of the tea allows oxygen to change some of the components in the tea leaf, giving it a different color and flavor. Green tea has more tannins and therefore is slightly bitterer than the other two types. Oolong tea is the next most bitter, and black tea is the least.

The amount of tannin in tea has much to do with how readily the brew clouds when chilled. Green tea clouds the most easily when served as iced tea (which it seldom is) because it is high in tannins that precipitate (form a cloud of visible particulate matter) when chilled. Oolong tea has more stability than green tea, but black tea is best—although even so it is not too dependable. One can make a fairly strong solution of black tea, put it into a refrigerator, and find that it has clouded. Adding a bit of acid to tea retards clouding.

Most operations use tea bags. One tea bag can be used to make a single order of tea. The way to make tea is absolutely not to put boiling hot water in a warm cup and place the tea bag on the side. Use a small, heated, two-cup pot; put in the bag and then pour boiling water over it, filling the pot.

Tea flavors are best extracted just below boiling. By the time a cup of hot water reaches a patron, its temperature is so low that it cannot extract the full flavor of the tea. An additional pot of boiling hot water may be brought to the patron so that the tea can be properly diluted. Tea should never be boiled; as with coffee, the flavors escape easily when the brew gets too hot.

A teaspoon of tea (which is about what a tea bag holds) can produce two cups of strong tea. A single ounce of tea is equivalent to 18 teaspoons, and between 5 and 8 ounces are needed for 100 portions. A bag holding 1 ounce of tea should produce 1 gallon of strong tea. To make tea in quantity, put the tea in a cloth bag and allow it to steep in water that is just below the boiling point. The Tea Council recommends the 1-2-3 method of making iced tea: for a gallon of strong iced tea that is to be diluted in crushed ice, use

1 quart of boiling water over
2 ounces of tea; steep for 6 minutes; then remove the bag, and pour the brew into
3 quarts of cold water.

For larger quantities, multiply the quantity of tea needed for 1 gallon by the number of gallons needed. Make sure that the boiling water completely covers the tea. Do not refrigerate. Such a brew is good for about 4 to 6 hours. Pour it over ice cubes or crushed ice. Many operations today use instant tea to make iced tea.

Cocoa

Most operations make cocoa from a packaged mix containing cocoa, sugar, and dry milk. Cocoa is a by-product of chocolate. Some of the fat is extracted from the cacao bean—breakfast cocoa must be at least 22 percent cacao fat—to make a drier product that is ground into a fine powder. Hot water is added to the packaged mix in the specified proportion. Cocoa that is advertised as Dutch process (Houghten brand) has been treated with alkali. This process smooths the flavor and makes the cocoa more soluble. The result is often considered a richer cocoa. About one heaping teaspoon of unsweetened breakfast cocoa is enough for one cup. Blend in about 2 teaspoons of sugar, and then add hot milk.

□ Summary

The recipe is a control factor to ensure that foods meet desired standards for quantity, quality, and cost. The form for a recipe should give the name, the code number, the total yield, the number of portions, the portion size, the ingredients (in order of use), the weight and measure of each ingredient, the equipment needed, the cooking time, portioning, plating, and garnishing directions, and suggestions for substitutions or changes that might be made. In addition, ingredients should be grouped as they are used, and instructions should be given for their use.

Weighing or measuring is a vital step in good recipe production. Cooks should also know how to make calculations for increasing or decreasing recipes. To convert temperatures from Celsius to Fahrenheit, multiply the Celsius amount by ⅝ or 1.8 and add 32. To change temperatures from Fahrenheit to Celsius, subtract 32 from the Fahrenheit amount and multiply the result by ⅝ or 0.555.

A short order cook must also know a lot about how foods react in handling and cooking.

Starch thickens liquids when moisture and heat are present. Thickeners include flour, cornstarch, tapioca, and arrowroot. A special starch called waxy maize or converted starch is used for pies. Starch breaks down in hot acidic solutions. Most starches are added to liquids in the form of either a roux or a slurry.

Emulsions are mixtures of oil in water or other liquid. Some are stable, while others (such as some French dressings) are unstable.

To prepare vegetables properly, cooks need to know how to preserve their color, flavor, texture, and nutrients. Many red items contain a pigment called *anthocyanin*, which turns red in an acidic medium and dirty purple in an alkaline one. Other red items contain lycopene, a red pigment that is quite stable. White vegetables such as potatoes and cauliflower contain a pigment called *flavone*. Flavone turns white in an acidic medium and yellow in an alkaline one. Green vegetables get their color from a pigment called *chlorophyll*. Acids destroy this pigment, while alkalies preserve it. On the other hand, an alkaline medium destroys vitamins C and B and also gives vegetables a poor texture. Yellow vegetables get their color from a pigment called *carotene*, which, like lycopene, is very stable.

Vegetable texture depends on the degree of cooking given. In crisp vegetables, some of the cellulose remains uncooked. In completely cooked vegetables, all of the cellulose has been softened. Alkalies can speed the softening of cellulose and often give vegetables an overly soft, sloughy texture.

Cook tender, high-moisture vegetables in a small quantity of boiling salted water, as rapidly as possible. Brief steaming is also good. Members of the cabbage and turnip families should be cooked for a short time in plenty of water. Members of the onion family should be cooked for a long time to get rid of their strong flavor. Moist, starchy vegetables steam well and boil well. Dry starchy vegetables such as dry beans should be presoaked and then simmered until tender. Acids tend to keep them hard, while alkalies tend to speed their cooking. Again, however, adding an alkali such as a bit of soda destroys valuable vitamins. Pastas should be cooked by being dropped into boiling, salted water and cooked until just tender. Rice can also be cooked this way, or it can be boiled in just the right amount of water and then cooked covered until the rice is soft. Breakfast cereals are dropped into the proper amount of boiling water and cooked until just done.

Soft-cooked eggs should be boiled for about 3 minutes, medium-cooked eggs should be boiled for about 4 minutes, and hard-cooked eggs should be boiled for 12 to 15 minutes. Poached eggs should be cooked in simmering water that contains 1 T salt and 2 T vinegar per gallon of water. Fried eggs should be slid into a pan of hot, clarified butter and the heat should then be dropped so that the bottom does not crisp or turn brown. Over-easy eggs are flipped over for just a few seconds. Country-style eggs can be basted with hot fat or covered so that steam is allowed to cook the top. Scrambled eggs are eggs that are mixed in a bowl and then cooked. Special techniques must be used in making French omelets properly. Shirred eggs are baked eggs.

Dairy products are delicate items that need care in handling and cooking. Many curdle easily, and the proper techniques must be used to prevent this. Ripened and processed cheeses blend into a sauce more easily than does unripened cheese.

Animal flesh consists mostly of water, much of which can be lost by improper cooking. Thus, roasting and other cooking of flesh products should be done at low temperatures to avoid moisture loss. In some cases, such as in broiling or roasting small pieces of meat, the cooking temperature is elevated to achieve other desirable results. The white connective tissue, collagen, is dissolved by moist heat; the presence of acids speeds the reaction. The yellow connective tissue, elastin, must be tenderized by mechanical means. Aging tenderizes meat. Fish lacks connective tissue and therefore is usually quite tender; it should be cooked only until just done.

Most meat flavor comes from essential oils present in fat. Fat also contributes to moistness. Stocks are made from flesh and bones.

Coffee flavor is best extracted when water is heated to about 205°F (96°C). Special techniques must be used in making urn, coffee maker, vacuum maker, or other method coffee. All equipment must be kept scrupulously clean. Brewed coffee should be held at from 185° to 190°F (85° to 88°C).

Tea is the leaf of a camellia bush. There are three kinds of tea: green, oolong, and black. Green tea is unfermented; oolong is only slightly so; and black tea is fully fermented. Good tea results when good-quality tea leaves are used and freshly boiled water is poured over the leaves. Tannins can precipitate in tea, clouding it. When iced tea is made, the 1-2-3 method is recommended: 1 quart of water is poured over 2 ounces of tea, and (after steeping for 6 minutes) the brew is poured into 3 quarts of cold water.

Cocoa is a product made from the cacao bean (the source of chocolate). Breakfast cocoa is 22 percent cacao fat. Dutch process cocoa has been treated with an alkali to make it smoother tasting and easier to blend into a liquid.

──────────── □ CHAPTER REVIEW □ ────────────

1. Mark each of the following statements True or False:
   a. All one needs in order to produce a successful product is a good recipe, good equipment, tools, and utensils, and good ingredients.
   b. If the weights of ingredients in a recipe are given, the measures never should be.
   c. A standardized recipe should give a known quantity and known quality of food at a known cost.
   d. There are 8 quarts in a gallon.
   e. The eggs in a recipe listed by count are standardized as Medium size.
   f. To convert a recipe into a larger or smaller quantity, divide the present amount into the required amount.
   g. A liter of water weighs 1 kilogram.
   h. To change Fahrenheit to Celsius, multiply the Fahrenheit reading by 1.8 and add 32.

2. What is gelatinization in regard to starch? What is the result of the gelatinization of a starch in a liquid?
3. What does acid do to starch-thickened sauce?
4. What are the two major differences between waxy maize starch and cornstarch?
5. What is an emulsion? a stable emulsion?
6. Name some emulsions that occur in food production.
7. How does one get a bright red color in cooked beets? a dirty blue color? Would one get a bright, clear white onion if it were boiled in water containing soda? If not, what color would it probably be? What is chlorophyll, and how does one preserve it in cooking vegetables? What is the pigment in yellow or orange fruits and vegetables? Is it stable in cooking?
8. What is cellulose, and what part does it play in the makeup of a vegetable? What does cooking in moist heat do to cellulose? What does an alkaline reaction do to it in cooking?
9. Would you cook members of the cabbage family a long time? members of the onion family? Explain.
10. If you saw that bean soup was listed on the menu for tomorrow, how would you prepare the beans so that the soup would be ready by noon?
11. What does *al dente* mean, and to what food items is it applied in cooking?

12. Explain how one should prepare fried eggs sunny-side up, over easy, and country style for breakfast orders. How does one make scrambled eggs? shirred eggs? soft-cooked eggs?
13. What precautions does one have to take in cooking eggs?
14. What is iron sulfide? syneresis?
15. What happens to whole-egg protein at around 156°F (69°C)?
16. How should one prepare poached eggs?
17. How should one make a regular omelet?
18. Rank dry milk, fresh milk, and evaporated milk according to their cost and then again according to their stability in cooking.
19. What things can help curdle liquid milk?
20. How are the tiny fibers in flesh bound together? How can one tenderize meat with a lot of collagen? with a lot of elastin?
21. What does aging do to meat?
22. Where does the major flavor of meat come from—the flesh or the fat? How do essential oils contribute to the flavor of meat?
23. What is drip or purge?
24. What is coffee, and what happens to it before we get it as a ground product ready to use?
25. How does one make urn coffee, and how does one take care of an urn?
26. How does one make coffee in a modern coffee maker? in a vacuum maker? in a percolator? How does one make boiled coffee?
27. What is tea, and how should one make a good cup of hot tea?
28. How should one make iced tea for a large group?
29. What is cocoa? breakfast cocoa? Dutch process cocoa?
30. How does one make a good cup of cocoa with unsweetened cocoa, sugar, and hot milk?

CHAPTER FIVE

Breakfast, Lunch, and Dinner

□ The Short Order Shift

The shift of a short order cook usually extends over two meal periods. The shift hours (including a 30-minute break) might be 6:00 A.M. to 2:30 P.M. or 11:00 A.M. to 7:30 P.M. The first covers breakfast and lunch, while the second covers lunch and dinner. Sometimes a shift covers only one meal such as when a short order cook comes to work at 5:00 P.M., goes through dinner, and then continues with short orders until 1:30 A.M. Thus a knowledge of how to work at least one meal—and usually two—is necessary. As a matter of fact, most short order cooks should be able to handle any meal period.

Basically, the work is much the same for any period except that different specific items are prepared. In some operations, a California menu is used; this is a fixed menu from which one can order breakfast, lunch, dinner, or snacks at any time of the day. The cook must then cover all varieties of meal preparation during a single shift.

□ Breakfast

The breakfast shift sees almost all orders coming to the short order section. Here egg orders, waffles or hotcakes, grilled breakfast meats, hot cereals, and so on are prepared to order. It is fast work that requires a short order cook who knows how to prepare a large variety of orders well.

Eggs
One of the items most frequently prepared on the breakfast shift is eggs. Their preparation has been covered in Chapter 4, so Table 5-1 only summarizes some of the information previously discussed.

Breakfast Meats

Another common breakfast item is breakfast meats, with pork being the most common. Most operations use only the two top pork grades, U.S. No. 1 and U.S. No. 2, predominantly the first. Good fresh pork is a grayish pink color and has firm, fine-textured, slightly moist flesh and medium-soft, white fat. It should not be reddish in color and should not have a coarse or flabby texture.

Pork keeps well if refrigerated at about 34° to 36°F (2° to 3°C). About 1½ weeks is the maximum holding time for fresh pork, but cured or cured and smoked items can be held longer. Pork holds well frozen for about 3 months. Make sure that frozen pork is packaged in vapor/moisture-proof wraps and that as much air as possible is exhausted so that the wrap fits tightly around the meat. Do not refreeze. It is best to thaw pork in a refrigerator.

Cured pork is treated with common table salt, curing salts (nitrites or nitrates), sugar, and seasonings. There are two kinds of cures: dry and brine. When the curing medium is placed over the pork in a dry state to sink into the meat and pull out moisture (thus making its own brine), the technique is called a dry cure. Country-style cured pork is dry-cured.

TABLE 5-1. Egg Cookery

Type Preparation	Method
boiled eggs	Eggs cooked in boiling water to three stages of doneness: soft-cooked (3 min), medium-cooked (4 min), or hard-cooked (12 to 15 min).
coddled eggs	Eggs cooked by pouring boiling water over them in the ratio of 1 pint of water to one egg.
poached eggs	Eggs shelled in simmering water.
fried eggs	Eggs fried in about ⅛ in. of fat in a special egg pan: eggs can also be fried on a griddle.
shirred eggs	Baked eggs.
scrambled eggs	Eggs that are well mixed and then cooked in a sauté pan with some stirring. Sometimes eggs are scrambled by dropping shelled eggs onto hot grease in a pan and mixing rapidly as the eggs cook, in which case some white of egg shows.
French omelet	Well-blended whole eggs poured into a sauté pan containing a small quantity of fairly hot clarified butter or margarine and cooked fairly rapidly, with the eggs kept in a fairly tight, solid mass, and not divided as in scrambled eggs. The eggs are folded (they may be filled with a filling) and shaped; French omelets filled with a sweet filling are burned.
foamy omelet	Eggs whose yolks and whites are beaten separately and then blended, put into a pan, and baked.

Brine-cured pork is placed in a strong brine containing the curing medium and seasonings and allowed to soak in it until the meat absorbs enough to give the meat flavor and retard spoilage. Today much brine-cured pork is pumped, which means that the brine is forced into the meat through needles or that the brine is pumped into the arterial system and thence throughout the meat. Much cured pork is smoked to add further flavor and enhance keeping qualities.

Proper labeling is required of pork products. The label must state that cured and smoked products are cured and smoked. Products that do not weigh more than they did when they went into cure may be labeled "cured"; products that do not exceed original weight by more than 110 percent may be labeled "cured, water added"; and products that weigh more than 110 percent above their precured weight must be labeled "imitation." Cured items that contain a lot of moisture shrink more in cooking.

When beef is cured, it is called *corned*, as in corned beef brisket. Some corned and smoked beef on the market resembles bacon but is leaner. Hotel bacon is a bacon that yields 18 to 22 slices to the pound; to produce this many slices, the bacon must be small and must come from young hogs. Most operations purchase sliced bacon, but some may purchase bacon in slab form. If so, the rind must be removed by being cut away from the bacon, with no fat on the rind. The slab can then be sliced on a slicing machine. Where a large quantity of bacon is used, the operation may purchase sliced bacon in layered tray packs (see Fig. 5-1). Each layer fits pans of a certain size, so the layer on paper can be turned upside down on the pan bottom and the paper lifted, leaving the bacon nicely layered for ovenizing. Alternatively, the layer can be turned over a grill and the bacon fried there.

The federal government requires that all cured and smoked pork products be brought to an internal temperature of 142°F (61°C) to destroy *trichinae*. If the product is brought to an internal temperature of 155°F (68°C), it can be labeled "fully cooked."

Cooking Breakfast Meats It is common for the breakfast short order cook, when coming on shift, to go to the refrigerator first thing and take out a quantity of breakfast meats—almost as much as will be needed on the shift. The cook then partially cooks these in pans, on the grill, or in the oven. They are then held ready for finalizing as orders come in. This prepreparation saves time and makes the service faster. For cooking breakfast meats, the griddle temperature should first be set at 350°F (177°C) and then be held at 160°F (61°C) for service.

Ham and sausage should be lightly browned when served. Do not fully cook these meats too far in advance; otherwise, they will be too dry

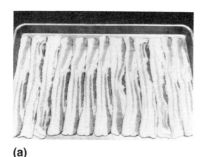
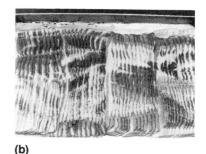

(a)   **(b)**

FIGURE 5-1.   Bacon strips in (a) *layer pack* so that they can be placed *en masse* on a pan to be ovenized or on a griddle to be fried. (b) *Shingle pack* is less desirable because it requires labor in separating the slices. (*Photo by Michael Upright*)

when served. Bacon should be crisp when served. All meats should be drained on paper towels before being served. Sausage patties should be brown and cooked all the way through. Do not allow breakfast meats to become too crisp or too brown. Turn pork links during cooking so that they color and cook evenly. If a product tends to curl in sautéing, place a hammer or frying lid on it. This will preserve the shape of the meat and ensure even and fast cooking.

Batter Items

A wide variety of batters are used for breakfast items such as hotcakes, waffles, and French toast. Some operations use prepared mixes that only require the cook to add water and mix. When mixing non-rich (low-fat and low-sugar) batters, mix as little as possible. In fact, in mixing muffin batter, mix only until the moisture is evenly distributed but some dry particles remain evident. Overmixing non-rich batters like waffles, hot-cakes or muffins develops gluten in the flour and toughens the product.

With the market changing rapidly, some operations may even use frozen items, such as fully cooked waffles, hotcakes, French toast, and even omelets. These can be conditioned for service by being dropped into a toaster, ovenized, put into a microwave, or griddled.

Carryover batters keep under refrigeration for about two days. Cover before storing, so the top does not dry out. Never freeze: eggs toughen if frozen and must be specially treated before freezing to prevent this from happening.

Waffles Waffles are a popular item. The waffle iron should be well seasoned, and the recipe should contain enough butter, oil, or melted shortening to make greasing the iron unnecessary. Several waffle recipes are listed in the appendix.

To bake a waffle, fill the lower grid to about three-quarters of its space. The temperature of the iron should be around 350° to 375°F (177° to 190°C). Close the lid, and do not reopen until checking for doneness. When a waffle stops steaming, it is done. Allow it to remain a bit longer if a crisper waffle is desired. Most waffle irons have automatic temperature controls, and some even have timers. Frozen cooked waffles are available that can be rewarmed in a toaster and served.

Hotcakes Hotcake (griddle cake or pancake) batter should be thin enough to pour. The batter is thinner and less rich than a waffle batter. Polish or French hotcakes (*blinis* or *crepes*) are thin unleavened batters, high in egg content.

Bake hotcakes on a lightly greased, seasoned griddle. If the ratio (by weight) of shortening to flour is 1:4 or higher, the griddle does not have to be greased. Pour about 2 ounces of batter onto a griddle heated to between 350° and 375°F (177° and 190°C). As the heat enters the batter, the cake's volume increases and bubbles appear on the upper surface. When the edge shows a slight drying, the cake should be deftly turned with a spatula or turner. Baking should be completed on this turn, since additional turning lowers quality. The cake rises slightly in the center after the first turn; when this recedes and the top becomes even, the cake is done. If the temperature is too low, the cakes will have poor volume and the texture will be poor. If the temperature is too high, the color will be too dark and the cake probably will be undercooked and raw in the center. A pitted top side after baking indicates too high a heat or too long a time lapse before turning.

Crepes, blinis, and plättar (pancakes) are unleavened griddle cakes made from very similar thin batters. The first is a traditional French product often used as a dessert; blinis are a Polish cake often served with sour cream. Both can be made on a griddle or in a small pan. *Plättar* (Swedish) are traditionally baked on a *plättar* pan, which is circular and is divided into small circular depressions. *Plättar* are traditionally served with a sweet lingonberry sauce, although cranberry sauce can be substituted for this.

The usual way of baking these three specialty pancakes is to start by rubbing a well-seasoned small sauté pan with an oiled cloth. Heat the pan until it is hot, pour in 1 or 2 tablespoons of the batter, and quickly roll it around to cover the bottom, producing a tissue-thin cake. The cake can be turned and browned on the top side if desired, but ordinarily the cake is browned only on one side. The unbrowned side is then either folded in with a filling or rolled over a filling. Fillings are usually sweet—

often preserves or fruit fillings. These cakes can also be served with fillings such as crab Newburg or creamed chicken, as a luncheon dish. They are not common breakfast items, but in some operations they may be placed on the menu.

Regular pancakes, blinis, crepes, and *plättar* can be purchased frozen and then rewarmed for service. Recipes for these items are listed in the appendix.

French Toast Cooks disagree about how to make the dipping mixture for French toast. Some want no milk or other liquid added: "straight eggs," they say. Others feel that adding some milk makes a better product. Some even recommend blending a small quantity of flour into the milk and then adding this to the eggs; the amount of flour can be increased until the liquid into which the bread slices are to be dipped forms a thin batter. This makes a tighter cover, reduces soaking, and extends the batter, lowering the cost.

There are also differing opinions about how to cook French toast. Some cooks prefer to seal the bread with egg dip and then deep-fry at 360°F (182°C), while others like to place the dipped bread on a well-greased griddle, fry one side, turn, and fry the other. In either case, the toast should be served golden brown. A frozen French toast is available that only needs rewarming.

The appendix includes a recipe for making French toast.

Cooked Cereals

It is usual for a facility to offer at least one cooked cereal on the breakfast menu. The most common one is oatmeal, but some operations vary the offering from morning to morning. The word *cereal* comes from the name of the Roman goddess Ceres, who taught agriculture to man. Store bulk cereals in airtight containers in a cool, dry place. Store packaged cereals tightly covered in their original containers. In warm weather weevils can develop from eggs laid in the raw cereals. In climates where this may be a problem, the cereals are stored in a refrigerator.

Cereals are cooked to gelatinize the starch and soften the cellulose. Whole-grain cereals, from which little of the cellulose has been removed, require longer cooking than do refined cereals. Some cooks soak whole-grain cereals overnight to speed cooking. Once the starch has gelatinized and the cellulose has softened, there is little advantage in further cooking. Because stirring is apt to produce a pastier cereal mass, as little stirring as possible is desirable. Cooking over hot water helps prevent scorching the cereal during cooking. Sprinkle or sift the cereal over very hot water. Add finely divided cereal very slowly, stirring constantly. Cover and cook until done. Some cooks boil the cereal for about 5 minutes and then place it over boiling water, covered, to cook until done. If the water in a bain-marie or steam table is hot enough, the cereal can be cooked there. Some operations cook cereals only in water; some, in part water and part milk; and others, only in milk.

Table 5-2 summarizes information on cooking some cereals.

Potatoes

Potatoes are often served as an accompaniment to the main breakfast dish. The most common form is as hash browns although sometimes french fries may be served. Occasionally a dish such as steamed finnan haddie (a lightly smoked and salted cod) may be served with a parsley buttered potato (boiled or steamed). Today many operations purchase hash browns that have been frozen in sheets for easy griddling. Squares are marked, indicating individual portions. These sheets can also be placed on well-greased baking sheets, drizzled with melted shortening or oil, and baked in a 375°F (190°C) oven until lightly browned.

For regular hash browns, the potatoes are pared and then boiled or steamed until done. The cooled potatoes are then finely chopped and cooked in a bit of oil or shortening until well browned. They may be turned in cooking so that both tops and bottoms are browned when the potatoes are served (see Fig. 5-2). A traditional recipe for hash browns is given in the appendix.

TABLE 5-2. Breakfast Cereal Cookery

Cereal (8 oz or 2 c)			Amount	Cooking Time	Yield
Type	Product	Salt	Water		
whole-grain, cracked, or ground	corn*	3 t	8–10 c	4–5 hr	8–10 c
	oats*	3 t	8–10 c	8 hr	8–10 c
	wheat*	3 t	8–10 c	8 hr	8–10 c
coarse	cracked wheat, hominy grits, oatmeal (steel-cut and Scotch)	3 t	6–8 c	1–3 hr	6–8 c
fine§	cream of wheat, farina, Ralston, cream of rye, cornmeal	3 t	8–10 c	¼–1 hr	8–10 c
flaked§	flaked wheat, Pettijohn's, rolled oats	3 t	6–8 c	¼–½ hr	6–8 c

*Soak in water 2 to 8 hr ahead of time.
§For quick cooking, follow directions on package.

Preblanched frozen french fries contain from 6 to 7 percent fat, but after frying they contain about 17 percent fat. French fries can be prepared from raw potatoes; this involves paring the potatoes and cutting them into ⅜- to ¼-inch-thick strips about 3 inches long. Hold these strips in cold water. To speed final cooking, preblanch them in 350° to 375°F (177° to 191°C) oil for 4 to 6 minutes; no color should show, but the potatoes should be almost cooked. Then drain, cool, cover, and hold under refrigeration for up to 3 days. Final cooking should be done at 350° to 380°F (177° to 199°C) for 2 to 4 minutes.

Dry raw potato strips that are wet, before adding them to hot fat. Potato strips may be blanched for 1 to 2 minutes under 7 to 10 pounds of steam pressure and then deep-fried. About 7½ pounds of raw potato strips is enough for twenty-five portions of about 3½ ounces each (about eight to ten strips).

Where orders are infrequent, it may be desirable not to preblanch the potatoes in hot fat, but to fry them from the raw strip stage. This is done by adding the drained and dried potato strips to about 375°F (190°C) fat and frying them for about 7 minutes or until they are tender inside, crisp outside, and well browned.

FIGURE 5-2.   An order of hash browns. Notice the symmetrical shaping and the well-browned, crisp tops.

Shoestring potatoes are cut about ⅛ to ¼ inch thick, while julienne potatoes are closer to ¼ inch thick. The length of both should be from 2 to 2½ inches. Long-branch potatoes are larger than french fries and may not be squared. Thus, one might cut a small round potato into four equal parts, a medium potato into six parts, or a large one into eight parts and then deep-fry the pieces. Soufflé potatoes are cut from pared potatoes into pieces 2½ inches long by 1½ inches wide by ⅛ to 3/16 inch thick. Potato chips are sliced 1/16 inch thick. Wafered or waffle potatoes are made by a device that cuts across the width of the whole pared potato to give a round slice with tiny lattice-work holes in it. Parisienne ball potatoes are cut from raw, pared potatoes with a round melon-ball cutter.

Shoestring potatoes are fried at a slightly higher temperature than french fries, and they are fried until they are crisp. Juliennes are fried in much the same way as shoestrings are. It is desirable to soak potato chip slices in iced water for about 30 minutes and then to dry them before frying. Soufflé potatoes should be potatoes that are high in starch, mature, and equal-sized. Crisp the pieces in ice water for 30 minutes; then dry, and deep-fry them in very hot fat. The steam formed in the first frying puffs out the outer wall, and the potatoes end up as a crisp, puffed product. Waffled potatoes are fried in much the same way as potato chips are.

□ Lunch

The luncheon job of a short order cook usually revolves around the preparation of light items—often snacks—although at times full lunch preparation may also be required. The variety of items may be large, ranging from salads to sandwiches, hamburgers, and hot dogs to grilled items to deep-fried items to such things as luncheon omelets and filled crepes. If the operation has a California menu—where breakfast, lunch, and dinner are available at all times—the variety may be even greater, and the cook may simultaneously be cooking an order of hotcakes and fried eggs, making sandwiches, and preparing a steak with French fries and a salad.

Of course, the kind of operation will dictate what is prepared. If it is a drive-in, the specialty item such as hamburgers, fried chicken, or tacos will be the major item prepared. If it is a coffee shop or family restaurant, the menu will be more elaborate and the items served will tend to be more like complete luncheons. Although the patrons will pay more for such a meal, they will still want fast service. Many patrons will be businesspeople who have only a short time for lunch. If it is a luxury restaurant, the short order cook can expect to grill more meat items and fill orders that are more typical of a main meal. Some operations are geared toward expense account luncheons, where the meal will be quite extensive. Most cafeterias do not feature many short order items for lunch, although some do. If so, a short order cook will be on duty to prepare hamburgers and other items to order.

Salads

The salads served for lunch are usually limited to a few: lettuce and tomato, tuna fish, chicken, shrimp, tossed green, plain lettuce wedge, or sliced tomatoes. Other possible types include fruit salad, cole slaw, pasta salad, or Waldorf salad. These salads may be large, serving as the main part of a light meal, or they may be small and accompany foods served. Thus, a hamburger steak served with french fries may be accompanied by a small lettuce-and-tomato salad.

A salad can be thought of as having four parts: an underliner, a body, a garnish, and a dressing. Often the underliner is a leafy green, but it is also common to see an attractive bowl or dish without such a green. The main part of the salad is the body. This might be the lettuce and tomatoes, the chicken salad, or other contents from which the salad takes its name. The garnish should contribute form, color, and texture and should be edible. It can be as simple as a sprig of parsley or a few mint leaves, or as elaborate as a radish rose. The dressing can be one of three basic types—French, mayonnaise, or boiled—or any of the many derivatives possible from these three.

Freshness is the primary quality factor required for a salad. Colors should be bright, and vegetables should be crisp. Cutting should be precise, and mixing should not produce a messy appearance. Items should be sharply distinct in the salad. Tired, wilted ingredients make for an insipid salad with little appeal. The dressing should be appropriate to the salad. A French dressing with strong garlic flavor would be out of place with a mixed fruit salad. Similarly, a heavy pasty dressing would be unsuitable on a light, tossed green salad.

Good *mise en place* is required in salad production. Greens should be prewashed and precut or broken apart. Many operations purchase already-prepared greens, so they only need rinsing and drying out before use, which saves time and labor. In some cases the salads may be premade and held in readiness for service. If this is the case, the pantry may well make these salads and send them to the short order section or have them in readiness to serve when they receive that section's orders. In other situations, the short order cook is expected to have such salads in readiness for pickup with the orders. If at all possible, salads should be made to order. If this cannot be done, it is advisable to make up the salads, place a thin film of plastic over them, and then store them in a refrigerator. Never add dressing to a salad until it is to be served. Many operations now serve the dressing on the side and let the guest add it. Some guests who are trying to reduce their fat intake wish to limit the quantity of dressing they use, since these preparations usually have a fairly high oil content.

In setting up the work center for salad making, follow the principles of motion economy discussed in Chapter 1. Set the most frequently used ingredients, tools, and seasonings closest at hand and the less frequently used items farther out. See that plates or salad dishes are on hand, and try to have storage space close by for the salads when made up (unless the salads are being prepared to order and need no storage).

Crispness is essential for many salad ingredients. Crisping an item involves following certain procedures. A vegetable or green becomes crisp because the tiny cells in the item fill completely with water. This water is pulled in from the outside by the cells through a process called *osmosis*. A cell's attraction for water is encouraged if the cell contains a higher concentration of salts than the outside environment does. If this occurs, the cell is "thirsty" and pulls the water in. However, if the outside environment has a greater concentration of salt than the inside of the cell does, the attraction is the other way and water leaves the cell, causing the vegetable or green to wilt. Thus, items to be crisped or refreshed should be dipped into fresh, cold, clean tap water. But do not soak just any item in the water and expect it to crisp: some will, but others will drown without crisping. Shake excess water from the item, and store the item in a plastic bag under refrigeration. Allow air to surround the item, since this enables it to "breathe." Again, never put salt, vinegar, or a salad dressing on a salad until the point of service. The dressing, salt, or vinegar pulls water from the vegetable or green, causing it to wilt.

Recipes for various salads are listed in the appendix.

Sandwiches

Sandwiches are made differently depending on whether they are made to order in small quantity or are made in large quantity. If in small quantity, a larger number of items must be on hand to provide ingredients for the various sandwiches offered on the menu. If in large quantity, only the ingredients needed to make up one kind of sandwich need be on hand. Thus, when making sandwiches to order, the cook must have a well-planned work area so that all the required ingredients are conveniently at hand.

Like salads, sandwiches are usually composed of four parts: the bread, the filling, the spread, and the garnish.

Bread should be fresh but firm enough to allow the sandwich to be lifted without bending or sagging. Store soft-crusted breads in their wraps at 75° to 85°F (24° to 29°C). Hard-crusted breads should be stored without wraps and are only good for sandwiches on the day they are baked. Breads can pick up odors in storage, so the storage place should be odor-free. Refrigerated bread stales faster than bread held at room temperature; freezing retards staling best of all. Some sandwiches can be made, wrapped, and then frozen, while others cannot (see Table 5-3).

The spread should suit the type of sandwich being made and should contribute to its flavor, richness, or moistness. Margarine or butter are the most commonly used spreads, but mayonnaise, salad dressing, cheese mixtures, peanut butter, jelly, and others are also used. The danger of undesirable soaking is increased when melted butter or margarine is used as a spread.

The kind of filling used gives the sandwich its name and character. Sliced meats and cheeses are most often used, but salad mixtures are also popular. Vegetable combinations such as lettuce and tomato also

TABLE 5-3. Sandwich Filling Ingredients and Freezing

Ingredients That Freeze Well	Ingredients That Freeze Poorly
cooked egg yolk	cooked egg white
peanut butter	cream cheese or cottage cheese
chopped or sliced cooked meats, poultry, and fish	process cheese
lemon juice, orange juice	chopped cooked bacon
butter, margarine	tomatoes, celery, lettuce, cucumbers, green peppers, radishes, carrots, watercress, onion, cabbage, apples
dried beef	
bread, buns	jelly, jam, preserves
baked beans	mayonnaise, salad dressing
crushed or chopped pineapple	sliced cheese
roquefort or blue cheese	cheese spreads
milk	nuts, whole or chopped
sour cream	chili sauce, tomato catsup
applesauce	whole frankfurters
horseradish	honey
	swiss or cheddar cheese
	liverwurst
	olives, sliced or chopped
	pickles, dill or sweet
	pimiento
	prepared mustard
	sweet relish

NOTE: Freezing adds nothing to sandwich quality. Thaw sandwiches under refrigeration 24 hours prior to use; once thawed, they should be eaten; palatability is lost on standing. Keep thawed sandwiches refrigerated until used.

TABLE 5-4. Yields of Some Common Sandwich Materials

Item	Portion[*]	Quantity for 100 Sandwiches
butter or margarine	2 to 3 t	2 to 3 lb
jelly or jam	2 T	3 qt (1 No. 10 can)
spread-type filling	2½ T	1 gal
peanut butter	1½ T	2½ qt
mayonnaise	2 to 3 t	1 to 1½ qt
lettuce	1 leaf	5 medium heads or 5 to 7½ lb
American cheese	1 to 1¼ oz	6¼ to 8 lb
meat	1½ to 2 oz	9½ to 12½ lb

[*]Two slices of bread per portion; rough-textured bread requires more spread than smooth-textured bread.

frequently appear on menus. Filling mixtures should spread easily and should be of good consistency for eating—neither too dry nor too moist. Messy fillings should be avoided. Freshness is an important quality factor in sandwiches. Greasy bacon or limp, wilted lettuce can ruin a sandwich. Meat, cheese, and other sliced ingredients should fit the bread and be sliced evenly. Most fillings should be well chilled when used.

Typical garnishes include pickles, olives, and potato chips. Like salad garnishes, they should be edible and should suit the item.

For quantity sandwich making, arrange the bread slices, the spread, and the filling in an efficient work center, with a cutting board in front of the worker. Have the tools also close at hand. Pick up sixteen slices, using both hands, and deposit them on the board in a 4 × 4 arrangement. Spread each slice with butter or margarine using an *S* motion. Spread the filling on the eight slices in the middle two rows, using an *S* motion. Then pick up the slices in the outer two rows, using both hands, and close up the sandwiches. Eight sandwiches are now complete. The same sequence can be repeated until there are twenty-four sandwiches stacked in eight stacks of three sandwiches each. The sandwiches may then be cut through in the center or on a diagonal. Figure 5-3 shows these motions being made. Some cooks like to use an electrical knife for cutting the sandwiches. Tables 5-4 and 5-5 list some quantities of ingredients to use in sandwich making.

The amounts of ingredients needed to make twenty-five sandwiches vary, but usually 1⅓ to 2 pounds of bread (depending upon slice thickness), about ¾ pound of softened butter or margarine, and about 1½ quart (2¼ to 6 pounds) of filling are needed. Usually a 1- to 1¼-ounce slice of cheese and a 1½- to 2-ounce slice of meat are used per sandwich. For twenty-five sandwiches, this computes to 1 pound 9 ounces to 2 pounds for cheese and 2 pounds 5 ounces to 3 pounds 2 ounces for meat.

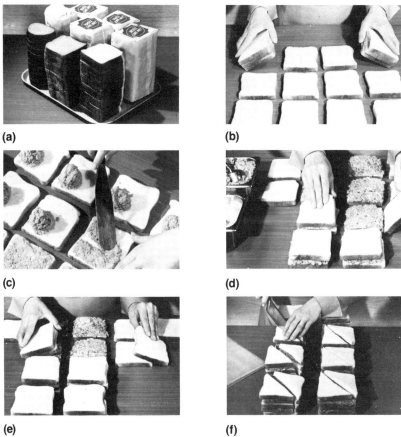

FIGURE 5-3. One-worker methods for making sandwiches in quantity: (a) Split bread wrappers in the middle, and place each half loaf open-side down on a tray. Remove the wrappers as the bread is used. (b) Pick up four slices of bread in each hand and, starting from the center out, line the slices up to form four rows on the working surface. (c) Spread the filling with a spatula in one motion: with the tip of the spatula, press the filling lightly, moving from the upper right to the upper left corner; complete the *S* motion to the lower right and then to the lower left portions of the slice. (A left-handed person should reverse this procedure.) (d) Using both hands, cap the sandwiches. (e) An alternative method in which the worker tops completed sandwiches and adds another row of fresh bread simultaneously. This may be repeated until three tiers of sandwiches are laid out. (f) Each stack may be cut with a single knife stroke.

At times a savory butter is used as a spread for meat or fish sandwiches. Recipes for savory butter and for several sandwich fillings are given in the appendix.

To make a grilled cheese sandwich, begin by putting a slice of cheese weighing about 1¼ ounces between two slices of bread that have been lightly brushed on the outside with melted butter or margarine. Then place the sandwich on the griddle with a hammer to weigh it down, and lightly toast it on each side. A recipe for toasted cheese sandwiches is included among the sandwich recipes in the appendix.

Luncheon Entrées

The short order section may have to prepare some light luncheon dishes such as spaghetti with Italian sauce, baked beans, etc. Recipes for a few of these dishes are given in the appendix as examples of what the short order cook might be expected to prepare.

TABLE 5-5. Amounts Obtained per Pound of Sandwich Material Used

Ingredient	Quantity per Pound or Other
bacon, sliced	18 to 25 slices; 2½ c cooked and chopped
butter or margarine	2 c
cheese, cream or cottage	1 pt
cheese, Swiss or cheddar	16 slices about 4 × 4 in., ³⁄₃₂ in. thick; 1 qt ground
date and nut filling	1 pt (scant)
eggs, hard-cooked	10 large eggs, chopped, equals 3 c
fish, flaked	2½ c; each portion about 1½ oz or 2 T
jelly, jam, or preserves	1¾ c
lettuce	1 medium head yields 16 leaves about ¾ oz each, leaving about 3 to 4 oz of heart
meat	chicken, sliced, 12 to 16 portions, 1½ to 1 oz each; ham, beef, or other, 8 to 12 portions, 2 to 1½ oz each; ground, cooked meat, 3 c
olives, drained, chopped	3 c
peanut butter	1⅞ c
tomatoes, fresh	18 to 32 slices, 6 to 8 slices per tomato, ³⁄₁₆ inch thick; a large tomato (5 × 5), about 2 to 2½ per lb will give about the right size slice for a regular sandwich
vegetables, chopped or diced (celery, onions, carrots, peppers, etc.)	2½ to 3 c

☐ Dinner

In some operations, the work during the dinner shift in the short order section changes dramatically, becoming largely a fry cook job dealing with fried, broiled, or griddled items. It may also involve the preparation of cooked dishes such as stews, fricassees, pot roasts, and Swiss steaks. In other operations, the menu and the work change little from those for lunch or even breakfast.

To be prepared for all possible work conditions, therefore, a short order cook should learn how to handle the moist-heat cooking problems of braising, fricasseeing, stewing, poaching, and so on. In addition, good information is needed on how to deep-fry many items, how to roast meats, poultry, and fish, and how to perform other tasks. In small operations that offer anything more than a very limited menu but have no separate cooking section, the short order section must carry all of these tasks if such items are to be produced.

Griddled or Sautéed Items

When one thinks of dinner-time griddle cooking, one thinks immediately of steaks, but many other items are also cooked on the griddle for dinner, including Salisbury steaks, fried liver and onions, and hamburgers.

As discussed in Chapter 3, griddle cooking and sautéing are very similar. In sautéing, a thin layer of oil is put into a well-seasoned pan before the item is cooked, but almost the same results can be achieved by using sufficient oil in griddling. Griddling can also be used in place of deep-frying. Thus, cod cakes that are breaded and then deep-fried can instead be griddled as breaded items. The same is true for breaded veal cutlets.

In this section, therefore, while only griddling is specifically discussed, sautéing could be used as a parallel process, and in some instances so could deep-frying.

Steaks, pork chops, lamb chops, veal steaks, and the like can be griddled effectively on a griddle heated to about 375°F (191°C). Have the griddle well-seasoned and lightly greased; then place the item firmly down on it. A hammer or cover can be used to weigh down the item so that it cooks faster. When the meat is browned on one side, turn it over without piercing the flesh (using tongs or piercing the fatty tissue with a fork) and allow it to cook on the other side. Cooking should continue until the desired degree of doneness is reached. Thin items can be cooked at a relatively high heat, and unusually thick ones should sometimes be cooked at a lower one.

Various recipes for griddling or sautéing dinner menu items are listed in the appendix.

Broiled Items

Steaks, chops, ham, and other items may be broiled. The amount depends on the type of operation and on the volume of demand. Where a facility specializes in serving broiled items—even hamburgers—the amount processed in this way is large, while other operations may do little, if any, broiling.

Pan-broiling consists of putting a meat item into a pan with no added fat and cooking it at fairly high heat, pouring off fat as it collects. Only well-marbled meats can be processed in this manner.

In regular broiling, well-marbled items—rib steaks, strip loin (N.Y.) steaks, tenderloins, and chops—are first dipped into oil, and the excess oil is allowed to drain. The item is then placed on a preheated broiler grid, set at a 60° angle, and pressed firmly down on the grid. When it is about one-quarter done, the item is moved, but not turned over, and again pressed firmly down on the grid. This sets a crisscrossing pattern as was discussed in the section on broiling in Chapter 3. When the steak is about one-half done, the steak is turned over, and at the three-quarters done stage the angle change is repeated on that side. When fully done, the item is placed on a warm plate and brushed liberally with seasoned butter.

Steamed, Simmered, and Poached Items

With many patrons seeking to reduce their consumption of fried foods, the popularity of steamed, simmered, or poached items is increasing. Many tasty, appealing foods can be prepared in these ways.

Simmering involves maintaining the water temperature in a pot at 212°F (100°C), without letting it boil. Just a slight bit of movement occurs: that is all. Simmering yields a tenderer product than does boiling and usually extends over a long cooking period, since a lot of tough items are cooked in this way to make use of moist heat as a tenderizer.

Stewing hens (fowl) are often simmered until tender, and then the meat is used for items such as chicken salad, chicken à la king, and creamed chicken and mushrooms. Usually these are prepared in the cooking section; but if not, the short order section may have to do it. Each fowl normally weighs 4 to 5 pounds when ready to cook.

One of the best ways to cook fish is to poach it in a flavorful court bouillon (fish stock), cooking it only until it flakes. Overcooking gives a dry product. Low-fat fish that do not broil or bake well can be cooked very satisfactorily by this method.

The appendix includes recipes for several items that can be produced by steaming, simmering, or poaching.

Deep-Fried Items

Various deep-fried items are made in the short order section, ranging from meats to fish to poultry. Deep-fried shrimp is the No. 1 selling seafood item. Batter-fried fish with french-fried potatoes (fish and chips) is another very popular menu item. And deep-fried chicken is also a good seller.

Good deep-fried foods are produced when the cook uses a good-quality frying fat, keeps the fat and the frying equipment clean, uses sound frying techniques, and properly prepares the items to be fried. While the trend today is toward reducing fat in the diet, deep-fried items retain widespread popularity.

Broiler chickens weigh about 3 to 3½ pounds each. To cut one into parts, lay the chicken on its breast and then cut with a sharp knife down along each side of the backbone. Remove the backbone and save it for stock. Turn the bird over and cut through the wishbone to the breast-bone. Then pick up the chicken and pull it apart at the breastbone. Remove the breastbone and cartilage. Separate the breasts from the leg quarters by following the natural seams between the two. Remove the wings. If more separate parts are desired, cut the legs from the thighs where they join. This gives eight parts. If ten parts are desired, cut the breasts in two (see Fig. 5-4).

Recipes for deep-fried fish and chicken are provided in the appendix.

Roasting or Baking

Normally, the short order section does not prepare roasts; most operations have them prepared in another section and sent in to the short order section for plating. Occasionally, however, the short order cook may have to prepare them, so some knowledge of how to do this is valuable. And in any case, short order cooks have to know how to carve roasts.

Savarin, the great epicure, once said, "A good roast cook is born." While he was a highly respected man in the field of foods, he may have erred here: good roasts are not difficult to prepare if the rules are followed. Roasting consists of putting meats into an oven to cook by dry heat. Seasoning is best done after the roasting has been completed, and usually the sauce or gravy contains enough flavor to make any further seasoning unnecessary.

It is important that meats be roasted at a low temperature to achieve their best flavor and tenderness while retaining maximum juiciness, although in some cases searing at high heat at the start of roasting is done to develop a caramelized flavor and to improve appearance. The fat side of the meat is placed uppermost during roasting. Since most of the fat on a chicken or turkey is on its back, these poultry are roasted breast-side down.

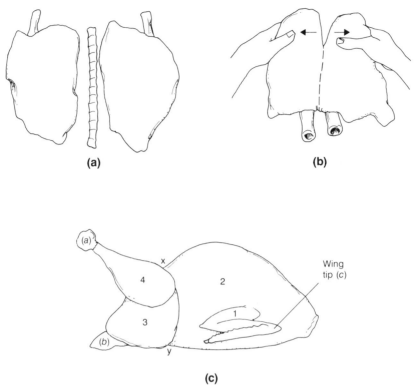

FIGURE 5-4. Cutting up a chicken: (a) Separate the backbone by cutting down along the backbone through the ribs and thigh bone on either side. (The inside of the chicken is shown face up; skin-side is down.) (b) Cut the chicken through the wishbone up to the breastbone, and pull the two halves apart. Remove the breastbone along with the cartilage. (c) Cut along the *x-y* line, where the leg and thigh separate from the breast, to divide each half into quarters. Then cut the quarters into parts 1, 2, 3, and 4 to separate a wing, a breast, a thigh, and a leg. Sometimes the leg knuckle *(a)*, tail *(b)*, and wing tip *(c)* are removed and used for stock.

Racks are used to keep meats out of their own juices (except for those that must be rolled in their juices for basting during roasting). Most roasts are cooked uncovered, but occasionally a roast such as leg of veal that lacks fat is cooked covered so that the resulting steam can keep the meat moist.

A *mirepoix* is often added to a roast to give it added flavor. Sauces, gravies, and the natural juice *(jus)* from the meat are produced from meat drippings left in the roasting pan. In order for the cook to use these drippings, the roasting pan must be deglazed with a liquid such as water, tomato juice, or wine.

It is wise to set a meat thermometer into the deepest part of the roast to ensure that a correct internal temperature is attained. Remember that the interior temperature of meat rises after its removal from the oven, so roasts must be removed before the desired temperature is reached; thus, for example, to have an 18-pound rib of beef cooked rare (140°F or 60°C), remove it from the oven when the internal temperature is around 125°F (46°C).

At times roasting may be called baking. Thus we may "bake a ham" or "bake a chicken," but we will "roast a turkey." Thus one will note in the appendix a recipe for "Baked Chicken" and one for "Roast Turkey." Note also "Baked Stuffed Pork Chop." Why these terms are used this way is unknown but it seems to be traditional in cooking terminology. The procedures for both are, however, identical.

A turkey can be roasted in the same way as chickens are, but it will take about 2 hours of preliminary roasting before the turkey can be turned breast-side up and then roasted for a final 45 minutes to 1 hour; the bird should be basted every 15 to 20 minutes. When a thermometer in the thickest part of the breast or thigh registers 170°F (79°C), the turkey (or chicken) can be removed from the oven. An additional rise in internal temperature will occur thereafter, ensuring a well-done bird. Geese and ducks do not have to be roasted breast-side down, since they have enough fat on the breast to keep it moist.

Recipes for roasting or baking chicken, stuffed pork chops, and rib of beef are given in the appendix.

Carving

The way to carve poultry, fish, or meats depends a lot on the layout of bone and muscle structures. Cooks should be familiar with these so that they can carve properly. To make the standard carving stroke start at the heel of the knife; then, with a steady, even motion, cut down and through to obtain a clean cut. Cutting across the grain of the meat gives a tenderer, better-looking portion. Often during carving, excess fat, gristle, and other substances need to be removed. Figure 5-5 details how to carve a turkey.

Select a knife suited to the particular carving need. Thus, for roast beef, use a long-bladed (12-inch) roast-beef slicer (see Fig. 5-6). Have it very sharp so that only a small amount of pressure is needed to cut through the meat. Forcing the blade through can shred tender meat and reduce the number of portions, as well as yielding unattractive slices. Meats should not be carved until after the final rise in temperature following oven removal has occurred. At that point, the meat is firmer and gives better slices.

Hams and other legs can be carved as shown in Figure 5-7. Sometimes boned meats can be sliced on a slicer. This method is quicker than hand-slicing and has been shown to give more portions. When carving a flank steak, corned beef brisket, or other thin cut, try to cut on a diagonal to get wider slices. This technique also increases tenderness. Except in the case of such items as roast beef, several small slices usually appear to provide a bigger portion than a single large slice. They also can be grouped together into a better-looking portion.

In serving, use a portion scale frequently until matching the correct amount to serve becomes almost automatic. Make sure, too, that the sliced meat is hot and is put onto a warm plate. In some cases, carved meat is held in rich stock in the bain-marie or steam table, which helps

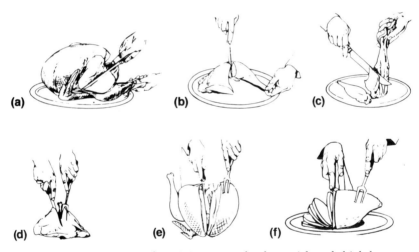

FIGURE 5-5. Carving a turkey: (a) Remove the drumstick and thigh by pulling the leg away from the body. The joint connecting the leg to the backbone often snaps free or may be severed easily with the knife point. Cut the dark meat from the body by following the body contour carefully with the knife. (b) Place the drumstick and thigh on the cutting surface, and cut through the connecting joint. (c) Tilt the drumstick at a convenient angle, and slice down toward the cutting surface. (d) Hold the thigh firmly on the cutting surface with a fork, and cut slices evenly and parallel to the bone. (e) Hold the turkey breast firmly on the cutting surface with a fork, and carve away the breast from the ribs on each side of the keel bone by cutting along the keel bone and the rib cage. (f) Hold the breast firmly on the cutting surface and carve thin, even slices against the grain of the meat.
(*Courtesy National Turkey Federation*)

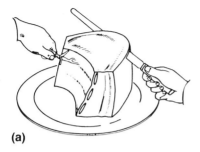

(a)

(b)

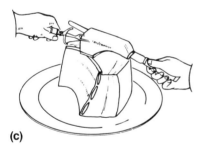

(c)

FIGURE 5-6. Carving a rib roast: (a) Place the cooked rib on the cutting surface, with the small cut surface up and the rib side to the carver's left (for a right-handed person). With the guard up on the fork, insert the fork firmly between the two top ribs. From the outside edge, slice inward across the grain toward the ribs. Make even slices of ¼ to 1 inch thick, depending on the portion size desired. (b) Release each piece by cutting close along the rib with the knife tip. To release a group of slices in one pass, cut the slices in series, leaving them in place, and then free them all with one cut. (c) Remove a slice by inserting the knife blade under it and placing the slice on a prewarmed plate. Cover with *jus* and serve. (*Courtesy National Live Stock and Meat Board*)

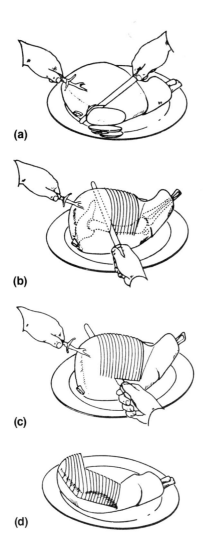

(a)

(b)

(c)

(d)

FIGURE 5-7. Carving a ham or other leg: (a) Place the leg on the cutting surface, fat-side up, with the shank end to the carver's right (for a right-handed person). The thin side of the leg, from which the first slices are made, will be nearest to or farthest from the carver, depending on whether the leg is from the right side or the left side. Using a standard carving knife or a ham slicer and fork, cut several even, clean slices perpendicular to the cutting surface. (b) Turn the leg so that it rests on the surface just cut. Holding the leg firmly with the fork, cut and remove a small wedge from the shank. Then cut a series of thin slices down to the leg bone. (c) Release the slices by cutting along the bone at right angles to the slices. (d) For additional servings, turn the leg back to its original position and slice at right angles to the bone. (*Courtesy National Live Stock and Meat Board*)

it stay warm and moist. Ladling a hot sauce or gravy over the meat can also help it maintain a proper temperature. Today, however, many patrons like to have these served on the side of the meat, so this is not always a desirable way to increase or hold the meat's temperature.

□ Summary

Breakfast eggs are often the most important items prepared by the short order cook, with breakfast meats perhaps the second most important. Cooks should know how to handle meats and eggs well and how to anticipate their reactions during cooking. Breakfast meats are often given some precooking so that they can be processed more rapidly. A well-seasoned griddle should be used for cooking eggs and meats; its temperature should be between 325° and 350°F (161° and 177°C).

The cook also needs to be able to produce batter items such as waffles, hotcakes, and French toast. Standardized recipes should be used. Hot breakfast cereals thicken because the starch in them gelatinizes in the presence of moisture and heat. Add the uncooked cereal to rapidly boiling water, stirring it in well.

The most common breakfast potato is hash browns, with french fries next. Hash browns are prepared on the griddle, while french fries are deep-fried.

Luncheon items range from salads to sandwiches to luncheon entrées. Because of the wide variety, good organization is essential to producing good-quality orders as rapidly as needed. In some operations, luncheon preparations are simplified because a simplified menu is used.

The method of making sandwiches differs according to whether they are produced in quantity or singly. In either case, a well arranged workplace is needed. Sandwiches have four parts: bread, spread, filling, and garnish. The bread should be fresh and suited to the type of sandwich being made. Good storage is needed for bread; hard-crusted breads should be used the same day as made. Softened margarine and butter are the most commonly used spreads. The kind of filling used, which gives the sandwich its name, can differ from slices to mixtures. Freshness is an important factor in these. Garnishes should be edible and should suit the item.

Only a few salads may be made in the short order section, since the pantry produces most of them. Salads have four parts: underliner, body, garnish, and dressing. The underliner is frequently a leafy green, but other bases may take its place. Good work organization is needed to produce salads quickly. Freshness is an important factor, and salads should be made as close to service as possible.

Prepared or grilled special luncheon entrées may have to be produced. If the operation is large, other sections will be responsible for some of the preparation, but in smaller operations the short order section must do it all.

Dinner cooking often involves preparing a lot of griddle or broiler items. Some deep-fried products such as deep-fried fish and shrimp may be involved, too. Meat carving may be a task of the short order cook. In addition, the work may require some knowledge of braising, steaming, simmering, and poaching. The work requirements for dinner may be simple or quite varied and complex, depending on menu demands.

□ CHAPTER REVIEW □

1. An order comes in for shirred eggs and bacon. How would a short order cook go about preparing this order?
2. How can a cook tell whether an egg is fresh or not?
3. Breakfast link sausages are on the menu. How would these be prepared?
4. What causes hard-boiled eggs to have a dark color and a sulfury flavor? (See also Chapter 4.)
5. What can overmixing a waffle batter do to it?
6. How would you prepare a waffle to order if the batter were already mixed?
7. What are crepes, blinis, and *plättar*?
8. How would you go about preparing an order of French toast? How would you cook it?
9. Describe the proper way to cook a breakfast cereal.
10. How do short order cooks prepare french-fried potatoes? Could you argue that another way is actually more often used? Why would one way be correct and the other way less correct?
11. What are hash brown potatoes, and how are they prepared?
12. Lunch is a midday meal. What kinds of foods are most popular at lunch, and why?
13. Name the four parts of a salad.
14. How does one crisp salad greens? What is osmosis?
15. What are the four parts of a sandwich? What part gives the sandwich its name?
16. If you were asked to set up a fast sandwich-making station, what would you do to make it most efficient?
17. What is the difference between a toasted cheese sandwich and a grilled cheese sandwich?

18. Indicate how you would make a hot beef sandwich.
19. What luncheon entrée dishes might one have to make in the short order section? (The range is wide, but narrow it down to typical kinds of menu items.)
20. The menu calls for turkey à la king. What are its main ingredients, and how is it prepared?
21. A student in a short order cooking class must be prepared to know the preparation of major dinner items. What types of foods might this cook be expected to prepare?
22. How would you describe the differences between sautéing and griddling?
23. How would you prepare an order for sautéed fillet of sole?
24. List some good techniques to follow in producing broiled items.
25. What treatment does a lean meat item require in order to be broiled successfully?
26. What general rules must be observed in order to make good deep-fried items?
27. What is the difference between a breaded-fried and a batter-fried item?
28. How would you divide a whole chicken into sixteen parts and have a backbone for using for stock? Would you remove anything else for stock?
29. How do steaming, simmering, and poaching differ?
30. What is a court bouillon, and how is it used in cooking fish?
31. What is braising? What kinds of meats, fish, and poultry are usually braised? What is long-time, moist-heat cooking, and why is it done?
32. Indicate how you would prepare a pot roast.
33. What is roasting?
34. How would you carve a prime rib roast of beef? a turkey?

CHAPTER SIX

Safety and Sanitation

□ Safety

Safety is crucial to all cooks. The short order section presents many opportunities for inadvertent accidents to occur. Sharp knives, hot fat, heated utensils, slippery floors, moving mechanical equipment, and other factors can contribute to accidents. Cooks need to be trained to work safely, and then they must use their training to avert accidents. Some people are accident-prone, because they are not watchful and cognizant of the dangers that create accidents. People who know what the dangers are and how to avoid them tend not to have accidents.

A number of factors can create accidents. Equipment may be poorly constructed or improperly installed. Proper safeguards against accidents may not have been taken. Short order cooks may not have been trained to plan and act with safety in mind. Pressures in the workplace can also increase the accident rate. When one rushes at work, one raises the likelihood of causing or encountering an accident. Thinking while working is the way to avoid accidents. One may also become more accident-prone as one tires. Records show that most accidents occur during the later stages of shifts, when workers are tired, rather than at the beginning.

Foodservices have a high accident rate. In fact, the accident rate per 1,000 workers is higher in foodservice than in mining. This is because there are so many chances for accidents. Grease and other slippery things can get dropped or spilled on floors, inviting slips and falls. Heavy weights must be lifted. Hot materials must be handled. Mechanical equipment—often cutting types—must be operated. Knives must be wielded. At times, cooks come under pressure and abandon precautionary measures that prevent accidents.

The federal government has passed a law designed to reduce hazards in work areas and thus to reduce accidents. The Occupational Safety and Health Act (OSHA) gives broad coverage to safety matters, and employers must adhere to its code or be fined. Operations can even be shut down for repeated or major violations. In addition, local and state laws

159

often require that other specific safety measures be taken. Cooks may be charged by these to ensure that safety measures are implemented and that safety rules are observed. Human failure is the largest cause of accidents; and unless cooks themselves work for safety, no law or precautionary measure can keep accidents from happening.

Cuts

Among the most common accidents in foodservice work are cuts. There is a saying: "The dull knife cuts; the sharp knife doesn't." This refers to the fact that using a dull knife requires force, which creates an extra hazard. A sharp knife moves easily through material and thus gives better control. Safety-minded cooks make sure that they use the proper knife for a particular purpose and that it is sharp. It is also important that a cook know how to use knives properly. Using a boning knife takes special motions and a lot of wrist action. Using a mechanical slicer to carve a roast requires even pressure, faithful use of safety guards, and a healthy distance between the hands and the cutting blade.

In a previous discussion of knives and how to use them, it was noted that the fingers of the hand holding the food should remain bent down so that the knife rides against them (see Figs. 2-23 and 2-24). As cutting occurs, the holding hand is moved backward slowly so that the knife continues to make up and down motions in cutting through the material. Keeping the holding hand in this position is important in avoiding cuts. When cutting an unstable item, first cut a portion from the bottom so that it will rest more securely on the cutting board. Cut away from the body when using cutting tools. The proper way to carry a knife in hand while walking is to keep the knife tip pointed toward the floor. If a knife or other sharp instrument falls, let it fall. Get out of the way so that it does not hit a foot or leg. Do not grab for it. This often results in the grabber's catching the blade and receiving a nasty cut.

Knives should not be left out when not in use. They should be washed immediately after use, dried, and stored in their proper place. Putting a knife or other sharp tool into water where it cannot be seen is taboo, since it can cause a severe cut. Treat all sharp tools as you would knives; make sure that they are kept sharp, too.

Grinders, choppers, and slicers are also high-hazard items. One should always use a stamper (mallet for pushing food through the machine) to move food to be cut or ground through them. Use proper care in disassembling such equipment. Do not put a slicer or the rotating cutting mechanism of a rotating chopper into a pot sink filled with water and leave it there. Set them up where they can be seen. Hidden in the water, they become high-hazard items.

Another potentially dangerous piece of equipment is the cutting saw, with its rotating blade. One should be well trained before using it. When using a cleaver, know where the holding hand is and take care that the cleaver does not meet it. Never put any glassware into a sink. It can easily get broken, and then some unsuspecting victim can suffer a bad cut. Watch for nails and other sharp items when unpacking boxes, crates, and cartons. Use proper tools for such unpacking, and be careful.

Burns

Other top lost-time offenders in foodservices are burns and scalds. Since so much cooking equipment is used and so many hot things are handled, this is not surprising. Heat is an almost constant accompaniment to the work done. Lift hot things carefully. Do not try to lift extremely heavy items filled with hot things; get someone to help. Use dry cloths, towels, or hot pads to separate the hand from hot handles and other things. Before lifting anything hot from the fire, know where it is to go and make sure that the way is clear of hazards. Do not let handles on hot utensils project out from the heat area, and always assume that the handle itself is hot. Some cooks put a pinch of salt on the tip of very hot handles to signal that they are hot and should not be touched.

Cooks should know how to work safely around hot ovens, griddles, or steam equipment. The inexperienced cook can get a severe burn or scald from lifting the lid of a boiling pot or steam-jacketed kettle by hand, instead of using a long fork or other tool to lift the lid (see Fig. 6-1). When the lid is lifted by hand, the steam rushing up and out of the pot can catch the arm. Remember that lifting hot things situated above shoulder height or below knee height is more difficult than lifting things situated at central body height. One has less strength (and thus less control) toward these extremes, so handling hot things at these levels is more dangerous.

Hot grease, oil, or fat is another cause of burns. Because these materials' temperature can rise far above the scalding temperature of boiling water or free steam, the burns they produce can be deeper and more painful. Whenever one is handling such material, special care must be taken; it is not something to fool with. Remember also to use frying equipment properly. Do not overload it, and make sure that foods are not too moisture-laden when put into the hot fat. Keep equipment in proper order, and turn off the heat when the fryer is not in use. Be especially careful when working around hot fat or oil. Make certain that handles do not protrude, that the container holding the hot fat is sitting securely and not on the edge of a counter or shelf where it can fall and spill. Remember that oil and fat has a flash point of around 600°F (312.4°C).

FIGURE 6-1. The proper way to lift the lid of a kettle that is boiling hard: use a long-handled fork or other instrument. (*Photo by Michael Upright*)

When draining equipment filled with hot grease, oil, or fat, use proper methods and check to see that everything is in proper order before trying to perform the operation. In one bad accident, a cook connected a deep-fryer filled with hot oil to a pump, in order to drain it; but the cook failed to fasten the hose of the pump securely, with the result that the force of the pump blew the hose free from its connection and hot oil sprayed over several workers. It is always wise to let the material cool down before attempting to transport, filter, or drain it—if that is possible.

Many cooks work in short sleeves, but this is not the safest way to dress. Long sleeves are a better protection against burns and scalds. Remember, too, not to overfill containers with hot items. This leaves room for splashing.

If one gets a burn or scald, putting the injured part under cold water or covering it with ice can help relieve the pain. Strong tea contains tannin, a substance that keeps air away from a burn and thus makes it less painful. The juice of an aloe plant contains a large quantity of tannin, and a broken leaf rubbed over a burn or scald can help give relief. Of course, a first-aid unit should always be kept in the kitchen.

Mechanical Equipment

Almost any piece of mechanical equipment can be an accident hazard, because it is being driven by a force that is not controllable at a moment's notice. Cooks should never put a hand or scraper in the bowl of a mixer or near the agitator while it is mixing. Moreover, no part of the clothing or other items should be positioned where they might get caught in the mixer. Make sure that the bowl and agitator are firmly in place before starting the mixer. A dough divider or rounder is another potential hazard. Know how to reach quickly for the turn-off switch on all automatic machines. Be sure to know how to operate the equipment, and see that it is assembled and used properly.

There are times when accidents have results that are noninjurious and even funny, but they should still be recognized as teaching a serious cautionary lesson. Once your author was working as a pantryman and needed to make several gallons of mayonnaise. His mixer was not available, but the one on the chef's wooden worktable was free, so he asked the chef is he could use her mixer. She said yes but asked that he be careful, because she had just scrubbed the table and it was nice and clean, and she did not want it soiled with a lot of oil blobs. After promising to be careful, the pantryman tied a towel around the mixer as a safeguard, so that oil could not splash onto the machine as it was being fed into the mayonnaise. Unfortunately, however, the mixer was near an open window, and a sudden draft blew the cloth into the mixer. The mixer picked it up, along with about 1¼ gallons of mayonnaise. The chef saw the mass coming and turned to run, but she was too late: it caught her square between the shoulders. At that point, everyone could agree that she was a "well-dressed" woman! Luckily for your author, she took it all in good humor. Still, the point should not be lost that—had the material in the equipment been hot, or had someone slipped and fallen in the residue of the mayonnaise explosion—a far from amusing outcome might have resulted.

Falls

The most frequent accident in foodservice is not a cut, as one might think, but falling. A blind corner where two people run into each other, slippage, hurrying, floor obstructions, and just plain carelessness are frequent causes. All spills of liquids, foods, grease, or other items should be cleaned up immediately. Often floors are wet, which makes them slippery; workers should be trained to use special care when this is the case. Cooks have been seen to come to work wearing open-toed sandals with leather bottoms. Leather footwear is slippery on a wet floor, so a cook's shoes should have composition and not leather soles.

In one study in which an operation bought two pairs of shoes per person, the cost of the shoes was more than made up for in higher productivity and reduced complaints of tiredness and backaches. The shoes were designed to fit up to and around the ankles, with a good last and a high-quality leather top that was quite pliable and flexible. Two pairs were purchased for each person, to allow each pair of shoes to be worn one day and rested the next, thus prolonging the shoes' working life.

Often cooks wear shoes with too high heels. In many work areas, the cook works on slatted duckboards, and such heels can slip through the slats and cause tripping. Duckboards should be made of wood or a hard, nonslipping composition. Some types have an abrasive surface that prevents slipping.

Cooks should not put objects on the floor where they can be tripped over, and electrical cords should not cross walk areas. Good lighting should be provided throughout the work area, in hallways, and on stairways. Poor lighting is often the cause of cuts and bruising, as well as falls. Handrails should be present on all stairways. Torn or loose carpeting and other surprise factors can cause a fall. Nonskid flooring should be provided. Cooks should remain alert at all times. Many falls are caused by inattention. It is a poor practice to carry anything that obstructs one's view. Instead, a cart or tray should be used.

Fires

There are three kinds of fires: Type A fires result from the burning of combustible materials such as paper, wood, or rags; Type B fires involve grease, gas, or petroleum; and Type C fires are electrical. Each requires different treatment in order to be extinguished. Types A and B should be smothering. A fire extinguisher that creates a blanket of CO_2 is good for smothering a Type A fire, but it may spread a Type B fire, if it is water-based. A blanket, a cover, or some other item can be thrown over a fire in some situations to put it out. Type C fires should not be fought with water or a water-based fire retardant. Faced with such a fire, first shut off the electricity to the affected unit *immediately*; then use the appropriate fire retardant. Usually foodservices have the kinds of fire extinguishers needed to put out each of these three kinds of fires, and cooks should be trained in their use.

Dealing with fires is not only a matter of knowing how to put one out properly; it also involves preventing them from happening in the first place. Cooks should be taught that fires result when there is something to burn, when there is sufficient heat to cause a fire, and when oxygen is available to keep the fire burning. Removing any of these three lowers or removes the risk of a fire. It is a good idea to have fire-retardant blankets placed at strategic intervals throughout the kitchen; then, if someone should catch fire or if a fire should start, these blankets can be used to smother the flames.

The first few moments are the most important in extinguishing a fire. Equipment should immediately be turned off, if it is an equipment fire, to remove the source of fuel. The next thing to do is to sound the alarm. Then use an extinguisher. Sometimes a small bit of soda thrown on a grease fire will smother it. The heat of the fire breaks down the soda which then emits carbon dioxide. Salt can help smother flames but creates no effective gas. Grease fires are most dangerous if they get up into the hood filters and into the ducts that exhaust air out of the kitchen; a terrible fire can occur here, especially if grease has been allowed to build up in the ducts. Good housekeeping is therefore an important factor in fire prevention.

All cooks should have a deep concern for their own safety and for the safety of others. Everyone in the kitchen should know how to get out of the building and how to help others do so, if such help is needed.

Explosions and Electrical Shocks

The most common location of an explosion in a food facility is in a place where gas is used; for some reason the gas escapes, and suddenly it is ignited. Cooks should therefore use special care in operating gas equipment. All gas equipment should be properly vented; and when such equipment is turned on, the cook should see that ignition is proper. If it is not, it should immediately be turned off and allowed to sit awhile before the cook tries once again to ignite it.

Rare explosions can also occur. It is possible for a moist product (such as a slice of apple surrounded by batter) to explode in hot fat. Steam builds up under the batter, creating a force that, if suddenly released, can throw a mass of hot fat or oil out of the fry kettle. Steam equipment can also be the cause of very hazardous explosions. Safety valves on such equipment should be checked to ensure that they are working properly and are not encrusted with debris that interferes with proper functioning. Cooks should know how to use steam equipment correctly and should check to see that safety catches and other parts of the unit are properly used.

Electricity is excellent for providing power for equipment, but it also can be dangerous as a source of electrical shocks. While many of the circuits may carry only 120 v of electricity—which is not as life-threatening as a voltage of 208 v or higher—cooks should have respect for even these voltages. If a cook is standing in a wet area or has wet hands and thus is well grounded, even a 120-v shock can be fatal. The cook should inspect equipment to see that wires are not exposed. All equipment should be grounded so that a malfunction that allows the equipment itself to become electrified does not cause it to hold the full charge. Grounding may not prevent shocks, but it can help to reduce the intensity of one. Cooks should also know that most metals, water, and other liquid substances are good electrical conductors. Never handle electrical equipment with wet hands or when standing in water. Cooks should also know where the shut-off switch is for electrical equipment, so it can be turned off immediately. They should never touch metal when touching anything electrified. Knowing is preventing.

General Precautions

As noted, accidents result more frequently from human failure than from equipment or facility failure. Cooks need to know how to prevent accidents, and then they must use such information to prevent accidents. Cooks need to be constantly alert and not daydreaming while working. Often cooks stand too near ranges or other hot equipment or try to pass other workers in spaces that are too crowded to allow safe passing. Keeping the workplace tidy and well organized can also be an important safeguard. Standing erect, having good posture, and using the body in an efficient and controlled manner are important. Good work habits are an asset, and knowing how to do a job before starting to do it is very valuable. Being alert, cooperating with others, and being watchful are necessary traits of a cook who is accident-free.

Finally, cooks should take precautions to ensure that accidents do not occur to patrons. Carelessness in this area can cause a serious accident to occur to a guest, which may place the entire operation in jeopardy. Huge lawsuit settlements can wipe out a business and cause a number of workers to lose their jobs. Then, too, cooks should know that they can be personally liable for carelessness that results in injury to another person (who is often a fellow worker).

□ Sanitation

Sanitation is a way of life. It is the quality of living that is expressed in the clean home, the clean farm, the clean business and industry, the clean neighborhood, the clean community. Being a way of life, it must come from within the people; it is nourished by knowledge and grows as an obligation and ideal in human relations. (*Credo of the National Sanitation Foundation, Ann Arbor, Michigan*)

Today patrons of foodservices are concerned about sanitation. They want their food to be clean and sanitary. They know that disease can be caused by food, and they do not want to have their foodservice cause them problems in this area. The U.S. Public Health Service has identified some forty diseases that can be transmitted in food. This is about two-thirds of all diseases known to be harmful to man.

A number of organizations work to see that food is safe and healthful for patrons in foodservices to eat. The U.S. Public Health Service has established a code that serves as a model for states and communities to use in setting up regulations to ensure that proper food handling occurs in foodservices and that the food served is safe and clean. This code covers not only the sanitary conditions that must exist in these facilities but also the hygiene of workers, their freedom from disease, and the ways in which they perform their work. It is said that problems that result in the eating of harmful food are caused 95 percent of the time by human failure and only 5 percent of the time by equipment failure. Thus, the Public Health Service program is directed largely at cooks and workers, to make certain that they use good food-handling procedures.

The National Restaurant Association has been a leader in promoting good sanitation. It has realized that the industry's interest lies in seeing that high sanitary standards exist. The National Sanitation Foundation has taken the lead in ensuring that foodservice equipment manufacturers meet high standards for equipment, so as to reduce potential hazards in that area. All states have agencies and regulations requiring that foods be handled in a safe manner and that proper sanitary standards be met. Local communities also set up bodies and regulations to promote sanitation in foodservices.

It is in an operation's best interest to have a clean and sanitary facility. Patrons avoid operations that appear unsanitary, unclean, messy, or disorganized. The outer areas must be kept up and must be neat and orderly; the interior should be inviting; and the food must be above reproach when it comes to being sanitary and wholesome.

While the management of a foodservice bears a large share of the responsibility for seeing that food is safe and healthful to eat, workers (and especially cooks) also carry a part of this responsibility. They should observe the rules for safe and sanitary food handling. Workers must be committed to sanitation, must know how to obtain it, and must take the necessary steps.

Unsatisfactory Food

Food can become unsatisfactory for service as a result of any of a number of factors. Sometimes the food is not properly prepared, is messy, and is served very unattractively. At times it may not be the food itself that causes rejection but the kind of service given with the food. However, some food becomes dangerous to serve because it contains harmful substances. In some instances, the food itself may naturally contain harmful substances, as poisonous mushrooms do. At other times, harmful chemicals may get into the food. Certain kinds of microorganisms may be in the food that are dangerous in themselves or that produce harmful substances as by-products. Food can spoil because of the action of bacteria, molds, yeasts, and other microorganisms. Chemical changes can occur that cause the food to be unpalatable or downright harmful. Many different spoilage reactions can occur, such as actions from yeasts, bacteria, or molds. All of these can be prevented by one means or another, and good sanitation involves knowing how these changes can occur and how they can be prevented.

Microorganisms

The main groups of microorganisms that cause food deterioration are bacteria, parasites, viruses, yeasts, and molds. These organisms differ considerably from one another in some respects, but they also have some remarkable similarities that can lead to their control or eradication.

Bacteria Many species of single-celled microorganisms exist. These living things are so small that a thousand of them clustered together may not be visible to the naked eye; they average $\frac{1}{25,000}$ inch in size. These microorganisms, which are neither plant nor animals, are called *bacteria*.

Some bacteria are harmless, they neither do good nor harm. Others are beneficial: they do such things as breaking down substances in the soil so that plants can get food. One beneficial type of bacteria is put into Swiss cheese to make the holes and give flavor. Others, however, are harmful.

Usually, harmful bacteria are categorized as being either *intoxicants* or *infectants*. An intoxicant is a bacterium that gets into food and creates a toxin that is injurious to humans when they eat the food. The bacterium itself may no longer be in the food (perhaps being destroyed when the food was heated), but the toxin is still there and causes the problem. An infectant is a bacterium that gets into the food and is taken into the body while still alive, infecting the body so that illness occurs.

Intoxicants *Staphylococcus* is a common intoxicant. Most people carry these bacteria in their bodies. Sneezing or coughing can spread them, and a small pimple or a festering cut can contain a lot of staph. Human feces also contain staph. These bacteria are also found in the air and on our hands, so they can easily get into food. If staph gets into food and the conditions are right for its growth, in about 4 hours it can generate enough toxin to make a person ill. Such illness usually occurs within 1 to 6 hours and is evidenced by nausea, vomiting, diarrhea, fever, and abdominal cramps.

Clostridium botulinum creates a terrible toxin. The amount that can fit on a pinhead is enough to paralyze a person and cause death. It cannot grow with air present, and it cannot grow in an acidic medium. Thus, it most often appears in nonacidic canned foods. Drugs are now available that can counteract the toxin, if they are administered soon enough.

Clostridium perfringens resembles *C. botulinum* in that it grows best in an airless, nonacidic environment. The bacteria are attracted to proteins and are found most often in meat dishes. Although not fatal, *C. perfringens* can cause serious illness. The clostridium family is found in the soil and in the intestinal tract of humans and animals.

Infectants Many contagious diseases, including diphtheria, scarlet fever, strep throat, and typhoid fever are caused by infectants—bacteria that get into food and drink and from there into the body, where they cause problems. Some, such as the *salmonella* group, cause food poisoning, evidenced by diarrhea, vomiting, abdominal cramps, headaches, and fever. Salmonella are found in eggs, in the intestinal tract, and in feces. Recently there has been much publicity about the amount of salmonella found in the intestinal tracts of chickens. Fortunately, cooking the chicken destroys them; and since they are infectants, they must be alive in the food when consumed in order to cause trouble.

Shigella are infectants that cause diarrhea. The bacillus lives in moist foods that contain meat, eggs, or other proteins. Again, the basic contaminant exists in fecal matter. Illness occurs one to four days after infection.

Streptococci can cause strep throat, scarlet fever, and other illnesses. People who contaminate food or drink can be carriers, but there are other ways of getting the infection. Some strep infections are mild, while others can be fatal.

Parasites Federal law requires that all cured and smoked pork products be heated to an interior temperature of 155°F (68°C) to ensure that *trichinae*—small larvae found in pork, bear, rabbit, and some other animals—are destroyed. Tapeworm is another parasite; it can get into beef, fish, or poultry from uninspected sources. Taken into the body as a tiny egg, the tapeworm then hatches and lives in the intestine. Tapeworms can grow several feet long.

Viruses Structurally, viruses are even simpler microorganisms than bacteria. The most common dangerous virus found in food is the kind that causes hepatitis. It usually comes from fecal matter and can result in a fatal infection. Some individuals can be carriers of hepatitis.

Other potentially harmful viruses are also found in food, including one that comes from birds. Therefore, it is not desirable to keep live birds close to food preparation and service areas.

Yeasts There are many different yeasts. One is the kind bakers use to make bread. Brewer's yeast and champagne yeast are used for fermenting alcoholic beverages. Because brewer's yeast is high in nutrients, it is consumed by some individuals for its nutritive value.

Yeasts are everywhere. When they get into food, they cause it to ferment—to break down constituent carbohydrates into alcohol and carbon dioxide. While fermentation is a desirable process in some instances, it is highly undesirable in others; thus, fermentation may force a cook to discard a food as inedible.

Molds Like bacteria and yeasts, molds may be harmless, beneficial, or harmful. One special mold is used to make Roquefort cheese and blue cheese, and in fact the drug penicillin is refined from a closely related mold. Molds grow from spores that are always in the air ready to land on some moist food product and start growing. Some molds can develop poisonous toxins, but these are not common. When some food gets moldy, it should be thrown away.

Prevention

Undesirable elements get into food in a number of ways. The things that carry them to the food are called *vectors* or *carriers*. Air and water can be vectors, and thus foodservice operations try to ensure that air is clean and water is purified so it will be safe to drink. Raw sewage is disposed of in treatment plants in a manner that destroys harmful microorganisms. Utilities add chlorine to their water supply to oxidize and destroy pathogens (disease-producing organisms). Humans can be carriers. The pus in pimples or festering sores are filled with staph. People even carry pathogens in their breath. And as noted, feces are a major producer of pathogens; thus, it is a rule to wash one's hands well after visiting the rest room. Rodents such as mice and rats and insects such as flies and cockroaches can contaminate food, too.

To stop the spread of disease, contact with the vector must be broken. This is often hard to do, but the process of sanitation is dedicated to doing it. Operations try to keep roaches, flies, and other insects away from food; rats and mice are also unwelcome feeders. And all people in contact with food are instructed to be clean, wear clean clothing, and handle food in a clean and sanitary manner.

An important early step in practicing sanitation is to see that sanitary food is purchased. Purchases should be made from purveyors who have clean establishments and who carry food of approved sanitary quality. Their trucks are clean, their drivers are clean, and they handle food in a sanitary manner.

Once the food is received, the operation is responsible for seeing that it is stored and handled properly. The oldest foods should be used first. The principle of First In, First Out (FIFO) should be practiced. Foods should be stored off the floor and away from walls, and proper storage temperatures should be maintained. Pathogens are most active at about 100°F (68°C). The Public Health Service says that life begins after 45—45°F (7°C), that is—and from then on up to about 140°F (60°C), food is in the danger zone. Pathogens are not destroyed at temperatures below 45°F (7°C), but their rate of growth is slowed down. Above 45°F (7°C), growth speeds up and continues to flourish at temperatures up to 125°F (52°C). Above 125°F (52°C), most bacteria begin to die.

When milk is pasteurized, holding it for 30 minutes at 145°F (68°C) is sufficient to kill off pathogens but not heat-loving bacteria. That is why modern pasteurized dairy products develop a bitterness as they age, instead of souring. The souring (lactic acid-producing) bacteria are killed off, and only the heat-loving bacteria are left to alter the dairy product. Sterilization occurs within 10 minutes of boiling at 212°F (100°C), but at higher steam pressure temperatures the kill-off rate is much faster. No bacteria or other organisms remain alive after complete sterilization. This treatment must occur in canned foods and some other processed foods.

Freezing does not destroy microorganisms but it does halt their growth. Food held for a long time in frozen storage can eventually become sterile because the microorganisms slowly die off. The interior of meat itself is sterile but becomes contaminated when some part of the outer surface comes into contact with an outside vector. Ground meats usually contain a fairly large number of microorganisms and so must be watched much more closely than meat in large pieces.

Some fruits and vegetables—Irish potatoes and yams, for example—are quite stable and hold well at room temperature, although the best storage temperature for them is at or around 60°F (16°C). Other items such as cabbage, turnips, carrots, and apples hold very well under refrigeration. But some highly perishable fruits and vegetables hold for only about three days, even under good refrigeration (about 35° to 38°F, or 2° to 3°C). It is usual to store tropical fruits and some vegetables such as tomatoes at room temperature; this treatment helps them retain their quality, but it also increases their perishability.

Cooked foods that are to be stored in a cold place should be cooled as quickly as possible and then placed under refrigeration. It is best to wrap or cover them. It is also desirable to avoid storing food in too large a pack, in order to accelerate its rate of cooling. Some operations have a rule that no food put into pans can be more than 2 inches deep.

Spreading food out speeds cooling and guarantees a better holding temperature. In some studies, a warm pudding (such as chocolate pudding) has held a critical interior temperature for several days.

Foods can be cooled more quickly if they are placed in a draft, and sometimes a fan is used to blast air at cooling food in order to cool it more quickly. Stockpots are often placed on a rack or trivet in a sink, and running water is allowed to flow around and under them to speed cooling. When items are air-cooled, it is wise to set them on racks so that air can circulate underneath them. Studies have shown that hot food cools down just as rapidly to about room temperature outside refrigeration as under refrigeration, so there is little value in putting hot food into a refrigerator. The only advantage of immediate refrigeration is that it ensures that the food will not be forgotten and allowed to stand out longer than it should.

Some foods, including meats, eggs, and dairy products, must be given special handling. Store them at 40°F (4.5°C) or lower. Ordinarily, refrigerated units are set to hold a temperature of slightly less than 40°F (4.5°C). Remember that some foods—such as apples—give off odors and so should either be wrapped with an air-proof wrap or stored separately from other foods.

It is best to keep frozen foods at 0°F (−18°C) or below. This helps them hold their crystalline structure and prevents the crystals from changing into larger ones, which would cause a deterioration in food quality. All frozen foods should be thawed under refrigeration, if possible. Sometimes well-wrapped meats and other items can be thawed more quickly under running water or in front of a fan; this is only an emergency method, however. No food, once frozen, should be refrozen. Refreezing destroys texture and flavor, and it can be dangerous in that intoxicants may have developed while the food was unfrozen, building up toxins or infectants to a point where they are now harmful. Figure 6-2 indicates some critical temperatures in food handling.

How Microorganisms Grow

For microorganisms to grow, certain conditions must exist. Microorganisms need food, moisture, temperature (warmth), proper pH (acidity, alkalinity, or neutrality), air (or lack of air), and time.

Food is required by all forms of life, and the microorganisms in human foods are there because they like the same foods people do. Some are especially attracted to certain food items, just as some human beings are. Staph bacteria, for example, love cream fillings, which have everything they like best: protein, carbohydrates, and certain vitamins and minerals.

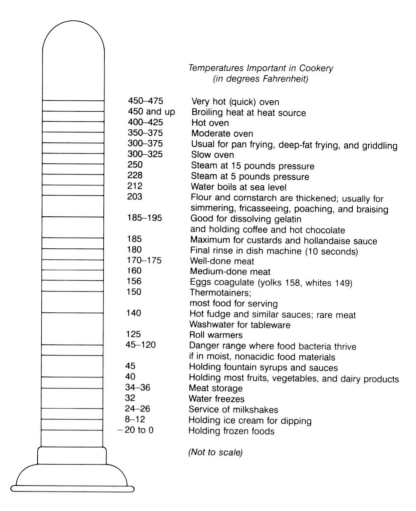

Temperatures Important in Cookery
(in degrees Fahrenheit)

450–475	Very hot (quick) oven
450 and up	Broiling heat at heat source
400–425	Hot oven
350–375	Moderate oven
300–375	Usual for pan frying, deep-fat frying, and griddling
300–325	Slow oven
250	Steam at 15 pounds pressure
228	Steam at 5 pounds pressure
212	Water boils at sea level
203	Flour and cornstarch are thickened; usually for simmering, fricasseeing, poaching, and braising
185–195	Good for dissolving gelatin and holding coffee and hot chocolate
185	Maximum for custards and hollandaise sauce
180	Final rinse in dish machine (10 seconds)
170–175	Well-done meat
160	Medium-done meat
156	Eggs coagulate (yolks 158, whites 149)
150	Thermotainers; most food for serving
140	Hot fudge and similar sauces; rare meat Washwater for tableware
125	Roll warmers
45–120	Danger range where food bacteria thrive if in moist, nonacidic food materials
45	Holding fountain syrups and sauces
40	Holding most fruits, vegetables, and dairy products
34–36	Meat storage
32	Water freezes
24–26	Service of milkshakes
8–12	Holding ice cream for dipping
−20 to 0	Holding frozen foods

(Not to scale)

FIGURE 6-2. Important temperatures (in degrees Fahrenheit) for various foodservice purposes. (*Modified from Lundberg and Kotschevar,* Understanding Cooking, *Marcus Press, Holyoke, Mass., 1985*)

The way to stop microorganisms from growing is to take away their food—in other words, never to let them get into the food. Good food handling, which involves having everything clean and using good handling procedures, is the way to accomplish this. Knowing what contamination is and how it can be spread is essential if one is to keep microorganisms out of food.

Microorganisms cannot grow easily in dry food, in foods that are high in salt or sugar, or in foods that contain chemicals such as nitrates, nitrites, or sodium benzoate. Some chemical preservatives are allowed in foods because there is no proof that they are harmful (at least not up to this point) but some of these are suspect. Thus, nitrites and nitrates may cause fats to break down during frying into *carcinogenic* (cancer-causing) substances. However, if one consumes a food fairly high in ascorbic acid (vitamin C), the vitamin in the stomach seems to retard the formation of these carcinogens. Thus, some experts say, eat bacon or ham for breakfast if you want, but at the same time eat a grapefruit, drink some orange juice, or consume something else that is high in ascorbic acid.

Some molds are very tenacious when it comes to establishing a foothold on moisture-lacking food. As a result, mold is sometimes found on foods that normally keep rather well. For example, a country-cured and smoked ham can get moldy on the outside. However, this can be wiped away or the moldy part trimmed off, and the ham can then be used. Often such pieces of meat are wiped down with a cloth that has been soaked in vinegar, because the acid in the vinegar discourages the growth of the mold. Some items that are high in sugar, such as jellies or jams, can also mold. Using food up as quickly as possible or holding it at a temperature that discourages the growth of microorganisms helps prevent microorganism growth in these situations.

Temperature, as we have seen, is critical to microorganism growth. The optimum temperature for growth for most such organisms is around 100°F (38°C), which also happens to be close to the temperature at which we like to keep our bodies. Moving in either direction away from this ideal temperature begins to lessen the rate of microorganisms' growth. Thus operations can do a lot to control these organisms just by controlling temperatures.

As was noted in connection with the clostridium family of bacteria, an acidic medium discourages the growth of many microorganisms. While some microorganisms tolerate (or even prefer) a somewhat acidic environment, acids discourage most growth; and in items that are highly acidic, such organisms simply will not grow. Pickles, for instance, keep well because they have a high acid content. Most organisms prefer the neutral range—neither acid nor alkaline. While some grow fairly well in mild alkalinity, most are discouraged as the degree of alkalinity goes up.

Again in connection with the clostridium family, it was noted that, if air (oxygen) is present, the microorganisms cannot grow; they require a space completely sealed off from air. Other organisms, however, cannot grow without air. Thus, controlling microorganism growth is a matter of properly keeping air out or keeping it in. However, this is not the most practical nor the best way to control microorganisms in short order work.

Bacteria grow by a process called *budding*. For example, a single oval-shaped bacterium gradually enlarges, and then a noticeable depression becomes evident in the midsection of the organism; the depression continues to constrict until it finally pinches the one oval into two ovals. Now these two ovals can both bud or separate, producing four. Then these four can separate to yield eight, and these eight can separate to make sixteen; then thirty-two; then sixty-four; and so on, until in a short time millions of bacteria can have been produced from just one. Some parasites, including certain protozoa, can also bud, as can yeast. Molds produce spores, which look like tiny particles of dust but are capable of "seeding" and causing new molds to grow. Mushrooms also propagate in this way. While the budding or beginning of growth in molds takes very little time, some time is required before the growth becomes significant. Thus, shortening the time between the contamination of the food and its cooking, its other preparation, and its consumption can make a difference in the amount of microorganism growth secured. Serving food as soon as it is cooked is a good rule.

Getting Rid of Unsanitary Vectors

Another way to prevent contamination of food is to keep certain vectors away. This means that vermin such as rats, mice, flies, roaches, weevils, and ants should not be allowed to be around food. Flies carry millions of harmful bacteria on their legs and bodies; so do cockroaches and other insects. When they crawl over food, they contaminate it. Eradicate them. They have no place in a foodservice building.

Mice and rats are also disease carriers. Rat urine has been found to carry hepatitis. Once rats or mice get into a building, it is extremely difficult to evict them, but perseverance can force them out and keep them from coming back. Often professional eradicators are the best way of getting rid of insects, rats, or mice.

Cleaning and Sanitizing

Another way of avoiding contamination is to keep things clean. Microorganisms and certain vectors do not stay in clean places. They need filth to live, so when things are clean they do not prosper.

There is a difference in meaning between the words *clean* and *sanitary*. *Sanitary* carries with it the connotation that the substance or thing is completely free from any harmful substance and possesses no objectionable qualities of filth or uncleanliness. *Clean* means that the item has no soil on it. Thus, any item may be clean without being sanitary: all soil may have been removed, but microorganisms still are on it. Often, however, getting something clean is synonymous with getting it sanitary, because removing the soil also removes the harmful organism. Sometimes items are cleaned and then sanitized. This happens in an industrial-strength dish machine. First the soil is washed off, and then during the final rinse period 180°F (82°C) water is run over the dishes to sanitize them.

One way to get rid of soil on things is to dissolve it. For this purpose hot water is used, because things are more soluble in it than in cold water. In addition, fats are melted by hot water. Soaps and detergents are also used to dissolve soil. These products contain additives that increase water's natural solubility, pick up soil and carry it away, and hold the soil away from the item so that it cannot reattach itself to the item. Sometimes a wetting agent is used to get a better runoff of soil during the final rinse. Normally in cleaning, detergents or soaps do about 30 percent of the job and friction by the washer does the remaining 70 percent. Using too much detergent or soap retards the cleaning action, since the excess foam impedes cleaning. Thus, dishwashing compounds may foam very little but still have good cleaning action because they give great solubility.

Exposure for 10 seconds in a hot water rinse at a temperature above 180°F (82°C) is usually sufficient to destroy pathogens. Sanitization is promoted by adding chlorine- or iodine-containing substances to this rinse water. Such a sanitizing medium, along with a good wetting agent, provides appropriate conditions for the final sanitizing process. Some soaps and detergents are antagonistic to bacteria and other microorganisms, so they actually function to some extent as a microorganism-destroying agent.

Cleaning agents, sanitizers, and other cleaning supplies require proper care. They should not be mixed with foods. Some washing machine powders can be confused with dry milk powder, and this has led more than one cook to add it to food by mistake.

Cooks should learn how to clean all kitchen things properly and should understand that, without cleaning friction (often called "elbow grease"), good cleaning cannot occur. The detergent or soap cannot do all the work; scrubbing and force are essential to getting things clean. Moreover, because cleaning does not sanitize, sanitizing may have to be done after cleaning. Normally, dishes, silverware, and pots and pans are not toweled after being cleaned and sanitized. Such toweling usually just smears undesirable extraneous substances onto the dishes after their surfaces have been cleaned and sanitized.

Poisons

Poisons and chemicals that act like poisons can get into foods, making them unhealthful. One widely recognized danger is lead poisoning, which can come from lead dissolved out of lead pipes. Other hazardous chemicals that can get into food include the following:

1. *Antimony:* Antimony is a poisonous constituent of graniteware. When food is stored in such ware, the antimony can be dissolved out of chipped or cracked areas.
2. *Copper:* Acids can dissolve copper, which produces a poisonous substance. The action of carbonated beverages can do the same thing. Thus, one should never use a copper utensil whose copper is exposed to the food being prepared. Copper utensils are lined with tin so that this reaction cannot occur under ordinary circumstances.
3. *Cyanide:* Some silver polishes contain cyanide. This is an extremely powerful poison, and a small amount of it can cause death.
4. *Zinc:* Zinc can cause health problems through "heavy metal poisoning"—a poisoning similar to that caused by lead. Zinc is a metal used to coat galvanized utensils and metal work surfaces.

Other poisonous substances can also get into foods—usually as a result of careless handling. Amateurs should not be entrusted with applying poisons in foodservice areas. This job should be left to professionals. Any poisonous substances that must be kept in a foodservice operation should be kept in a locked storage area that is isolated from food. Access to this storage area should be restricted to those who know how to use the poisonous substances properly.

Food Storage

Good food storage practices prevent food contamination and microorganism growth. Cleanliness is an important factor: all food storage areas should be kept scrupulously clean. Temperature is another significant factor: as much as possible, keep stored foods out of the food danger zone (45° to 125°F or 7° to 52°C). To this end, move foods into refrigerated or frozen storage, or use them as soon as possible.

Many foods do not support the growth of microorganisms, because they do not contain enough moisture. Such items include flour, cereals, rice, and other grains; dried beans, peas, and other legumes; crackers; sugar and salt; oils and shortenings; and unopened canned or bottled goods. Some of these can be attacked by rodents and insects, however; and in some areas of the South, flours, cereal, and dried fruits must be stored under refrigeration during summer months to keep weevils and other insects from them.

All dry foods should be stored in a cool dry place, off the floor, away from the wall, and not under sewer pipes. Once opened, dry foods should be stored in containers with tight-fitting covers.

Perishable foods should be refrigerated or frozen. Overcrowding such foods in the refrigerator can block air circulation, which may speed deterioration. Some foods such as fruits and vegetables need to respire; that is, they need carbon dioxide and oxygen in the air to remain in good condition. Blocking air off from them hastens loss of quality. Reclosing refrigerator doors as soon as possible after opening is a good idea. Thus, workers should not leave walk-in refrigerator or freezer doors open while inside. Since all doors have safety catches on them, there is virtually no chance that a worker might get caught inside and be unable to get out. The exterior bottoms of containers should not touch foods, as might happen if containers were stacked. It is desirable to have separate places for cooked and raw foods. Cover all foods before storing them. When placing chilled foods out on counters for service, make sure that they hold only a limited amount—such as the amount needed for the serving period. Piling food on until it is thickly massed in the container may cause cooling problems. Give refrigerated spaces good *mise en place*, and see that the refrigerated area is kept scrupulously clean.

When air cools, it loses moisture, which often collects on the refrigeration pipes in refrigerator and freezer units. Foods under refrigeration or in frozen storage can lose moisture, too, unless they are packed in vapor/moisture-proof wraps. Moisture can also build up on refrigeration coils, causing the coils to lose efficiency and making it more difficult to maintain desirable temperatures in the space. Therefore, such frost should be removed by proper defrosting methods when it begins to build up noticeably. Chipping the frost off is not a proper method.

Cross-contamination is a process in which one item, such as the surface of a worktable, or food, becomes contaminated and then itself contaminates another food. Thus, if one cuts up chickens on a meat block and fails to clean it properly afterward, the next time the meat block is used—say, for cold cuts—some of the cold meat may get contaminated with salmonella.

In handling foods, it is desirable to use tongs, plastic gloves, or utensils as much as possible, to avoid touching food by the hands. In circumstances where foods must be handled by the hands, the hands must be clean. All utensils, cutting boards, and tools should be clean and sanitized. Always wash raw fruits and vegetables thoroughly, and if appropriate, scrub them. Then rinse after such washing and scrubbing. Keep foods in the workplace covered as much as possible. Make sure that stocks, sauces, gravies, and other items made from stocks are heated to a temperature above 170°F (77°C) before using them. Such items are highly perishable, and bacteria and other microorganisms love to grow in them. Carryover foods should never be mixed with fresh ones. Pork should always be cooked to an interior temperature of 160°F (71°C) or more to ensure that any trichinae present are destroyed.

Special Food Handling

Certain foods are especially susceptible to contamination or make wonderful hosts to microorganisms once the food is contaminated. These need special care in foodservice operations.

Sandwiches Cold sandwiches often contain fillings that microorganisms flourish in. Because sandwich making requires considerable use of the hands, there is an additional chance of contamination. Being cold, sandwich fillings cannot benefit from heat as a way to destroy any harmful organism that gets into the sandwich. Sandwiches often must stand for some time before being consumed; thus, it is very important to see that, during such standing, they are refrigerated. The best approach is to make sandwiches to order and serve them immediately. All perishable materials used in the sandwich should be kept under refrigeration until the last possible moment.

Salads Many of the items used in salad making are attractive to microorganisms; and once there these grow quickly. While salad dressings are acidic, which discourages organism growth, the acidity of the main acidic ingredient such as mayonnaise is reduced by other foods present, so bacteria find it a very hospitable place to grow. Salads containing meat must be given special care, especially those with poultry meat. Like sandwiches, salads are usually served cold, so there is no chance to use heat to destroy microorganisms in the food once it has been prepared. Clean hands, sanitary work methods, good food protection, and sanitary equipment and tools are needed. Refrigerate salads as soon as they are made.

Pastry Pastry cream is composed of milk, eggs, starch, and sugar. This makes it an ideal medium for microorganism growth, and indeed it has been responsible for many cases of food poisoning over the years. Other, similar items such as soufflés and puddings are also excellent mediums for growth. In many operations, such items are always kept refrigerated, and some operations do not include them on the menu during the summer months.

Sanitized, clean equipment and tools should be used in preparation and service. The pastry cream should be brought rapidly to cooking temperature and the thickening process should continue long enough to cook the product thoroughly. The hands should never touch the cream, which should be cooled down and chilled as soon as possible after cooking. Sometimes the cream is blended with whipped cream and used as a filling for cream puffs or eclairs. This product, too, is highly susceptible to contamination and subsequent rapid organism growth. All cream-filled products should be refrigerated. Some operations refuse to offer them for sale during the summer months.

Poultry and Eggs Sanitation is important when handling raw poultry, since salmonella bacteria are found in the birds' intestinal tracts. These can be spread on cutting boards or utensils, from which they contaminate other products. Cooked poultry (especially poultry salads) need special care during preparation and handling. Such products should always be refrigerated.

Eggs, too, can be the source of salmonella poisoning. At one time, processed eggs (frozen or dried), were used to make such items as mayonnaise and salad dressings. The result of using such eggs was a lot of salmonella poisoning, since the processing often did not destroy the salmonella. Today it is safe to use processed eggs, because the federal government requires pasteurization of all such items. Egg salads and egg salad sandwiches need as much care as meat or poultry salads and sandwiches. Hard-cooking usually destroys salmonella, but other contamination can occur, and the eggs, mayonnaise, and so on provide a good culture for microorganisms.

Dressings Among the most dangerous items cooks prepare (as far as food poisoning potential is concerned) are bread stuffing or dressing and other stuffings or dressings. Special care must be taken with the preparation and handling of all ingredients. In quantity work, dressings or stuffings are seldom put into a bird for roasting. Instead, they are baked separately in a pan. The cook should make the dressing and then refrigerate it immediately if it not to be baked at once. Often there is carryover dressing or stuffing; this should be cooled down rapidly and put under refrigeration. It is also important to see that the interior of the dressing completely cools down so that the dressing does not remain warm inside while under refrigeration. If this does occur, the warm spot inside provides a marvelous growth medium for microorganisms. If a bird is stuffed for roasting, make certain that refrigerated stuffing is put inside, and if the bird is not immediately to be roasted, refrigerate the whole thing. Never allow warm dressing to be put into a bird, and never allow a stuffed bird to stand at room temperature. If some of the dressing in a stuffed bird is not used, remove it from the bird and put it into a pan. Cool it down, cover it, and put it under refrigeration. Take no chances.

Gravies and Sauces Anything with a stock or broth base is a good medium for microorganism growth. Certain bacteria love such foods.

Thus, gravies and sauces made from stock or broth and thickened with starch are hazards requiring special care. Bring them to temperature quickly when reheating, and do not allow them to stand around at room temperature. Cool and refrigerate as quickly as possible after use.

Certain sauces—hollandaise sauce, its derivatives, and others made similarly—have been known to cause food poisoning. The eggs may not have cooked completely, leaving salmonella in the product; and the sauce's level of acidity is insufficient to stop bacterial growth. Thus such a sauce, if left out at a favorable temperature for bacterial growth, can be the source of serious food poisoning. Always refrigerate such sauces when they are not in use. Some operations make and use these sauces but consider them too dangerous to be carried over. Consequently, any unused quantities are dumped after service.

Buffets The large amount of cold food presented on a buffet raises the need for special care to be taken in the food's preparation and handling. The buffet format often results in items' being left open and out of refrigeration for an extended period of time; in part this is unavoidable, since preparation, decoration, and assembly take time. However, when not being worked on, foods should be kept under refrigeration. It may also be desirable to place certain highly perishable foods on beds of ice. If the buffet is to last a long time, redishing should be done so that chilled foods can be brought to the buffet during the dining period.

Fish and Seafood Consumption of marine products is on the rise because patrons think that eating them reduces their intake of fat and cholesterol. This popular notion is true of fat, and indeed the kind of fat seafoods provide is relatively healthful (unless they are cooked in the wrong kind of fat). It is not true of cholesterol, however, because seafoods such as shrimp, crab, and oysters contain more cholesterol per pound than beef, veal, pork, or lamb.

The enzyme defenses of fish and seafood against spoilage and bacterial onslaught are weaker than those in meat. At the same temperature, fish and seafood deteriorate a lot faster than meats or poultry. It is therefore important that fish and seafood be kept well refrigerated. Upon arrival at the foodservice, they should immediately be moved into refrigeration, and it is advisable to place them on a bed of ice. Oysters, clams, crabs, mussels, and lobsters should be alive, if in the shell. Gaping clams, mussels, or oysters have died and should be discarded. There is a move afoot at the federal level to put unprocessed seafood and fish under the Inspected and Passed program now used to ensure that meat and poultry meet sanitary and safety standards.

Personal Hygiene

To produce clean and sanitary food, short order cooks must maintain high standards of cleanliness and sanitation toward their work and toward themselves. Dirty cooks create dirty food. Personal cleanliness carries over to good grooming (see Fig. 6-3). Men should be clean-shaven, and people with acne should not work around food. Teeth should be clean and sparkling. An unkempt head of hair, greasy and flecked with dandruff, is unacceptable. Dirty hands and dirty fingernails invite food contamination. Women should not wear too much makeup and should apply it tastefully. There should be no body odor and not too strong a perfume. The clothing worn should be appropriate and clean. Poor-fitting clothes create an impression of sloppiness. Crisp, well-pressed uniforms indicate that the wearers care about how they look. A worker with a dirty shirt, collar, or cuffs, wrinkled and baggy clothes, tie on crooked, and unshined shoes makes patrons want to get up and leave. Even a visible hosiery run or crooked hosiery seams can make some patrons uneasy about an operation's standards of cleanliness and hygiene. Cooks with their bodies and their dress should show that they care about themselves and how they appear.

All people harbor bacteria in their noses, mouths, and throats, and these are easily spread by sneezing or coughing. The nose and mouth should be covered when sneezing or coughing. Disposable tissues or handkerchiefs should be readily available. A worker with a cold can easily spread it. Colds are accompanied by staph in the nasal, mouth, and throat passages, and this is often the origin of staph that gets into food and causes food poisoning.

Frequent bathing, careful grooming, and regular hair washing should occur. Frequent hand washing is desirable while at work. Touching the body and then touching food transfers microorganisms to the food. Open sores or pus, as noted, carries staph, which can be the source of a toxin that makes patrons ill. A cut or sore should be covered by a clean, neat bandage. The hair is a common cause of contamination, so all workers should wear a hair net or a hat. Flouncy hairdos are not appropriate around food.

The feces of the body carry many microorganisms that can cause health problems, including staph, salmonella, and hepatitis. It is therefore very important that cooks wash their hands carefully after visiting the rest room.

Short order cooks should also have good carriage and posture, carrying the head high and standing erect. A slouched-over worker makes a poor impression. Smartness and alertness in using one's body signals professional pride and a desire to serve. Cooks should never smoke or chew gum while on duty. Furthermore, workplaces and worktables are no place to sit.

FIGURE 6-3. Two well-groomed short order cooks in uniforms. (*Photo by Michael Upright*)

Good personal hygiene includes getting enough sleep, routinely seeing the doctor and the dentist, staying away from work when sick, and avoiding poor personal habits such as picking the nose or biting fingernails. A minimum of jewelry should be worn—and not only to avoid flashiness. Long necklaces or other jewelry can get caught in moving parts and cause bad accidents.

Legal Responsibility

By inviting the public to eat at their facilities, foodservices assume an ethical and moral responsibility to serve patrons safe food and to ensure that they are free from harm when on the premises. These obligations are reinforced by legal responsibilities to observe and maintain good safety and sanitary practices.

A foodservice is liable if a patron has an accident in the operation that can be traced to a fault of the operation or one of its workers. The same holds true for food that harms someone. Lawsuits sometimes conclude in such a costly judgment or settlement in favor of the offended patron that the foodservice must close its doors and go bankrupt, in which case employees lose their jobs.

When a patron enters a foodservice operation to eat, there is an implicit understanding that the person's health will not be put at risk and that sound, nonharmful food will be served. The patron understands this, and so does the facility. The federal government has enacted the Uniform Commercial Code, which all states have also adopted. Its Section 2-314 recognizes an implied "warranty of merchantability" that the operation, by being in business and serving patrons, will and does provide safe premises and serve food "fit for human consumption." This code provision has been the basis of many lawsuits against substandard businesses. No one has to state that safe foods will be served and that the premises will be safe: it is implied by the mere fact the business exists to serve the public.

☐ Summary

Safety is a matter of being alert and knowing how to prevent or avoid trouble. There are many chances for accidents in the short order section, and cooks need to take proper care. Training is needed to learn how to work safely, and then cooks need to use this training. Most accidents are caused by human error, rather than by equipment failure or other error. Many federal, state, and local regulations work to ensure that foodservices establish and observe good safety and sanitation standards.

Knives are a common cause of accidents in the short order section. Basic rules have been formulated to avoid such accidents, and cooks should know and follow them in handling knives and other sharp instruments. Cooks must also know how to handle mechanical equipment that might cause cuts.

Burns are other common causes of accidents. Grease or steam burns can be much more painful than hot water burns because their temperature can be so much hotter than that of water. Mechanical equipment is driven by automatic force, and such force can be the cause of a serious accident if the cook does not handle the equipment properly because the force cannot be shut off instantaneously. Falling is the most common cause of accidents in the short order section. Floors often get wet or slippery, and the cook may then slip and fall. Good shoes should be worn to give the feet as secure a base as possible. Electrical shocks from exposed wiring or other causes should be avoided through good work practices. Poor lighting can result in various types of accidents.

There are three kinds of fires: Type A fires are caused by combustible materials; Type B fires are caused by ignition of grease, oil, or petroleum products; and Type C fires are caused by electricity. All fires should be smothered to reduce the amount of oxygen getting them. Combustible materials should not be left lying around. If a fire does occur, the cook must react to it quickly. Explosions are uncommon in the short order section, but they are most likely to be caused by gas equipment, when gas escapes and is ignited. Workers should know how to use gas equipment and how to avoid gas buildup.

Good work habits, being alert, and knowing how to work provide a safeguard against accidents. The cook who does not know how to work properly is often the one who causes an accident. Some cooks are accident-prone, because they do not follow good work rules. Cooks must also be careful not to cause accidents to others. If a patron is injured through the negligence of a cook or other worker, the foodservice operation may be in serious legal trouble. Cooks can also face legal proceedings personally if they cause an accident.

Patrons place heavy emphasis on getting clean and sanitary food, as well as on having it be highly palatable and attractive. The National Restaurant Association and various governmental agencies work to ensure that food is sanitary. Food often deteriorates and becomes unsafe because it gets contaminated by bacteria, parasites, viruses, molds, or yeasts. Intoxicants are microorganisms that get into food and build up a toxin that makes one ill. An infectant is a microorganism that gets into food and then continues to grow after being ingested, causing a health problem.

Contamination is introduced into food by vectors, which may be human beings, flies, roaches, rats, or mice. The best way to prevent contamination many times is to cut off the vector's access to the food. Clean people are less likely to cause contamination than people who are not clean. Keeping insects and animals out of food spaces is essential to combatting contamination.

Another important step in avoiding contamination is to see that uncontaminated food is purchased. After cooking, foods should either be cooled as rapidly as possible or be served. Frozen foods should be held at temperatures of 0°F (− 18°C) or below. Most refrigerator temperatures are slightly above 32°F (0°C).

Microorganisms do not prosper at temperatures below 45°F (7.5°C). Their growth is also slowed at temperatures around 110°F (42.5°C), and they begin to be destroyed at temperatures above 125°F (57°C).

Cooks should know the difference between *clean* and *sanitary*. *Clean* means free from soil. Something may be clean but not sanitary, because harmful (but invisible) microorganisms may remain on it. *Sanitary* means that an item is safe to use; it has no harmful materials or microorganisms on or in it. Items are cleaned by using water and then a detergent or soap plus friction to remove the soil. Detergents or soap do about 30 percent of the cleaning job, while friction does the remaining 70 percent.

Certain metals can react with food or be dissolved into food, causing poisoning. Good storage often prevents contamination. Clean storage spaces and proper storage procedures can protect food from contamination.

Certain foods require special care in their preparation and handling. These include sandwiches, salads, cream pastries, poultry, eggs, dressings, stuffings, gravies, sauces, buffet foods, fish, and seafood.

Short order cooks should not only produce clean food, they should be clean and well groomed themselves. They should bathe frequently and see that their hair is washed frequently. Clean, properly fitting clothing is important. Good carriage and good body posture also help create a good impression. Cooks who do not meet high standards of hygiene and grooming cause patrons to avoid the operation.

Besides having a moral and ethical responsibility to see that safety and sanitation standards are high, a foodservice has a legal obligation. Lawsuits resulting from accidents or from contaminated food can be extremely costly to an operation and may even bankrupt it. The federal government has enacted and all fifty states have adopted the Uniform Commercial Code; Section 2-314 of this code provides patrons with an implied "warranty of merchantability." This means that an operation, simply by being in business and serving patrons, accepts responsibility for providing safe premises and for serving food "fit for human consumption." Failing to meet these responsibilities gives the patron the basis for legal recourse against the facility. When someone patronizes a foodservice, there is an implied promise that the person will be safe and will not be served harmful food.

□ CHAPTER REVIEW □

1. Why should a worker be interested in safety? Give more than one reason.
2. What are some factors that cause a person to be accident-prone?
3. What is OSHA?
4. List safeguards that should be observed by workers in order to prevent cuts.
5. Why is a burn from hot grease or steam often much more severe than a burn from hot water?

6. Set up a safe procedure for draining fat from a deep-fat fryer. (Refer to Chapter 2 for methods of removing fat from fryers and filtering it.)
7. How can one treat a burn or scald?
8. List some good rules to follow in handling mechanical equipment. Why and how is a hammer or mallet used on grinders and rotary cutters?
9. Falls are the most common type of accident in foodservices. What are some of the factors that cause this to be true?
10. How does one put out a Type A fire? a Type B? a Type C?
11. What is the primary cause of explosions in foodservices?
12. What are some precautions workers should take in working around electrical units?
13. What are some good general safety rules to follow in doing work?
14. What percentage of failures in sanitation is due to faulty equipment, and what percentage is due to human error?
15. Identify some important features of each of the following bacteria, and indicate which are infectants and which are intoxicants:

Staphylococci   Streptococci   *Clostridium perfringens*
Shigella   *Clostridium botulinum*   Hepatitis

16. Which of the items in question #15 could you not identify? Is it a bacterium?
17. Name two parasites that cause health problems by getting into food. Why should pork always be cooked well done?
18. Mark each of the following statements True or False:

   a. Freezing destroys all bacteria.
   b. All fresh fruits and vegetables should be held under refrigeration at a temperature slightly above freezing.
   c. It is all right to let foods stand out at room temperature for 5 hours, but afterward one *must* refrigerate it if the food is to be safe.

19. Name some good ways to cool down foods quickly.
20. Name some good rules to follow when handling foods and placing them into refrigeration.
21. List eight foods that require special handling, and identify the most important special steps that should be carried out in each case.
22. What is the difference between *clean* and *sanitary*?
23. Name some heavy metals that can get into food and cause poisoning.
24. Where should poisons be stored in foodservices?

CHAPTER SEVEN

Meeting Nutritional Standards

History has it that "Methuselah ate what was on his plate" and lived to a remarkable old age. Today's patrons of foodservices are a bit more concerned than Methuselah was about what is on their plates, even though they might like to duplicate his longevity. They ask for food that is healthful as well as appetizing and appealing, and they have specific ideas about what is healthful and what is not. Items low in salt, high in fiber, rich in vitamins and minerals, low in calories, and low in fat and cholesterol are requested. Foods high in salt, low in fiber, lacking a good nutrient yield of minerals or vitamins, high in fat (especially saturated fat), high in calories, and high in cholesterol are rejected.

Today foodservice patrons show a greater degree of concern for the safety, purity, and healthful qualities of the food they eat than did past patrons; and this sentiment is growing as people realize how closely their health is tied to the quality of the food they consume. Table 7-1 indicates that heart diseases, malignancies, cerebrovascular disorders (mostly strokes), and arteriosclerosis (problems in the arterial system, such as hardening of the arteries) are the first, second, third, and fifth leading causes of death among people over 55 years of age. These are all diet-related problems.

Although patrons want foods that promote health, they do not especially want foodservices to emphasize nutrition and diet on the menu itself. There have been some notable failures in foodservice organizations that have tried to do this. Patrons want good food that meets their expectations for promoting health.

Actually, certain studies have found that not everyone is even interested in healthful foods. Thus, in a study by M. Pratscher, T. Lydecker, J. Weinstein, and L. Bertagnoll in *Restaurants and Institutions* (1987) patron interest in healthful foods was listed in certain areas as follows:

189

TABLE 7-1. Leading Causes of Death Among People 55 Years Old and Older

Cause	Percentage
1. Heart problems*	45
2. Malignant neoplasms*	15
3. Cerebrovascular diseases	15
4. Influenza and pneumonia	4
5. Arteriosclerosis*	3
6. Accidents	3
7. Diabetes mellitus*	2
8. Bronchitis, emphysema, and asthma	2
9. Cirrhosis of the liver*	1
10. Kidney infections*	1
11. All other causes	9

*Could be diet-related.
SOURCE: Adapted from 1984 data of the National Center for Health Statistics.

Interested in low-sodium (low-salt) food, 63.5%
Interested in low-fat, low-cholesterol food, 61.7%
Interested in low calorie food, 58.0%

It can be inferred that the others surveyed were not interested or had no opinion. Another study, *Consumer Nutrition Concerns and Restaurant Choices*, published by the National Restaurant Association in 1986, showed that patrons had the following dietary concerns:

Weight conscious	25%
Health conscious	17%
Total	42%

Want traditional food	43%
Uncommitted	12%
Not in any group	4%
Total	58%

Thus, more than half of those surveyed had few or no dietary concerns. However, it has been found that ignoring the wishes of the 42 percent who do have such concerns can be harmful for business. Many of these people feel very strongly about their food needs and refuse to patronize operations that ignore them. The foodservice industry has found that it pays to heed the demands of this growing group and to make sure that foods meet their expectations. Research has shown that younger people are less concerned than older people about what they eat. People also tend to be more concerned about what they eat for breakfast or lunch than about what they eat for dinner. Evidently when people go out to dinner, they cast some of their concerns aside and eat more as they would like to but know they should not.

While the National Restaurant Association estimates that 42 percent of all the money in the United States spent on food is spent at foodservices, this amount purchases probably only about 25 percent of all the food consumed in this country. If this is true, the foodservices in this country have approximately a 25 percent responsibility for the nutrition of the nation's people, which in turn affects their health and productivity. Thus, it is not only a matter of good business sense to heed the demands of a significant group of patrons for healthful foods; the foodservice industry has a moral and ethical responsibility to serve foods that promote good health.

If the foodservice industry is to discharge this responsibility properly, it must recognize and apply principles of good nutrition. Management must write menus, purchase foods, and ensure that it is properly prepared to be nutritious. Cooks must know how to handle and prepare foods so that they do not lose the nutrients they contain.

□ Basic Principles of Nutrition

People need some forty nutrients in order to live. Authorities usually classify nutrients according to whether they are carbohydrates, proteins, fats, vitamins, or minerals. Water might also be considered a nutrient, and alcohol also burns in the body to give energy, although it is not treated as a nutrient.

Carbohydrates

Carbohydrates comprise a family of food substances including sugars, starches, and dextrins. When eaten, they break down to produce energy, allowing the person to do work or generate heat. Most of the energy a person gets from food (about 55 to 65 percent) should come in the form of carbohydrates, and it is better for these to be starches than to be sugars. This means that, of a 2,400 daily calorie intake, one should get between 1,320 and 1,560 calories per day from carbohydrates; not more than one-fourth of these carbohydrate calories should come from sugars.

Carbohydrates burn cleanly in the body, breaking down into carbon dioxide and water. The body uses the water and exhales the carbon dioxide, so everything is used or removed. This is not true of other fuel nutrients, as we shall see.

Proteins

Like carbohydrates, proteins are organic substances but they contain nitrogen, which the body uses in making flesh, blood, antibodies, bones, hormones, and other body substances. The body can also take a protein, remove the nitrogen, and then use what is left for energy, just as it does with a carbohydrate. However, the burning is not clean, and the kidneys must get rid of the excess nitrogen by eliminating it in the urine. A person who eats too much protein and then breaks it down into fuel risks overworking the kidneys, which have to filter out these nitrogen fractions and get rid of them.

Proteins are made up of similar substances called *amino acids*. Some amino acids must be in a person's food to sustain life. Others can be made in the body. Those required in food are called *essential*, while those the body can make are called *nonessential*. A food that contains all of the essential amino acids in good quantity has a *complete* protein. If some amino acids are lacking, the protein is *incomplete*. In some instances, two foods that have incomplete proteins can be combined to produce a complete protein. For example, combining cereals and legumes (such as split peas or beans) in a meal supplies all essential amino acids in good supply. A meal of Boston baked beans and brown bread is thus protein complete, as is a meal of cornbread and split pea soup. Many people in the world don't get much food that in itself contains complete proteins. Instead, they depend largely on a combined diet of cereal and legumes. Thus, Mexican people combine corn tortillas and pinto beans, the Chinese consume soybean items and rice, and the people of India eat chapatas (bread) or rice with dahl, a lentil-like legume.

Almost all animal substances contain complete proteins. Thus, milk and milk-based products, eggs, meats, fish, and poultry are all complete. Most cereals and vegetables contain incomplete proteins, although the protein of the soybean is almost as good as that of beef. About 12 percent of a person's total calories—or 300 out of the daily total of 2,400 calories—should come from protein.

Fats

The average American's diet receives about 40 percent of its calories from fats, but the percentage should be 30 percent or less. Besides eating too much fat, Americans also eat too much of the wrong kinds. Saturated fats are more or less the hard or solid fats, and in the body they are thought to contribute to the buildup of a substance called *cholesterol*. Vegetable oils contain no saturated fat, so margarines and other things containing them can be labeled "No Saturated Fat." Nutritional authorities have identified two other kinds of fat as being of dietary importance: *monounsaturated* fat and *polyunsaturated* fat. These two fats may actually help the body get rid of cholesterol, by picking it up in the bloodstream and carrying it to the liver where it is broken down. Nutritionists recommend that people eat less beef, veal, mutton, and lamb and eat more fish and vegetable oils in order to increase the proportion of monounsaturated and polyunsaturated fats (versus saturated fats) in the diet.

The reason people are advised to eat foods containing little or no cholesterol is that cholesterol is a major constituent of a plaque or waxy substance that gets into the arteries, clogging them and eventually causing strokes, heart attacks, and other problems. The idea is that, by reducing cholesterol intake in the diet, a person can lower the level of cholesterol in the body. But, the best a person can achieve in lowering cholesterol by diet is about a 10 percent reduction. Beyond that, drugs must be used to lower the cholesterol level further. Today anyone who has a cholesterol level of 210 milliliters per 100 centiliters of blood is thought to have a high cholesterol level and is considered an at-risk person. Table 7-2 gives the cholesterol content of some common foods. The American Heart Association wants Americans to reduce their daily intake of cholesterol in foods to 300 milligrams or less per day. As the table shows, eating just one egg almost uses up this daily amount. In this regard it is important to realize that cholesterol is only found in animal foods and not in vegetable or cereal ones.

The breakdown of fat in the body differs from the breakdown of carbohydrates or proteins. Fat has many more carbons and hydrogens to burn than either carbohydrates or proteins do, and it has fewer oxygens to help such a breakdown. Fat begins to burn in the body by breaking apart into small fractions, but soon it stops unless it receives additional oxygen to continue the breakdown. This oxygen must come from carbohydrates, so carbohydrates are essential in order to have a complete breakdown of fat. Otherwise, the small particles of separated fat form ketones, and if too many of these pile up in the body a condition called *ketosis* occurs, in which the individual goes into a coma and may die. Diabetics who burn too much fat without carbohydrates' being present are susceptible to ketosis, so most diabetics' diets call for about 45 percent of the total calories to come from carbohydrates. Anyone who is dieting should make sure that some carbohydrates are in the diet; the usually recommended quantity is not less than 400 calories per day, but, of course the exact quantity depends on how much fat is to be burned.

Whatever nervousness people may feel about fats, they are needed in moderate amounts for good nutrition. Fats and fatty substances perform important functions in the body. One fat is known to be essential for good human nutrition. Others act as storage agents for extra nutrition. It is known, for example, that elderly people who get too

TABLE 7-2. Cholesterol Content of 3 Ounces of Some Common Foods

Food	Cholesterol	Food	Cholesterol
beef, cooked, lean	77 mg	liver, chicken	480 mg
veal, cooked, lean	86	abalone	200
rabbit, domestic	52	lobster	96
salmon, cooked	40	oysters	67
sardines	100	pork, cooked, lean	77
kidney	690	turkey, light meat	65
heart	274	turkey, dark meat	86
crab	138	haddock	51
scallops	75	herring	83
lamb, lean, cooked	83	brains	810
chicken, light meat	54	sweetbreads	396
cod	72	shrimp	160
flounder	43	clams	92
liver, beef	372	milk, whole	14
American cheese	75	milk, 2%	7
cream cheese	48	milk, 1%	4
Mozzarella	30	milk, skim	2
Swiss cheese	84	ice cream	20
yogurt	6	egg, one large (1½ oz)	250

thin lack the extra calories needed to get over a period of stress nutrition in which the extra calories stored in fat are vital. Fats also act as lubricants and as padding around organs. The only trouble is that too many people store far too much of this emergency energy fuel.

Calories from Fuel Nutrients

The three major nutrient groups that provide energy for running our bodies are carbohydrates, proteins, and fats. Per gram of pure substance, carbohydrates contribute 4 calories, proteins contribute 4 calories, and fats contribute 9 calories. In calories per pound, this works out to 1,816 calories for 1 pound of a pure carbohydrate or a pure protein, and 4,056 calories for 1 pound of pure fat. Thus, fats are more than twice as fattening as carbohydrates and proteins. Yet carbohydrates are often (wrongly) accused of being fatteners.

Carbohydrates and proteins are found in foods that contain a lot of other nonfattening substances such as fiber, minerals, vitamins, and water. Fats and related substances remain in foods in almost pure form and thus yield their calories directly and undilutedly. To get the best yield of healthful substances, one should eat foods that are high in calories and high in protein but low in fat per quantity of vitamins and minerals. The secret of good nutrition is to get the maximum yield of vitamins and minerals for the carbohydrate, protein, or fat eaten. Thus, the same number of calories in 1 teaspoon of butter, if eaten in raw spinach salad instead, would contribute a far greater quantity of valuable minerals and vitamins.

Alcohol can be burned in the body for fuel or energy. In fact, alcohol yields 7 calories per gram—a figure almost as large as the one for fats. Most alcoholic beverages do not contribute much to nutrition other than calories. Furthermore, alcohol has been shown to harm brain cells and to contribute to serious diseases such as cirrhosis of the liver. Today's nutritionists say that it is best to limit one's consumption of alcohol to about 200 or so calories per day, which works out to a maximum of about 2 ounces of pure alcohol per day. Some studies show that a bit less than this per day may help reduce heart and other cardiovascular problems.

The number of calories per day one should get varies. More are needed in cold weather than in hot weather. Men typically need more calories than women because of their bigger body size; moreover, women by nature seem to conserve energy better than men and so need fewer calories per pound of weight. Infants require a tremendous number of calories per pound of body flesh; children need somewhat less. As people enter adolescence and then maturity, their caloric needs stabilize until they reach the age of 45 or so (provided that their life-styles remain the same). After 45, many individuals find that they need fewer calories to meet their needs, and many start to gain weight that may be detrimental to their long-term health. Some nutrition authorities say that one should strive to maintain the body weight one has at 21. This might be hard to do, but it is a goal and can lead to better health.

Calories are consumed to fuel body actions. One of these is called the *basal metabolic rate* (BMR), which is the minimum amount of energy required to run the body if one lies still, breathing but not moving. As one moves about and increases activity, more and more calories are needed. Thus, a bedridden patient requires little above the BMR (about 1,200 calories per day), but a football player playing a rugged game might in this short period consume 4,000 calories or more. Any movement of the body requires calories, so the greater the amount of body action, the more calories are expended. This is why exercise is an important factor in reducing one's weight together with reducing food intake. The calories a person has stored in fat must be burned in order to get rid of this fat.

If the calorie intake from a diet is less than what the body burns, the difference is usually made up by calories from stored fat. However, correct dieting procedures are necessary to ensure that the body uses up fat and not protein. Otherwise, the body may lose valuable muscle tissues instead of undesirable weight bound in fat. Indeed, some individuals have actually suffered heart attacks because their dieting program led to withdrawal of valuable protein substances that the heart needed instead of burning the unwanted fat in the body.

To control calories and lose weight, one must reduce the calorie or energy intake to less than what one is using. This is easier for young people to accomplish than for older ones, because young people burn more calories per pound of body weight and are more active than older people. The more exercise one does, the greater one's calorie needs are. Cutting down on intake of fats is important because it is one of the biggest contributors of calories. Cutting down on consumption of alcoholic drinks can also be important. It is also known that stepping up one's physical activity can do much to promote weight reduction.

Controlling one's weight is easy for some people and difficult for others. Some people can eat all they want of everything and not get fat, while others can eat very little and still find they are gaining weight. In part this is due to differences in people's BMR. In others, because of activity, sex, age, and other factors. But of course, a lot of people think they are dieting when they really are not: they still add a liberal amount of margarine or butter to their plain bran breakfast muffin, add sugar to their coffee, and add a bit of ice cream to the dish of sliced peaches that was supposed to be a low-calorie dessert for dinner.

In most cases, a person should not try to lose more than about 1 pound per week. This means that one has to eat about 500 calories less per day than one needs. In 7 days, this amounts to 3,500 calories, or about 400 grams. A pound is equivalent to 454 grams, so at 500 calories per day one is a bit under 1 pound per week in fat loss alone; however, fatty tissue in the body carries with it some water, and as the fat is lost, the water disappears, too. Thus, 3,500 calories amount to just about 1 pound of weight loss.

If one goes on a calorie reduction program to lose weight, one will find that first a gradual weight loss occurs and then it stops. This is because the body is adjusting to a lower calorie intake, and as one loses weight the body gets smaller and needs less energy to run it. When such a plateau is reached, it is necessary to reduce one's intake of calories even more or to exercise more.

A person who tends to gain weight on a particular schedule and menu of foods needs to change eating patterns. One cannot go on a weight loss program, lose weight, and then successfully resume the same old dietary pattern and lifestyle. This is why we say, "To lose weight, one has to usually change one's eating habits." And, as one has wisely said, "To change your eating habits is often harder than to change your religion." It takes willpower and knowledge.

It is not a good idea to use drugs to lose weight. Many tragedies have resulted from trying to do this, and many more people have found that in the end it does little good. Any weight lost is quickly regained once the drug treatment program ends. Many quack claims are made about how one can lose weight by going on this or that program. The only program that really works for almost everyone is to eat some of everything (but in smaller amounts) and to make pushing oneself away from the table the first step in a reasonable exercise program. Unfortunately people do not have an "appestat" inside to tell them when they have satisfied their calorie needs. Human appetites are built on the physiological need to eat until one is full. Thus the body demands more than enough food, because that enables it to store some of the excess as fat and save this up for a rainy day. The only trouble is that for many well-fed Americans the rainy day never comes, and as a result they are left with all that fat.

Maintaining a desirable weight has been found to pay dividends in health. Obese people have many more health problems than people who maintain a more moderate weight. By keeping one's weight under control, one also can be more active and look better. In America, the lean person is the social ideal, as is evidenced by the individuals who populate product advertisements.

Vitamins

Vitamins in the body act as regulators and help bodily processes occur. Thus, thiamin, pyridoxine, niacin and other vitamins work together to create energy. Without them people could not break carbohydrates down into water and carbon dioxide and thereby extract heat or energy. Some vitamins help build up or break down amino acids. Vitamin K helps cause the blood to clot. Vitamin A makes vision possible. Vitamin C keeps body tissues healthy and working. All over the body, vitamins are working to keep it alive and functioning properly. Thus vitamins are essential organic nutrients needed in tiny amounts to keep us alive. They are noncaloric. Some vitamins are needed in minute quantities, while others are needed in larger amounts. For instance, adults need per day only 0.000003 gram of vitamin B_{12}, but they need 60 milligrams (0.06 gram) of vitamin C. Vitamins are classified according to whether they are fat-soluble or water-soluble.

Fat-Soluble Vitamins Fat-soluble vitamins are found in fatty foods and can be stored in fatty tissues in the body. Since they are not soluble in water, they cannot readily be lost once they get into the body. They must be used up in the course of body processes. It is therefore not difficult to store a lot of these vitamins in the body, and when the store becomes excessive serious health problems can occur. Individuals have died from taking too much vitamin A to stop a cold or too much of some other fat-soluble vitamin to accomplish another result.

Vitamin A Vitamin A was the first vitamin identified; hence, it was assigned the letter *A*. Some Vitamin A is obtained from fats such as butter and fish oil, but a lot of it is made in the body from a substance called *carotene*. This is the yellow pigment found in carrots, yellow squash, peaches, and other similar-colored fruits and vegetables. Carotenes are also found in green vegetables, especially the leafy ones. Table 7-3 summarizes some of vitamin A's jobs in the body. An adult male needs 1,000 retinol equivalents daily and a woman needs 800.

Vitamin D Vitamin D serves mainly to help the body use calcium and phosphorus to make bones and teeth and to carry out other functions that these two minerals perform in the body. Table 7-3 summarizes vitamin D's main functions. People obtain some vitamin D from fats such as butter and fish oils. Margarine is fortified with it, as is pasteurized milk. The human body can make vitamin D through the action of the sun's ultraviolet rays on cholesterol or ergesterol underneath the skin. People with dark skin make less vitamin D in this way than do those with lighter skin, because the darkness of the skin causes the ultraviolet rays to be absorbed before they can penetrate to the layers beneath the skin where the cholesterol and ergesterol are stored. Smog, smoke, shade, and other factors that cut off the sun's rays reduce the amount of vitamin D made in this way. Adult males and females need 10 milligrams per day of vitamin D.

Vitamin E A lot of false or at best unsubstantiated claims have been made for vitamin E, such as that it counteracts senility, prolongs sex life, and reduces aging. None of these claims has been proved. Researchers believe that vitamin E acts in the body to prevent undesirable oxidations. This protects other body substances from being oxidized (taking on oxygen), which would destroy their ability to function in the body. People get a lot of vitamin E in vegetable oils. Men need 10 milligrams per day, and women need 8. Table 7-3 gives more information about vitamin E's functions.

Vitamin K Dark-green leafy vegetables and liver are rich sources of vitamin K. People also manufacture plenty of this vitamin in their digestive systems. Vitamin K's main job is to assist blood in clotting. Aspirin and certain other drugs may reduce vitamin K's ability to work. Table 7-3 specifies vitamin K's jobs.

Water-Soluble Vitamins While fat-soluble vitamins can be stored quite well in the body, water-soluble ones cannot be stored in any

TABLE 7-3. Fat-Soluble and Water-Soluble Vitamins

Fat-Soluble Vitamins

Vitamin	Function	Sources in Food	Effects of Deficiency	Recommended Dietary Allowance
Vitamin A (retinol) and provitamin A (carotene)	Essential to maintain functions of epithelial tissues, mucous membranes, and eyes. Promotes growth.	Vitamin A liver, cream, margarine, egg yolk Provitamin A dark green vegetables, deep yellow vegetables, apricots, cantaloupe	Stunted growth, night blindness, keratinized skin	(Adults except as noted) Female 800 R.E. (4000 I.U.) Male 1000 R.E. (5000 I.U.)
Vitamin D (ergocaciferol and cholecaciferol)	Promotes absorption and utilization of calcium and phosphorus in bone growth	Fortified milk and margarine, eggs, fish	Rickets, weak bones, bowed legs, poorly formed teeth	Children and adolescents 400 I.U.
Vitamin E (tocopherols)	Protects vitamin A, C, and unsaturated fatty acids from oxidation. Protects cell structure.	Vegetable oils, green leafy vegetables, whole grains, nuts		Female 12 I.U. Male 15 I.U.
Vitamin K (quinones)	Essential for clotting of blood	Green leafy vegetables, pork liver, soybean oil	Hemorrhages	Unknown

Water-Soluble Vitamins

Vitamin	Function	Sources in Food	Effects of Deficiency	Recommended Dietary Allowance
Thiamin (B_1)	Essential for carbohydrate metabolism	Pork, organ meats, whole grains, nuts, legumes, enriched breads, and cereals	Beriberi	Adult males and females 0.5 mg/1000 kcal
Riboflavin (B_2)	Essential for growth and reproduction, carbohydrate, fat and protein metabolism	Milk, cheese, meat, eggs, green leafy vegetables, enriched bread, and cereals	Cheilosis	Adult males and females 0.6 mg/1000 kcal

(continued)

TABLE 7-3. Fat-Soluble and Water-Soluble Vitamins (continued)

Water-Soluble Vitamins (continued)

Vitamin	Function	Sources in Food	Effects of Deficiency	Recommended Dietary Allowance
Niacin (nicotinic acid)	Essential for carbohydrate metabolism	Yeast, meat, poultry, fish, whole grains, nuts, legumes, enriched breads and cereals	Pellagra	Adult males and females 6.6 mg/1000 kcal
Vitamin B_6	Essential for metabolism of amino acids, fats, and carbohydrates	Liver, meats, whole grain cereals, soybeans, nuts, corn, potatoes	Anemia Nervous disorders	Adult males and females 2–2.2 mg daily
Pantothenic acid	Essential for metabolism of carbohydrates, fats, and amino acids	Liver and organ meats, whole grain cereals, nuts, eggs		Probably 4–7 mg daily for adults
Biotin	Important role in metabolism of carbohydrates, fatty acids, and amino acids	Liver and organ meats, nuts, legumes, eggs, mushrooms		Probably 100–200 μg daily for adults
Folacin (folic acid)	Required for normal growth and reproduction and to prevent anemia	Liver, dark green leafy vegetables, kidney, yeast, legumes, nuts	Anemia	Adolescents and adults 400 μg
Vitamin B_{12}	Essential in metabolism of carbohydrate, fat, and protein and to prevent anemia	Animal foods—liver, kidney, meat, milk, eggs	Pernicious anemia	Adolescents and adults 3 μg daily
Ascorbic acid (vitamin C)	Essential for healthy tissues, promotes wound healing, maintains healthy blood vessels, assists in tooth and bone formation	Citrus fruits, strawberries, cantaloupes, green peppers, kale, broccoli, cabbage, tomatoes, potatoes	Scurvy	Adult males and females 60 mg daily

SOURCE: Dunn, M.D., Fundamentals of Nutrition. New York: Van Nostrand Reinhold, 1983.

appreciable quantities; therefore, one has to consume them almost every day in order to feel well. Excess water-soluble vitamins are removed by being excreted via the urine. It does little good to take excess or huge amounts, because the body will simply pass the extra amount out of the body. It also may be harmful. Most of the water-soluble vitamins belong to what is called the B-complex. Only vitamin C does not belong to this group.

Thiamine Table 7-3 lists the functions thiamine performs in the body. Often people do not get enough of this vitamin because they do not eat enough whole-grain or enriched cereals. Meat, fish, and poultry also supply a fairly good quantity, and pork is especially rich in thiamine. Legumes such as beans and peas are fairly good sources, too, as are peanuts and some other nuts. Often thiamine is called "the energy vitamin," because its main job in the body is to release energy. Men need 1.4 milligrams per day, and women need 1.1.

Riboflavin Adults need between 1 and 2 milligrams of riboflavin per day. It is found in milk and its derivatives. Dark-green leafy vegetables are also good sources of the vitamin. In a balanced diet, there should be no problem obtaining sufficient riboflavin. This vitamin can be destroyed by light, which is why in the past milk was delivered in opaque or colored milk bottles. Table 7-3 lists riboflavin's jobs.

Niacin Niacin is also known as *nicotinic acid, nicotinamide,* and *niacinamide*. These substances have no relation to nicotine found in cigarettes. It is a very important vitamin and works with thiamine and riboflavin to release energy. The human body can use the amino acid tryptophan to make niacin, so a diet that provides plenty of this amino acid obviates the need for niacin itself in the diet. A man needs 18 to 20 milligrams per day and a woman needs 14 to 15. Table 7-3 lists the jobs niacin performs in the body. Niacin is widely found in foods. Yeast is a rich source, but meat, fish, and poultry also provide good amounts. Foods that supply thiamine and riboflavin usually supply niacin, too. Enriched cereals have niacin added to them, and whole grains provide it naturally.

Pyridoxine (Vitamin B_6) Vitamin B_6 is involved in the body's use of amino acids, fats, and carbohydrates. It also helps to make nonessential amino acids. Table 7-3 identifies other jobs that pyridoxine performs. Adults need from 2.0 to 2.2 milligrams daily. It is found in liver, meats, whole-grain cereals, wheat germ, soybeans, peanuts, corn, and many vegetables including potatoes. Some people do not get enough of this vitamin, because they do not eat a balanced diet.

Pantothenic Acid The first part of the name *pantothenic acid* means in Greek "from everywhere." It is widely distributed in plant and animal tissues, so there is seldom a lack of it in the diet. Table 7-3 lists the jobs it does. No amount has been set for the daily intake.

Biotin Biotin works to metabolize carbohydrates, amino acids, and fats. There is no recommended daily intake, but people probably get enough from bacterial action in their intestines, without having to get any in their diet. It is also present in many foods. Table 7-3 indicates what it does in the body.

Folacin (Folic Acid) Folacin is found in many foods and occurs in good quantity in dark-green leafy vegetables. Folacin takes its name from the fact that leaves and blades of grass, or *foliage*, contain good amounts of it. Adults need 400 micrograms per day. Table 7-3 lists the functions it performs in the body.

Vitamin B_{12} At one time the disease *pernicious anemia* was dreaded, because it was almost always fatal. Then vitamin B_{12} was discovered, and soon thereafter it was found to cure this disease. Vitamin B_{12} is not found in plants, so strict vegetarians may lack it; it is found in animal foods. This vitamin joins with another component in the stomach to make the complete vitamin. If one lacks the necessary stomach substance, the vitamin cannot work; consequently, one can suffer from pernicious anemia not because one does not get vitamin B_{12} in food but because the other necessary part is lacking. Individuals who need the completed vitamin B_{12} can receive it by injection. Table 7-3 indicates what it does in the body.

Vitamin C (Ascorbic Acid) Scurvy is a disease that once attacked sailors, because they lacked fresh foods in their diets. For this reason, it was called "the sailor's disease." Then a British doctor discovered that lemons, oranges, and limes contained something (vitamin C, as later researchers found) that cured the disease, and the British navy began to provide lemons and limes to its sailors. This is why members of the British navy even today are called "limeys." A normal adult needs from 50 to 60 milligrams of vitamin C per day. A good supply is also found in cabbage, tomatoes, strawberries, cantaloupes, raw or lightly cooked vegetables, and potatoes. Table 7-3 lists some of its functions in the body.

Vitamin Losses in the Kitchen Vitamins can be destroyed by heat, by light, or by certain reactions of food. Water-soluble vitamins can also be lost as a result of soaking in water, boiling, or other contact with water. When frozen meat thaws and loses a lot of drip, a sizable quantity of the meat's water-soluble B-vitamins flow out with this drip. Because some vitamins are found in greatest quantity right under the skin of a fruit or vegetable, paring can contribute to a loss of vitamins.

Heat can destroy thiamine, pyridoxine, niacin, and some other B-vitamins, so as short a cooking time as possible is desirable to reduce such losses. Fresh vegetables usually have more vitamins than canned or frozen ones, but holding any of these too long in the steam table can cause sizable losses. To reduce leaching losses in cooking, vegetables are sometimes steamed. Microwave cooking also reduces leaching effects.

Riboflavin is destroyed by light. Vitamin C can be oxidized. Thiamine, some of the other B-complex vitamins, and vitamin C are all destroyed when cooked in an alkaline medium. Thus, it is not recommended that baking soda (which gives an alkaline reaction) be added to green vegetables to preserve their color nor to legumes such as peas or beans to speed their cooking. Overcooking meats can also cause them to lose B vitamins.

Most fat-soluble vitamins are rather stable in cooking. Since they are not water-soluble, they do not leach out easily when exposed to soaking, boiling, or other forms of water contact. They are also much more resistant to heat and chemicals than are the water-soluble vitamins.

Long-term storage or dehydration can destroy both water-soluble and fat-soluble vitamins. It is therefore recommended that vegetable supplies be used as soon as possible. Bright, colorful vegetables are richest in vitamins.

Minerals

People may need as much as 1 gram of calcium or phosphorus per day, but some other minerals essential for body functioning are needed in such minute amounts that they are called *trace minerals*. Minerals are inorganic, crystalline, homogeneous chemical elements. Minerals enter foods because plants pick them up from the soil and incorporate them into their tissues. People then inherit the minerals by eating these plants or by eating the flesh of animals that eat these plants. Table 7-4 lists the minerals that are needed in large amounts (macrominerals) and those that are needed in small amounts (microminerals) and indicates what they do in the body.

Each mineral has a specific function to perform, but they also have the following general or common functions:

1. Building a skeletal structure that supports the body.
2. Maintaining a proper acid-alkaline balance in the body.
3. Controlling the amount of fluids held in the body or excreted from it.
4. Helping to synthesize hormones, vitamins, enzymes, and other chemical substances in the body.
5. Helping body reactions occur, by acting as catalysts.
6. Promoting nerve impulses and muscular contractions and relaxations.

Calcium Our bones and teeth contain a lot of calcium. This mineral is found in good supply in milk and milk products, in dark-green leafy vegetables, in canned fish (the soft bones supply this), in broccoli, in legumes, and in some nuts. People need the equivalent of the amount of

TABLE 7-4.   Summary of Minerals

Mineral	Functions	Sources in Food	Recommended Dietary Intake
Macrominerals			
Calcium	Essential for normal growth, bone, and tooth formation. Promotes blood clotting process, healthy nervous system tissue, and normal muscle contraction.	Milk and milk products; dark green leafy vegetables; fish with bones; including salmon, dried beans, and legumes.	Daily 800 mg for adults 1200 mg daily for women during pregnancy and lactation
Chloride	Maintains water and electrolyte balance.	Common salts, milk, meat, eggs; packaged or prepared foods in relation to sodium.	1700–5100 mg daily for adults
Magnesium	Essential for regulating chemical reactions in the body. Regulates acid content of gastric juices.	Wholegrain cereals, nuts, legumes, green leafy vegetables, milk, meats, and seafoods.	Adult females (300 mg daily) Adult males (350 mg daily)
Phosphorus	Provides rigidity to bones and teeth. Essential for normal cell functioning and healthy blood supply.	Milk, cheese, meat, poultry, fish, and eggs. Wholegrain foods, nuts, and legumes.	800 mg daily for adults 1.2 grams daily for women during pregnancy and lactation
Potassium	Occurs in "intracellular" fluid and essential for growth. Lost during period of starvation, protein deficiency or injury. Affects ability of body for muscle contraction and nervous tissue response.	Lean meats, milk, fruits, vegetables, dark green leafy vegetables.	1875–5625 mg daily for adults
Sodium	Occurs in "extracellular" fluid. Essential for regulating acid-base balance and body-fluid volume.	Cheese, milk, shellfish, meat, fish, poultry, and eggs. Common salt.	1100–3300 mg daily for adults
Sulfur	Essential component of certain vitamins, amino acids. Contributes to rigid structure of hair, nails, and skin.	Adequate if protein is adequate.	Unknown

Microminerals

Chromium	Helps to maintain normal glucose metabolism.	Animal proteins, whole grain products, yeast.	.05–0.2 mg daily for adults
Cobalt	Essential component of B_{12}.	Animal products.	Unknown
Copper	Assists in prevention of anemia, normal development of bone and connective tissue, and maintenance of healthy nervous system.	Liver, nuts, legumes, some shellfish, and raisins.	2 to 3 mg daily for adults
Fluorine	Required for resistance to dental caries and developing strong bones.	Fluoridated water.	Probably 1.5–4.0 mg daily for adults
Iodine	Basic component of thyroid hormone. Deficiency produces goiter.	Iodized salt, salt water fish and shellfish.	150 µg daily for adults
Iron	Constituent of hemoglobin, myoglobin, and several enzymes. Essential for maintenance of tissue cells.	Organ meats, other meat, fish, poultry, eggs, legumes, whole-grain and enriched cereals and breads, raisins.	Adult Females, 18 mg daily Adult Males, 10 mg daily
Manganese	Essential for tendon and bone development, normal functioning of central nervous system and enzyme system.	Wholegrain cereals, nuts, legumes, coffee, tea.	Probably 2.5–5.0 mg daily for adults
Molybdenum	Essential component of two enzymes.	Beef kidney, cereals, yeast, legumes.	Probably .15–0.5 mg daily for adults
Selenium	Antioxidant to preserve cellular membrane.	Seafoods and meats.	Probably .05–0.2 mg daily for adults
Zinc	Essential component of enzymes, red blood cells. Necessary for growth, tissue maintenance, prevention.	Meats, milk, liver, poultry, eggs, seafood, wholegrain cereals, nuts.	15 mg daily for adults 5 mg additional during pregnancy and 10 mg for lactation

SOURCE: Dunn, M.D., *Fundamentals of Nutrition*. New York: Van Nostrand Reinhold, 1983.

calcium found in two glasses of milk, plus the additional amounts found in fruits and vegetables, every day. The recommended amount per day for adults is 0.8 gram. If the mineral fluorine is present in the diet, the body makes better bones and teeth. Elderly people can easily lose calcium from their bones, and they may lose so much that the bones become porous and break easily; this condition is called *osteoporosis*. Exercise helps the body absorb and store calcium.

Phosphorus The teammate of calcium in making bones and teeth is phosphorus. It too is found in milk but also in animal protein and in some plants. The same amount of phosphorus is needed by an adult each day as of calcium. Phosphorus can be present in an acidic form in the body, in which case it acts as an acid. But as a phosphate it assumes the opposite characteristics and acts as an alkaline substance. It is thus a helpful agent in maintaining a proper acid-alkaline balance.

Sodium Salt is about 40 percent sodium. The word *salt* comes from the Latin word *sal*, from which the English word *salary* and others are also derived. At one time salt was so valuable that people were given it as a part of their salary. Today, it remains a valuable substance in the diet, but to some people it poses problems. Most people do not lack sodium in their diets. The combination of natural sodium in some foods, plus that supplied by salt in processed foods, provides all that a person needs and more. It is said that individuals get about one-third of their daily sodium from that naturally found in foods, another third from the processed foods they purchase, and the final third from the salt shaker at the end of their hand.

Sodium also appears in many other substances such as monosodium glutamate (MSG, or Accent), baking powders, baking soda, headache remedies, and even drinking water. The estimated safe and adequate intake of sodium per day for adults is 1.1 to 3.0 grams. In this country the average intake is from 2.3 to 6.9 grams per day. Expressed in terms of salt (which, again, is only 40 percent sodium) the desirable intake is about 2.75 to 8 grams per day, and the average intake is 5.75 to 17.25 grams per day; but notice that this assumes the intake of no sodium from sources other than salt; 7 grams are considered a maximum.

The reason why many people try to avoid salt is that in some individuals it can cause hypertension or high blood pressure—a health condition that can lead to heart attacks, strokes, or other problems. Some individuals can consume a considerable amount of salt and incur no bad effects from it, while others must have none added to their food, must drink distilled water or milk from which the sodium has been removed, and must avoid like the plague any food that contains salt.

Chlorine As a free element, chlorine is a poisonous gas; but in the form of a chloride, it is an essential mineral found in table salt and other edible substances. It is a necessary constituent of hydrochloric acid, which the stomach's gastric juices rely on to help digest food. A considerable amount of chlorine is present in the drinking water of many municipalities, where it is added to the water to destroy harmful pathogens. Thus there is usually no problem getting enough chlorides in foods and elsewhere.

Potassium Human muscles need potassium to contract and relax. An individual who does not have enough potassium can suffer a heart arrest and die. Potassium helps keep the heart beating regularly, and it also works with sodium to create muscle action. Sometimes individuals are given what is called a *diuretic* to get rid of excess sodium in the body; but this medication can also get rid of potassium, so individuals who are taking drugs to reduce the sodium in their bodies often have to make sure that they do not lose too much potassium. Often foods such as bananas, which contain a good supply of potassium, are increased in the diet so that the individual gets more potassium.

Potassium and sodium work together: potassium pulls moisture and nutrients into cells, while sodium pulls moisture and waste out of them. This orderly and complementary arrangement keeps the cells functioning smoothly. Good sources of potassium are lean meats, milk, citrus fruits, dried dates, apricots, broccoli, tomatoes, bananas, and dark-green leafy vegetables. Cereals also contain potassium. We need per day about as much potassium as sodium.

Sulfur Sulfur is a component of the hard amino acids such as hair, skin, and nails. There is seldom a deficiency of sulfur in the diet.

Magnesium Magnesium helps form amino acids, works to release energy, promotes muscle relaxation, and helps transfer nerve impulses. An adult male needs 350 milligrams per day and an adult female needs 300. Tetany, a disease in which body muscles contract severely for a long time, can be caused by a lack of magnesium. The best sources are whole grains, bran, nuts, dried legumes, coffee, and tea. Vegetables and fruits are fair contributors. Fish contains some but not much.

Iodine Body cell speed is governed by a hormone called *thyroxin*, and iodine is an important part of this hormone. If iodine is not available, health problems can result, including *goiter*, an enlargement of the thyroid gland in the throat. *Cretinism*, a severe form of mental and physical retardation, occurs because of a near total lack of iodine reaching the fetus during pregnancy.

Today the use of iodized salt is encouraged. The federal government requires the following explanation on the labels of all iodized salt: "This salt supplies iodine, a necessary nutrient." Some people take sea salt, thinking that they get iodine from it, since seawater contains fair amounts of iodine. However, the iodine is lost as a gas when the water evaporates from the sea salt. Adults need 150 micrograms a day. Good sources are saltwater fish and vegetables grown in soil containing iodine. The Great Plains states' lack of soil iodine results in a fairly high incidence of goiter and cretinism in this region of the United States.

Iron Most of the iron in the body is found in the blood and in the red pigment called *myoglobin*, which gives flesh its red color. *Hemoglobin* is the substance in the blood that picks up oxygen in the lungs and carries it to the cells, where it is used to create energy. The blood then picks up and removes the resulting water and carbon dioxide. The carbon dioxide dissolves into the blood, creating carbonic acid (H_2CO_3), which is then carried to the lungs where it escapes as the gas carbon dioxide (CO_2).

Blood is made in the bone marrow; and once a cell is created, it lives for about three months. Worn-out blood cells go to the spleen, where they are broken down and the iron is saved to make new blood cells. The average adult male needs about 10 milligrams of iron per day, but women need 18 milligrams or more. The loss of blood during menstruation causes women to have this greater need for iron. Meat, fish, and egg yolks are good sources of iron, as are shellfish, legumes, dried fruits, nuts, green leafy vegetables, whole-grain cereals, enriched cereals, and dark molasses. Milk is not a particularly good source, but what iron it has is well utilized by the body.

A lack of iron in the blood can cause a health problem called *anemia*, in which the blood lacks the ability to pick up and carry oxygen; as a result, the person who has anemia feels tired and lacks energy. Too much iron, however, can be toxic.

Zinc Zinc works with a wide number of enzymes to promote body processes. Without zinc it would not be possible for people to make their bones and teeth. Zinc is also a part of insulin and is essential for making amino acids. It helps transport vitamin A around the body and plays an important role in the manufacture of sperm. It has also been helpful in the treatment of acne. Overdoses of zinc can be dangerous, however, and a well-balanced diet provides enough for a person's needs, without any supplements. The recommended intake per day for an adult is 15 milligrams. Zinc is found in a wide variety of foods; meats, fish, seafood, legumes, and milk are good sources.

Copper While the human body contains only about 0.1 gram of copper, it is an extremely important mineral, since it helps make hemoglobin and collagen (a substance that plays a major role in bone formation, acts to bind wounds, and does other body jobs). Copper is also a key constituent of the sheaths that cover nerves. There is seldom a lack of copper in the body. It is found in shellfish, grains, organ meats, dried fruits, fresh fruits, vegetables, and legumes.

Fluorine Like free chlorine, free fluorine is a toxic gas. But fluorides are extremely useful minerals. Many toothpastes state on the label that they contain fluoride, a substance added to decrease tooth decay. It has been found that children who drink water containing small quantities of fluoride develop larger and stronger mineral crystals in their bones and teeth and have fewer problems with their teeth throughout their lives. It has also been discovered that older people who continue to drink water containing some fluoride are more resistant to osteoporosis. In many communities, fluoride is added to the drinking water until the water has a fluoride content of 1 ppm (part per million). Despite the known value of having fluoride in drinking water, not everyone agrees that this should be done.

Selenium Selenium acts in the body as an antioxidant, much as vitamin E does, preventing undesirable oxidations. Some research indicates that it may also help prevent cancer. A lack of selenium can cause heart problems, but high amounts of selenium can cause health problems, too. About 0.05 to 0.2 milligrams of selenium per day is recommended for adults. This mineral is found in many foods in sufficient supply to make the chance of a deficiency very small.

Chromium Chromium is needed to help make insulin work in creating energy. If it is lacking, people develop problems much like those experienced by a diabetic. Between 0.05 and 0.2 milligrams is considered a safe and adequate daily intake. Good sources are meats, poultry, whole-grain products, and brewer's yeast.

Cobalt The major role of cobalt is to serve as part of the intrinsic factor for vitamin B_{12}. Even though this is the only physiological function of cobalt known, it is sufficiently important to cause this mineral to be recognized as essential. It is present in trace amounts in many foods, so there is seldom a lack.

Molybdenum This mineral is known to be a part of two important enzymes. Adults are thought to need from 0.05 to 0.15 milligrams daily. It is found in cereals, legumes, yeast, and some animal organs. There is seldom a lack.

Mineral Losses in the Kitchen While minerals cannot be destroyed, they can be lost through soaking, paring, or other ways of handling foods. And like vitamins, they can be leached out during cooking. In some cases chemical changes can make them unavailable for assimilation, despite their remaining in the food that is consumed.

Water

One can live for a fairly long time without food, but for only several days without water. It is essential in the diet if one is to have good health, and the average adult needs from six to eight glasses (1½ to 2 quarts) per day of water or its equivalent in liquids such as soup, tea, coffee, juices, and milk. Water is a structural component of carbohydrates, proteins, fats, and vitamins. Minerals need a certain level of water in the body in order to function properly. Water also acts to maintain even pressures in the body because its molecules resist crowding. It also helps the body hold heat or cool down, as needed. Water often carries nutrients such as calcium and magnesium; and in some areas of the country, people get a fairly good supply of valuable minerals from their drinking water.

The purity of the water supply is of growing concern in this country, and recently much stricter laws have been passed that are designed to ensure that the water remains safe and healthy to drink. Toxic chemicals and harmful substances have gotten into the water in many areas, and the good health of the nation is bound very closely to a high-quality water supply.

Fiber

Fiber is not considered a nutrient, but it is an essential component of anyone's diet. People need it to prevent constipation and to relieve intestinal pressure that causes hemorrhoids. It furnishes bulk to the feces and thus helps in their elimination. It can move foods more quickly through the digestive tract, reducing chances for bacterial action that may lead to appendicitis and diverticulosis. It binds up sterols in the digestive tract, which helps eliminate cholesterol. It especially aids in the digestion of starches, but it also helps digestion and absorption of other nutrients by keeping the foods from packing in the digestive system. Fiber is also thought to reduce the likelihood of cancer in the digestive system, especially colon cancer.

Fiber is mainly composed of a substance called *cellulose*, which is the fibrous part of fruits and vegetables making up their skeletal structure. People cannot digest it, so it remains unchanged in their digestive tract; but ruminants such as horses, goats, cattle, and rabbits can digest it.

The amount of fiber we should consume a day is somewhat confused by how we present the amounts. There are two kinds of ways to state the amount of fiber in foods: *crude* fiber and *dietary* fiber. Crude fiber is the amount left in food after a laboratory test has been made to see how much fiber is in the food, and dietary fiber is the amount of fiber that actually exists in the digestive system. Dietary fiber is from three to five times crude fiber. Up to now the amount of fiber in foods has usually been stated on food labels in crude fiber but there is a tendency today to state it now in amounts of dietary fiber. About 15 grams of dietary fiber a day should be consumed. More is often recommended. The amount averages from six to 20 grams. The amount of crude and dietary fiber in several foods is listed in Table 7-5.

□ What Is a Good Diet?

Individuals can use several methods as guides in selecting foods to ensure that their diet is balanced. One is to keep track of the amount and type of each food consumed and then to check tables of nutrient values to ascertain the quantity of nutrients present in what was consumed. This is a laborious process and not one for the amateur—although, since it now can be done by computer, the job is much easier.

Another approach is to follow what is called the *Exchange Method*. Originally this was developed to help diabetics select an adequate diet that also met their special needs. It has since been expanded and is now used for many other specialty diets and even for normal diets. Foods are divided into various groups, and one selects an appropriate number of portions or exchanges from among the various groups. The theory is that this will enable one to select sufficient portions of various foods in the groups to achieve a balanced diet, since the number to select from each group is prescribed. It is a good method and has been used by many people successfully.

TABLE 7-5. Crude and Dietary Fiber per 100 grams (3.6 oz.)

Food	Crude Fiber (g)	Dietary Fiber (g)
Shredded wheat	2.3	12.3
Stewed prunes	0.8	8.1
Tomato, raw	0.3	1.5
Kellogg's All-bran	2.4	28.0
Natural oats, dry	11.9	45.6

Another method is to use what is called the *Four Food Group Plan*. It was developed by the USDA and has been modified several times; but today it consists of foods arranged in four basic food groups, from each of which one is to select a certain number of portions. Sometimes it is called the 2-2-4-4 Plan, because it prescribes selecting two portions from a milk group, two portions from a meat group, four portions from a fruit and vegetable group, and four portions from a cereal group each day. Table 7-6 indicates how this is done.

If one eats only the portions and kinds of foods that are in the four groups, one will obtain about 1,200 calories a day. One can add calories by eating more of the various groups or by consuming such items as butter, oils, fats, cakes, and pastries. Sometimes these other foods are classed together as a fifth group.

TABLE 7-6. Structure of the Four Food Group Plan

Food Group	Adult Portions per Day	Examples of Portion Size and Kind	Main Nutrients Provided
milk and dairy products	2	1 c (8 oz) milk or yogurt; ½ c evaporated milk; ⅓ c instant dry milk; 1½ c cottage cheese; 1 c milk pudding; 1½ oz cheese; 1⅓ c ice cream	protein, calcium, B-complex vitamins (especially riboflavin and B_{12}), zinc, protein, vitamin A, and vitamin D
meat or alternatives	2	2 to 3 oz cooked lean meat, fish, or poultry; 2 eggs; ¼ c tuna or peanut butter; 1 c cooked legumes; ½ c nuts	protein, thiamine, riboflavin, niacin, iron, zinc, vitamin B_6, and some other B-complex vitamins
fruits and vegetables	4	½ c cooked or raw fruit or vegetable; ½ c juice; 1 orange, peach, or apple; 2 large or 3 small plums; 1 banana or wedge of lettuce; 1 c salad; 1 medium potato	vitamins A and C, folacin, minerals, fiber, and vitamin K
cereals (whole-grain or enriched cereal products)	4	1 slice bread; ½ to ¾ c cooked cereal, pasta or rice; 1 c (1 oz) ready-to-eat cereal; 2 T flour; ½ English muffin, hamburger bun, or hotdog bun	carbohydrates, niacin, iron, thiamine, zinc, fiber, magnesium, protein, and riboflavin, if made from milk. (Some fortified products include vitamins B_{12}, A, C, and D, plus some minerals such as calcium.)

□ Nutrition in the Short Order Section

The preceding discussion about dietary matters was general and broad, covering much general information in a simple, summarized form. Perhaps it is more than one needs to carry out good nutritional practices in preparing and serving food, but it is minimal if one is to have some general knowledge of nutrition. The short order cook should put such information to work to ensure that the foods served are healthful and meet good dietary standards.

The first thing that can be done is to place healthful items on the menu. To avoid fats, one can reduce or eliminate fried, sautéed, and deep-fried foods. Instead, foods may be broiled, poached, steamed, or simmered. Menu items that contain a lot of fat can be eliminated or modified. Many dishes are as tasty and appealing when made with low-fat items as when made with higher-fat items. A fruit plate served with low-fat cottage cheese is not very different in flavor from one made with a 4% milkfat cottage cheese. The menu can also feature specific dishes that meet the needs of patrons. Placing scrambled eggs made from the product called Egg Beaters on the menu offers a healthful substitute for the high-cholesterol egg items on the breakfast menu. Offering a leaner ground-beef patty in hamburgers may attract patrons even though the price is slightly higher than for higher-fat hamburgers. A good first step is simply to look at what is on the menu and ask, "How can I prepare this item so that it will taste as good as it does now but will not contain things that my patrons would prefer not to consume?" There are many other possibilities for menu improvement, although the short order cook may not have a very large voice in these decisions.

The short order cook may not have much say in the purchasing area either, but this is a significant area for improving the healthfulness of foods served. One can specify leaner meat items, purchase skinless chicken (since the skin contains most of the fat), and specify a pure vegetable deep-frying oil rather than one that contains animal fats (and thus more saturated fats). Purchasing more whole-grain items might also be wise and would certainly be more nutritious. For example, one could offer hamburgers on a whole-wheat bun as well as buns made of white wheat flour.

In any purchasing program, one should be sure to buy from a purveyor who has a clean operation, clean trucks, and clean personnel, and who sells foods that meet high standards for cleanliness, sanitation, and quality.

Many improvements can be made in handling, cooking, and serving the food, too. Care can be taken to trim meats of excess fat. One can also use Teflon-coated pans or a butter-flavored vegetable spray instead of large quantities of fats or oils for frying foods. Sending foods to patrons unsalted, with instructions that no foods are salted in the kitchen because many patrons want them that way is another healthful step to take. Offering a salt substitute at the table as well as real salt is another way of accommodating patrons with low-sodium needs.

Cooking foods only as much as required is also recommended. Today's trend toward just barely cooking vegetables is a good one from the nutritional standpoint. It also leaves the vegetable with more texture, which may be desirable.

Cooks should use judicious judgment before deciding to serve fatty items such as melted butter over a steak or a rich sauce over a chicken breast. A minimum amount should be used; and if possible, sauces should be served on the side. When serving salads, offer the dressing on the side and let the patron add the amount desired.

Another safeguard is to keep foods as fresh as possible. This means using items as soon as one can and keeping foods refrigerated and safe from dehydration and other deterioration. Covering food is another way to help preserve its freshness. Preparing foods as soon as possible before cooking is also advised. Avoid cooking too much food and then having to hold it at steam-table or bain-marie temperatures, since this results in loss of many of the nutrients. In some cases, foods may be partially cooked and then held for final preparation; when this is done on some perishable foods such as vegetables, they should be cooled as rapidly as possible after the preliminary cooking. Try not to blanch, soak, or in other ways cause a leaching of vitamins and minerals from food items.

In many kitchens the water in which vegetables, meats, fish, or poultry are cooked is utilized for soups or other kinds of stock. The liquid from canned vegetables can also be saved and added to the stockpot. In a study to see how much calcium could be extracted from boiling bones, it was found that adding a slight amount of vinegar to the simmering water helped extract sufficient calcium to produce a stock higher in calcium than milk is. Thus, adding a bit of vinegar to the stockpot may be advised; it does not remain too long, and it boils off so that little or no afterflavor of vinegar remains.

As a final admonition, however, do not overdo a healthful food program. Numerous operations have found that too much stress on nutrition turns patrons away. Foodservices that went too far in trying to impose healthful foods on patrons have dismayed their patrons and ended in failure. Remember, too, that only slightly more than 42 percent of the patrons in one survey said they were concerned that the foods they were served meet dietary requirements. The other 58 percent consisted of patrons who did not care, were uncommitted, or could not be classified in the study's parameters. While paying attention to patrons' concerns about obtaining healthful foods has been found to be profitable, overemphasizing it can be bad for business. A solid program is one that meets the varying needs and desires of patrons, without restricting free choice.

☐ Summary

Many patrons who eat away from home are concerned about the healthfulness of the foods they consume. Our biggest killer diseases are food-related, and many individuals are more concerned with diet now than they were in the past. However, not all patrons who eat out are concerned. According to one recent study, only about 42 percent are concerned, while 58 percent are not. Therefore, foodservices must cater to both groups. The National Restaurant Association estimates that about 42 percent of this country's food dollar is spent on food away from home and that about 25 percent of the food consumed in this country is consumed at foodservices. This places a significant responsibility on foodservices to see that they satisfy high nutritional standards in the foods they serve. Thus, individuals in the foodservice industry need to know about nutrition in order to discharge their responsibility properly.

There are five categories of food nutrients, plus water: carbohydrates, proteins, fats, vitamins, and minerals. Alcohol is not considered a separate type of nutrient, although it does supply calories.

Carbohydrates are found in foods that are high in starch and sugar. About 55 to 65 percent of a person's total calories should come from them. The end products of burning carbohydrates in the body are energy, water, and carbon dioxide.

Proteins contain nitrogen and are needed by the body to make flesh, blood, antibodies, bones, hormones, and other body components. Proteins can be burned for energy, but this is usually not a desirable occurrence. Proteins are made up of smaller units called amino acids. The body manufactures some of the amino acids it needs but cannot manufacture others. The latter are called *essential* amino acids because they must be obtained in the foods people eat. If a protein contains all of the essential amino acids in good supply, it is called *complete*. Complete protein also can be obtained by combining foods that have complementary incomplete proteins in them.

About 30 percent of a person's total calories should come from fats—preferably from mono- or polyunsaturated fats rather than from saturated fats, because the former do not contribute cholesterol to the body. Cholesterol is a substance that forms part of a waxy plaque that can clog the arteries and cause serious health problems. Too much fat breakdown at one time can cause a health problem called *ketosis*. The way to avoid ketosis when one is burning a lot of fat is to have some carbohydrates in the diet. The carbohydrates help the fat burn down to nonharmful products.

Carbohydrates and proteins each provide 4 calories per gram, while fats provide 9 calories per gram, and alcohol 7. Gender, age, our basal metabolic rate (BMR), and activeness all influence the number of calories a person needs. People also need more calories in cold weather than in hot weather. It is desirable to maintain one's weight at a certain level. Normally adults reach a desirable weight while in their early 20s, which can serve as a goal weight for the rest of their life. To lose weight, one needs to reduce one's daily caloric intake to a level below the level of energy (in calories) expended daily. Cutting down on food while exercising more can help a person lose weight. To lose about 1 pound per week—a good goal—one needs to eat 500 calories per day less than one uses. Using drugs to lose weight is not recommended.

Vitamins are substances found in food that the body uses to maintain and perform its vital functions. People only need a very small amount of them; but if they are lacking, the result can be life-threatening. Vitamins are usually classified according to whether they are fat-soluble or water-soluble.

Fat-soluble vitamins can be stored in the body. Taken in too large a quantity, they can do harm. Some people have actually died from overdoses. Vitamin A is an anti-infection vitamin, but it also helps improve vision. It is found in some fatty foods such as fish oils and butter, and it can also be made in the body from carotene—a substance found in yellow or orange fruits and vegetables and in dark-green leafy vegetables. Vitamin D enables the body to use calcium and phosphorus correctly. It is found in food but can also be produced when sunlight strikes the skin. Vitamin E is an antioxidant vitamin. Vitamin K helps the blood clot.

Most water-soluble vitamins are members of the B-vitamin complex. The exception is vitamin C. Thiamine, riboflavin, niacin, and pyridoxine are all B-complex vitamins that work to release energy and to metabolize amino acids and fats. Pyridoxine also works to make non-essential amino acids and to make healthy, red blood cells. Thiamine is important in helping maintain the nerve structure; a person who does not have enough thiamine can suffer from beri-beri. Riboflavin is necessary in the diet for normal growth to occur. Niacin is a vitamin that can cure pellagra. Pantothenic acid works to metabolize carbohydrates, amino acids, and fats, as does biotin. Folacin is needed to make healthy red blood cells, to avoid anemia, and to allow growth and reproduction. Vitamin B_{12} is needed to prevent pernicious anemia. The B-vitamin complex is found in meats, fish, poultry, and legumes. Dietary imbalances can result in a lack of thiamine, riboflavin, niacin, or pyridoxine. Pantothenic acid and biotin are found in good supply in so many foods that there is little danger of one having a deficiency. Folacin, which is found in the leaves and blades of plants, is usually not lacking in the diet either. Vitamin B_{12} is not found in plant foods, so vegetarians may lack it. Ascorbic acid or vitamin C is needed to prevent scurvy. It is also essential for good metabolism of amino acids, for wound healing, and for keeping the body tissues healthy.

A number of the B-complex vitamins can be lost in the course of preparation, cooking, or holding cooked foods. Some, such as vitamin C, can be oxidized. Others, such as vitamin C, thiamine, pyridoxine, and niacin, can be destroyed by heat. Being water-soluble, they can also be lost during soaking, boiling, or other contact with water. In contrast, the fat-soluble vitamins are fairly stable during handling and cooking.

Water is considered a nutrient. An individual should consume from six to eight 8-oz glasses per day. This volume need not be in the form of water as such; it can include liquids such as soup, tea, coffee, and juices. Water is important in the diet because it is the medium in which most body processes take place. The thirst mechanism in the body is controlled by a hormone called *aldosterone*. When the body lacks moisture, aldosterone is the signaler that sets up a thirst call; it also signals when to get rid of water in the body.

Fiber is not a nutrient. In fact, it is an indigestible substance that gives bulk to the feces. A lot of fiber in the diet comes from fruits and vegetables and is composed mainly of cellulose, a fibrous substance that forms the skeletal structure of plants. An adult needs perhaps 15 grams (½ ounce) of this fibrous material per day. It aids in digestion, keeps food from packing in the digestive system, and helps the body absorb nutrients. By giving bulk to the feces, it also aids in eliminating waste. A satisfactory fiber intake is said to reduce the risk of cancer in the digestive system.

Minerals, like vitamins, can be lost in cooking through leaching or through some chemical change that renders them unavailable. Unlike vitamins, however, minerals cannot be destroyed. It is therefore important that the soaking of foods be kept to a minimum in order to reduce the amount of mineral loss that occurs. For the same reason, as little material as possible should be removed during paring. Certain methods of cooking significantly reduce the leaching loss of minerals. Thus, rather than boiling, simmer, poach, broil, or steam.

Minerals are inorganic, crystalline, homogenous chemical elements that act to build the human skeleton, maintain a good acid-alkaline balance, control fluids, help make many body substances, act as catalysts, carry on the transfer of nerve impulses, and induce muscle contractions and relaxations. Calcium is important in the making of bones and teeth. It also is involved in blood clotting. A loss of calcium from the bones of elderly people is called *osteoporosis*. Phosphorus is a teammate of calcium in the making of bones and teeth and in cell maintenance. Sodium is an essential mineral, but many people get too much of it because they use too much salt in their food; salt is 40 percent sodium. The reason salt is not good for some people is that it elevates the blood pressure, and high blood pressure can cause heart attacks, strokes, and other health problems. Chlorine is an important component of hydrochloric acid, which is found in human gastric juices. It also supports some body oxidations, such as by helping to get oxygen to the cells. Potassium helps muscles contract and relax. A lack of potassium can cause heart problems because the heart muscles fail to function properly. People who take diuretics to get rid of excess sodium need to watch their body's potassium level, because diuretics can also force potassium out of the body.

Sulfur helps construct hard proteins such as nails, hair, and skin. Manganese helps make amino acids in the body. A lack of manganese can cause tetany—an ailment in which the muscles contract for long periods of time. Iodine helps make thyroxine, the hormone that governs the speed at which body cells work. Thyroxine is made in the thyroid gland in the throat; if there is a lack of iodine, this gland works too hard and swells, causing what is called a *goiter*. A lack of iodine during pregnancy may cause cretinism—serious mental and physical retardation—in the offspring. Iron is required in the blood to enable it to carry oxygen. If the blood lacks iron, one has what is called *anemia*. Zinc works with enzymes to promote various body processes. It is also important in the manufacture of many important body substances. Copper is important because it helps to make hemoglobin and collagen. Fluorine helps make stronger and larger crystalline components for bones and teeth, which makes them stronger and more resistant to decay and other problems. Selenium acts in the body as an antioxidant, as does vitamin E. Chromium helps insulin work in the body. Cobalt is a part of vitamin B_{12}. Molybdenum is an important part of two of the body's enzymes.

The nutrients in a diet can be monitored in any of three common ways: by using tables of nutrient values, by adopting the Exchange Method, or by following the Four Food Plan. The Four Food Plan is the simplest and easiest to use. In it, foods are divided into a milk or dairy group, a meat group, a cereal group, and a fruit and vegetable group. Two portions each of the first two groups and four portions each of the second two should be consumed daily in order to achieve a balanced diet of about 1,200 calories per day. Extra calories can come from foods such as fats, oil, sugars, pastries, jellies, and butter. Alternatively, more portions of the four prescribed groups can be eaten.

Various things can be done in short order cooking to meet patrons' desires for healthful foods. The first is to see that healthful foods are placed on the menu. This may mean replacing certain items on the menu with others or substituting certain ingredients in recipes for others. Foods that are made rich in fat by sautéing or deep-frying can be prepared differently. Low-fat items can replace high-fat ones. A no-cholesterol product called Egg Beaters can be used to replace regular eggs, and leaner meats may be offered. It is also advisable to ensure that purchasing is done with a view toward increasing the healthfulness of foods. A purveyor who sells safe, healthful, and high-quality food should be selected. It may be desirable to specify skinless chicken, well-trimmed meats, whole-grain items, and so on.

In the short order section itself, many things can be done during handling, cooking, and holding of foods to see that they retain maximum nutrition. Using Teflon-coated pans or a butter-flavored vegetable spray instead of fats or oils can reduce the amount of fat in fried foods. Not salting foods in the kitchen will please patrons who want less salt. Cooking foods only as much as required is recommended. In serving foods, one should avoid being too liberal in apportioning high-calorie items such as melted butter or rich sauces. Many sauces and salad dressings can be served on the side, for the patron to apply as desired. Ensuring that foods are as fresh as possible is a nutritional necessity. Utilizing the water in which vegetables or meats are cooked and the liquid from canned vegetables for stock is advised. Adding a bit of vinegar to a stockpot in which bones are being boiled can help extract calcium from them.

Overemphasizing nutrition, however, can do more harm to a business than ignoring it completely. Many patrons do not want foods that have been selected entirely on the basis of nutrition. They just want good, old-fashioned food. A moderate program—one that meets the desires of most patrons who are interested in nutrition, while not antagonizing the large number of patrons whose interest in nutrition is very low or nonexistent—is probably best.

□ CHAPTER REVIEW □

1. What are the three leading food-related causes of death among people 55 years old and older?
2. Are all patrons in foodservices interested in nutrition? If not, what groups are interested in it, and what groups are not?

3. How much of the U.S. food dollar is spent on food outside the home? What percentage of food consumed in this country is eaten outside the home?
4. What are the three fuel nutrients?
5. What other nutrients are there?
6. What kinds of foods are high in carbohydrates?
7. What percentage of a person's total calories should come from carbohydrates?
8. How are proteins used in the body? If the body wants to use proteins for energy, what does it have to do to accomplish this?
9. What is an essential amino acid? What is a complete protein?
10. What percentage of a person's total calories should come from protein?
11. What percentage of an average American's total calories come from fats? What *should* this percentage be?
12. Name some foods that are high in protein.
13. Do vegetable oils contain cholesterol?
14. What does cholesterol do in the body that is considered harmful?
15. What is ketosis, and what can cause it?
16. How many calories does a gram of pure carbohydrate have? a gram of pure protein? a gram of pure fat? a gram of pure alcohol?
17. What two things determine how many calories a person needs?
18. What does *basal metabolic rate* mean?
19. Why does a person lose weight?
20. Why does a person get fat?
21. Why will a person on a good weight-reduction program lose weight for a while and then suddenly stop? What must that person do to get beyond such a plateau and start losing weight again?
22. What is a vitamin?
23. Name four fat-soluble vitamins, and identify one major thing each does in the body.
24. The lack of what vitamin can cause a child to get rickets?
25. What vitamin helps the blood to clot?
26. What food is a good source of vitamin E?
27. What vitamin is known as the "energy vitamin"?
28. If a person's diet includes a lot of tryptophan, does that person need niacin?
29. Folacin is found in what kind of vegetables?
30. Vitamin B_{12} can help do what?
31. Why are British sailors called "limeys"?
32. What does light do to riboflavin?

33. How can one act to preserve nutrients during the handling, preparation, cooking, and holding of foods?
34. What is a mineral? Name three things in general that minerals do in the body.
35. What does the team of phosphorus and calcium do in the body?
36. What food contains a good supply of phosphorus and calcium?
37. Why is sodium harmful to some people?
38. How much salt is considered the right intake per day for an adult?
39. Chlorine is used to make hydrochloric acid. Where is hydrochloric acid found in the body?
40. What does potassium do in the body?
41. In what kind of amino acids is sulfur found?
42. What are goiters? What causes them?
43. What is cretinism, and what causes this condition?
44. What mineral in blood helps the blood carry oxygen?
45. What health problem is caused by a lack of iron in the diet?
46. Why do manufacturers add a fluoride to toothpaste?
47. How much water should the average adult have per day?
48. Why is fiber needed in the body? How much fiber should a person have per day?
49. What substance in fruits and vegetables makes up most dietary fiber?
50. What is the Four Food Plan, and how does it work?
51. What can be done to ensure that patrons who want healthful foods can get them?

CHAPTER EIGHT

Counter Service

□ Counter Work

In Chapter 1, where the job of the short order cook was described, it was noted that the short order cook sometimes had to do counter work as well as short order cooking. Such a job combination usually occurs only in small operations.

Counter service has the advantage of giving fast service to patrons who are not particularly interested in dining in style but who want fast and good service and good food. The patrons are usually business people who work nearby, shoppers, and walk-in passers-by from the street. Such fast service units are often located in high traffic areas. Counter service allows for fast turnover, so many more people can be served there than in seated table service. The menu is often simplified to the service of fountain items, hotdogs, salads, hot entrées, sandwiches, snacks, hamburgers, carbonated and other beverages, and desserts. Breakfasts and coffee break items are ordinarily a major part of the business. Dinner trade is casual and more relaxed. A lot of the items are purchased ready-made, such as cakes, pies, breakfast sweet goods, doughnuts, and even some wrapped sandwiches. Canned soups, canned chili, and other canned foods are used. In addition, many items are purchased in portions, ready to cook. Salad greens are obtained preprocessed and washed, ready for use. Almost no complicated food items are prepared. Salads are limited in number and simply prepared. The demand is for simple, good food, and it is made by busy people who want to consume the food rapidly and get on their way. There may be times in the afternoon when a shopper saunters in and has more time to spare; but for breakfast, coffee breaks, and luncheons, the pace is dominated by "order, eat, and get out in a hurry."

If a short order cook is to take orders, cook the food, serve it, make out the check, take the cash, and return the change, only a very limited number of patrons can be accommodated. Ordinarily, it might be possible for one counter person to serve twenty-five people at one time, but this is not true when the job is combined with short order cooking. Perhaps a maximum of fifteen patrons can be served at one time under the latter conditions, and that is assuming that some of the orders are as simple as coffee only, coffee and a doughnut or sweet breakfast roll, or a bowl of soup. It takes from 8 to 12 minutes to prepare a hamburger, and—while the cook should not simply be standing there watching the hamburger fry—there is a time factor involved in doing such a job right that reduces the amount of additional counter service the cook can do.

Doing combined cooking and counter service is fast work, and from the time one comes on shift until one leaves, it is go–go–go. People doing the combo have to have their wits about them, be well organized, know the job, and be able to work fast. The work takes stamina as well as ability. One can expect to be on one's feet 95 to 100 percent of the time. An observer seldom sees a stool for the cook to sit on in a short order section.

Handling the Counter Job
An individual who serves the public must possess certain talents and attributes. Such a person is often under stress and occasionally under severe aggravation when difficult patrons are encountered. To cope with the job, one must be able to handle pressure and be resilient and strong. The ability to see things in the long run rather than getting caught up in the moment is a good trait to possess. A good sense of humor is also a great asset in making it through difficult times.

One of the first necessities demanded of a short order cook who must also do counter service is a thorough knowledge of how to do the job, together with the ability to do it. Such knowledge and ability take learning and experience. There are certain ways of doing things, and the server should know these and follow them. For example, when one picks up a napkin for a patron seated at a counter, the napkin should automatically be picked up by the right hand and put down on the patron's left, not picked up by the left hand and then transferred over to the right hand (see Fig. 8-1). Similarly, forks are picked up with the right hand and put down on the patron's left. Conversely, knives and spoons are picked up by the server's left hand so they end up on the patron's right. The server should never touch the working parts of silverware (the parts that touch a patron's mouth) but always hold them by their handles. Glassware and cups should never be handled with the fingers on the inside surface, and plates should be handled so the thumb is not down on the upper rim of the plate.

Deftness and speed, of course, are special requirements. One cannot dawdle and still get the job done in a way that satisfies patrons or holds a job.

FIGURE 8-1. The proper way to pick up silver and napkins so that they are properly placed for a right-handed person.

Opening Up in the Morning

When the short order cook opens up in the morning, there may be one hour—from 6:00 to 7:00 A.M.—to get ready. Often the first step taken is to turn on fans or other ventilation. Next, check the menu to see what items are on it and how each is prepared and served. Look ahead and plan the sequence of work that must be done to have things prepared well and on time. If there is to be a roast for lunch, see that it is readied and goes into the oven at the proper time. If there are to be Swiss steaks for lunch, they must be floured, grilled, and braising in an oven or in a brazier on top of the stove by 9:00 A.M. The time requirements for getting many things ready must be known and followed. Note the kind of salads and sandwiches being offered, and see that the ingredients are prepared to go. Breakfast items must be brought out and placed in proper position so that they can be obtained quickly. Breakfast meats should be partially cooked ahead of time so that they are ready for last minute cooking. The short order cook should not "sandbag"—that is, overprepare just to be sure that the item will not run out. Instead, plan a run-out time. One of the rules to follow is: "Get everything you can in readiness, but not at any sacrifice of quality."

Preparations must also be made for service. For breakfast, butter, jellies, and jams must be set out (the butter on cracked ice). Ground coffee needs to be set out in sufficient portions for the meal. Cold cereals should be in place. What about fruits? Is the orange juice ready? Are half grapefruit to be served? If so, prepare some, place a plastic wrap over them so that they do not dry out, and put them under refrigeration. Is bread out and ready for toasting?

For lunch and dinner, plan ahead similarly, and see that needed items are on hand. Salad dressings should be out, and any preprepared salads and sandwiches should be under refrigeration. Rolls may have to be put into the bun warmer so that they are at a proper serving temperature when ordered. Are crackers ready for soups? Just checking through the menu and asking "What must be ready?" may make the job of serving just a bit easier.

If the cook must also act as cashier, there is the job of getting the opening bank (cash needed to operate during the day, consisting of bills, silver, and pennies) to do. This money may be stored in a secure place, or the cook may have the combination to the safe. (If the manager is there, this is probably not necessary.) If the manager is not present in the early morning, a group of checks to use for orders may be left in the safe, too. These are serially numbered; as they are used and cash is taken in, they are placed on a spindle so that the total cash taken in can be checked against check totals. Having them serially numbered makes it possible to confirm the existence of missing checks. In many cases, employees are responsible for missing checks.

The number of tasks that must be performed by the short order cook in the short period of this first hour is daunting. It may be that the first hour of a shift is the most challenging and the busiest.

Once all of these jobs are done, the short order cook has to consider a lot of other things. For instance, there is what is called *sidework*, which means checking to make sure that such things as catsup, Worcestershire sauce, A-1 sauce, and other condiments are available for service. Are salt and pepper shakers filled? Are menus clean and available? Is the backbar clean and the mirrors behind it sparkling? Are backbar displays arranged attractively? If carbonated beverages are to be served, is the carbonator turned on, and does the short order cook know how to connect a new CO_2 cylinder if the old one runs out? Does the cook know how to set the pressure to a proper level for good foam on carbonated drinks? Are napkin holders filled but not so overstuffed that patrons have to struggle to get a mangled one out?

Another important thing that must be known and performed speedily is how to clear dishes from patrons' places and put the dishes into tote boxes. A tote box (or bus pan) is a container into which soiled ware is placed for removal to the dishwasher; it is usually stored under the counter until full. Tote boxes should be situated at a point close to the origination of the soiled ware.

While one cannot do much to improve the efficiency of equipment placement in the short order section and its associated counter service, one can plan effective arrangements of utensils, food supplies, and other necessary but movable items. Study where silverware and napkins are placed. Where might glassware, ice, and water be set so that service is most convenient for the server? They should all be as close together as possible and also close to patrons. Where are the condiments needed for various foods? Are syrups, jellies, jams, and butter quickly available with the output of minimal movement?

When the short order cook works as a server, coordination is essential between service and cooking, and good *mise en place* must be performed in both the cooking section and the serving section. Clean up all work areas, and keep them clean and in order. Spills and other messes should be cleaned up as they occur. Do not let cleanup jobs pile up. Sometimes they can suddenly reach critical mass and swamp the striving short order cook, making it almost impossible to get the job done.

Taking the Order

After the preliminary time for getting things ready for opening is over, opening time finally comes. Thus, at 7:00 A.M. one goes to the front door and opens it. Perhaps several old steadies are out there waiting to come in and get breakfast. It's often nice to see them: they are friendly, everyone knows each other, and consequently there is no strain. However, these early-morning patrons are always in a hurry and have little time to waste, because they have to start work themselves at 8:00 A.M. Thus, the cook goes to work at once taking the orders and preparing them. In the meantime, another patron enters—this time a stranger. He sits on a stool and picks up a menu, opening it without looking around. He is still sleepy. As he sits down, the server should come over, greet the patron with a warm "Good morning," and put down a glass of water. After this, the cook may have to leave, because the first guests have now finished their fruit and want their main meal plus more coffee. After a quick swing around to do this, the server is now ready to take the last patron's order.

The server should stand in front of the patron, pencil and order check in hand. "And what may I bring you?" or "Is there anything on the menu you would like?" the server can ask. The patron may reply, "I'll take two over easy and a small glass of orange juice. Whole-wheat toast, and I like cream in my coffee." The server repeats: "Small glass of orange juice, cream with coffee, and two eggs over easy with whole-wheat toast.

Anything else?'' The patron shakes his head, and the server leaves, returning immediately thereafter with the orange juice, the coffee, and a small pitcher of cream. Before the cook-server goes into the kitchen, he or she makes out the first patrons' checks and leaves them with the patrons, saying, ''Thank you; have a good day. I hope I see you tomorrow.''

The server picks up two slices of whole-wheat bread, places them in the toaster, and then picks up the oil mop and greases a small portion of the griddle. Two eggs are quickly opened and put onto the greased spot. The toaster is then lowered. In a few moments the eggs are cooked underneath, and the cook grasps an offset spatula, slides it under the eggs, and neatly flips them over. After only a few seconds, the cook reaches for a warm plate and quickly slides the eggs into the middle of the plate. The cook-server next takes out the two slices of toast, stacks them one on top of the other on the cutting board, cuts both slices in two diagonally with a French knife, and places these on either side of the eggs. The cook-server quickly takes the order to the patron who by now has consumed the orange juice and almost all of the coffee and is waiting. The order is placed down, with the announcement ''Here are your eggs and whole-wheat toast.'' Quickly reaching under the counter, the cook-server puts two pats of butter on a small plate with one hand and with the other picks up a bowl full of small single-portion packets of jams, jellies, and honey. Both are put in front of the patron near the toast.

By now the first patrons are at the cash register, so the server moves over to take the cash, asking, ''How was your breakfast this morning? Everything all right?'' The reply is affirmative, and with a ''Have a good day'' from the server, the patrons disappear out the door.

This is the start. From now on the cook-server can expect to be really busy—taking orders, preparing them, serving them, taking cash, and cleaning up after a patron has finished. The pace is fast and the demands are heavy, but it can also be fun to a cook who knows the job and likes to be with people.

As noted, once guests are seated, they should be greeted as soon as possible and given a glass of ice water. Next they should be given a menu or allowed to pick it up from where it sits on the counter. Some patrons must be given time to study the menu and make up their minds. Others do not even look at the menu, because they are ready to give their order as soon as they sit down. It is a good habit in taking the order to repeat it to the patron. Check also at this time on specific details of an order, such as the doneness of meat, whether to include lemon with tea, and how the eggs should be fried. Knowing this beforehand is better than bringing the food to the patron and finding out that something is wrong because an ambiguity was not clarified when the order was taken. By repeating an order, the patron hears it and checks mentally to see if that was what was wanted. This allows a meeting of minds on exactly what is wanted.

Good serving is a matter of thinking ahead and remembering. While setting an order down before a patron, think about what has to go with the order: crackers for soup? steak sauces and tomato catsup for a steak or hamburger? milk for cereal? butter for rolls or baked potato? coffee now or later? Good servers learn to anticipate the needs of patrons so that patrons seldom have to ask for anything. What they need is always there or on the way.

Most of the orders going to patrons are delivered by what is called *arm work*; simply stated, this consists of carrying the dishes in the hands, using the arms to help carry the load. An experienced server can carry an amazing number of dishes by properly stacking them in the hands and over the arms. Arm work is faster than tray work; and trays are often a bother anyway in short order work, since often some landing space must be held open for them so that the server can put down the items and then serve them to the patron.

In clearing dishes from the counter, follow the same rules for handling dishes and silverware at service. See that tote boxes for soiled dishes and silverware are close at hand. Stack soiled ware in these tote boxes well so that a maximum quantity can be held and so that items are secure when the tote box is carried to the dish machine. Work fast but as quietly as possible. The sharp ring of dishes striking together is annoying to patrons, and furthermore, it is harmful to the dishes. Scraping them together can cause excessive wear to the glaze and can leave dark black marks on the dishes. It also can produce cracks or star cracks in dishes.

Patrons usually like to have soiled dishes moved from in front of them as soon as they have finished eating from them, so servers should remove these as quickly as possible, lifting them up and then quickly getting them out of sight by placing them down into tote boxes.

As the items are cleared, the server should ask, "Can I bring you anything else?" If the patron indicates that nothing else is desired, the server should make out the check and place it face down in front of the patron, with a polite "Thank you. I enjoyed serving you. I hope you come again." Although the server-cook may be as busy as the proverbial "cat on a hot tin roof," it is important to try not to say this in haste. Showing pleasure and ease in doing it leaves a better impression and really makes the patron feel welcome and appreciated. Remember, it is repeat business that makes for successful operations—and better tips. Patrons come back because they like the food, the place, and the service. Personal warmth and friendliness can do much to make a place successful and to raise the cook-server's income.

Tips

There is an old saying in foodservice work that the word *tips* is an acronym for "To insure prompt service"; in any case, this pretty well explains what tips are all about. Patrons are not obliged to give tips; they give them to express pleasure with the service. Often today a tip is calculated at about 15 percent of the total bill. Some patrons give less, and others give more. It all depends on the person's tipping habits and level of satisfaction with the service.

A foodservice can pay a cook-server less than the federally mandated minimum wage if tips can be expected to constitute part of the compensation. However, there is still a certain minimum base rate of pay below which employers cannot go. The rationale for this subminimum wage is that servers often get two to three times more in tips than what the employer pays as a wage. In some operations where seated service is provided and the average check is high, servers can make very big amounts in tips. Often management is actively interested in seeing servers make good tips, since such a result means that the servers are satisfying patrons. Low tips are therefore a sign that a server is not doing the job expected.

The Internal Revenue Service of the U.S. Treasury requires that employees keep a record of tips received and pay income tax on the total. While some amount out of the total might be hidden, the IRS has some very good ways of estimating what a server takes in in tips, and any flagrant underreporting draws its attention.

Cashiering

Taking cash is another job that involves following specific rules, and the cook-server must know how to do it properly. The job requires alertness and a quick mind with figures. Patrons come to the cash register with their check, put it down, and then reach for a billfold or pocketbook. The cashier should look at the check and state the sum, and then ask, "Did you enjoy your [main course item]?" At this point one can get valuable feedback from patrons, and the opportunity should not be missed to see how patrons are reacting to the food, the place, and the service. Any expression of dissatisfaction should meet with a tactful, proper reply from the cashier. If the matter needs greater attention, it might be well to call the manager in, but such an occasion should be rare.

In the meantime, the patron either has brought out the correct amount or has tendered an amount greater than the check and expects change. If it is the exact amount, count it out in front of the patron, say

"Thank you very much," and put the money into the till. If change is to be returned to the patron, pick up the bill, lay it on the ledge above the cash drawer (do not put the bill in the drawer), and count out the correct change. Leaving the bill on the ledge in full sight of the cashier and the patron leaves evidence of what was tendered in payment, so there can be no argument about what size bill the patron tendered. In giving the patron the change, first state the amount of the check, and then build up from there, giving back change until the proper amount is reached. After the patron takes the change and starts to leave, put the bill tendered in payment into the cash drawer. Often only bills up to about $10 are put into the till. Larger bills are put safely underneath the tray in the till drawer holding the money.

Money requires care in handling and good accountability. In some cases it might be a good precaution, when the server is busy waiting on patrons or preparing food, to have the cash register locked. The server can carry a key and quickly open it upon taking cash, relocking it when the transaction is completed.

Money is remarkably unclean, and handling it can soil hands. After handling money, one should always either wipe the hands with a moist cloth or wash and dry the hands. The same thing should be done after handling soiled dishes or other ware. Even after handling food, wipe the hands clean. Such cleaning of the hands should develop into a spontaneous habit.

It is also important for the cook-server to know how to operate the cash register. Some have a tab for every menu item (see Fig. 8-2); when punched, the tab writes out the item and its price. Most cash registers today also total the bill, and some automatically add the tax and other needed information. Some are connected to computers and record even more data. Proper operation of computer or electronically operated cash registers can simplify accounting, give better cash accountability, and provide lots of valuable information to management.

Guest Checks

Normally foodservices use guest checks in single form or in pads, and these checks are serially numbered. Management should issue the checks, recording who has which pads or checks and what the range of numbers on each is. Orders should be written on the checks as patrons give them. It is not wise to try to remember orders and write them up later. While some order takers may be able to memorize such orders quite well, during rush times one is sure to forget something or get orders mixed up, and then things can go to pieces.

Some guest checks may have on them the name of the restaurant, lines on which to write menu items, and that is all (see Fig. 8-3). Others

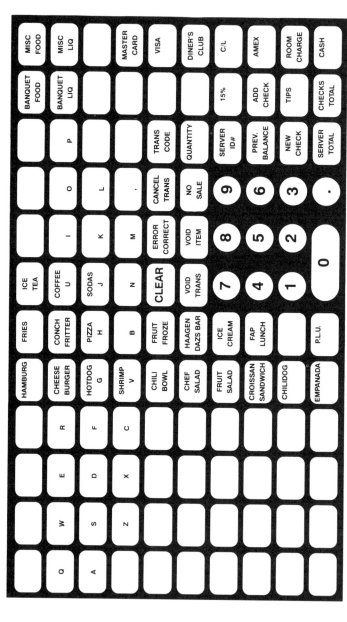

FIGURE 8-2. Some new cash registers can be programmed to print out the name and price of a menu item on a guest check and then keep this information in memory. The cash register is first properly programmed and an overlay made, such as presented here. Then the cashier simply presses the proper key and the register prints out and records the information.

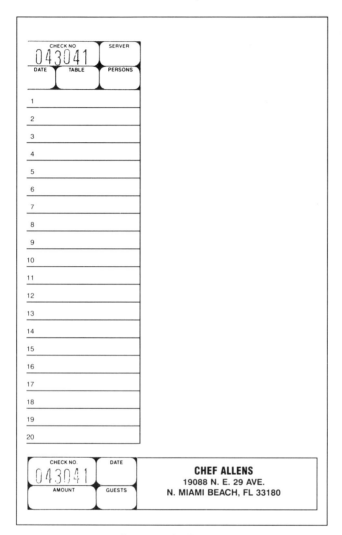

FIGURE 8-3. A simple guest check. (*Courtesy Chef Allens*)

carry much more information, and some may even have the entire list of available menu items printed on them. Usually checks are divided into columns so that the order taker can write in the quantity, item, and price. In some cases, prices will be extended (added up manually), and space for this must be provided. The check should be able to carry all the information needed to ensure that the order is prepared exactly the way a patron wants it.

Some knowledge of arithmetic is usually needed to handle guest checks properly, although this need continues to decline as more and more sophisticated features are added to cash registers. When working under more primitive conditions, servers often have to add up checks and calculate a sales tax or other tax. Thus one needs to be able to perform accurate computations, to make change, and to handle cash. An inability to handle mathematical problems can cause problems for the cook-server.

Closing Up

After the last delaying patron has departed, a number of things must be done before the cook can leave. The door should be locked, and a closed sign should be put up. Then the cash register must be attended to. A tape of the register should be taken, and the cash should be counted and recorded in a cash report. A bank may have to be prepared for the morning shift, and the money must be put away in a safe or a safe place. Guest checks need to be assembled, perhaps totaled, and bundled together for future verification and recording.

Coffee pots or urns may have to be emptied and cleaned. Side work such as filling sugar dispensers, salt and pepper shakers, and napkin holders; sweeping the floor; cleaning the tables, counters, and other tops; and so on may have to be done. Perishable food must be put away. Equipment may also need attention. The griddle may have to be scraped down, and a sandstone or other polishing device used to polish its surface. Then the griddle may have to be reconditioned so that it is ready to be put to work by the morning crew.

It is traditional that the night shift leave the place in good readiness for those who must come in in the morning and start all over again. The morning shift receives a big boost when the night shift fulfills this tradition efficiently and properly.

□ Fountain Work

Counter service often involves a lot of fountain work preparing malts, milk shakes, sundaes, sodas, and similar dishes. There is a lot of skill to managing a fountain effectively and to preparing the items well.

The proper kind of dish for the item, in clean and attractive condition, is needed if the fountain item is to meet a high standard. The fountain equipment must also be of high quality and in good working shape. It requires cleaning and frequent maintenance attention. Ice cream cabinets should hold reserve frozen supplies at about 0°F (−18°C), but for dishing they should be set at between 12° and 15°F (−9° to −11°C). The reason for this temperature difference will be discussed later.

A fountain should be equipped with a carbonation system—a system that adds sparkling carbon dioxide bubbles to water, giving the water a tingling, refreshing tang. It is used in making carbonated beverages, sodas, and the like. A tank filled with carbon dioxide gas under pressure is placed in a convenient spot, and a hose leads from it to a mixing device that mixes the carbon dioxide with water from the tap. The tap is able to produce a broad spray or, when turned another way, a very fine one. The very fine spray is used to give a final foam to a soda. Workers should know how to change the carbon dioxide tank, because it frequently runs out during work sessions. (If draft beer is served, a separate carbonation system is used to carbonate this beer.)

Most operations purchase their syrups and other fountain supplies, although some make their own; if so, the recipes should yield high-quality products. Usually one gets a more consistent quality by purchasing the syrups and supplies needed. Because some items (such as chopped nuts) can go rancid, not too much should be purchased at one time. It is advisable to keep chopped nuts under refrigeration. In addition, some kinds of fountain syrups can ferment, so these should be refrigerated, too. Often such items are stored in a refrigerated space in the fountain. High standards of sanitation must be maintained in handling supplies and in holding them.

Ice cream, sherbets, and ices are frozen mixtures made by mechanical freezers that whip air into them as they freeze. Desserts such as mousses, parfaits, frozen puddings, and frozen fruits are not whipped during freezing; they are whipped either before freezing or not at all. Slushes or granites are only partially frozen and are coarse and granular. There are many different kinds of ice cream. *Philadelphia* ice cream consists of milk, cream, sugar, flavoring, and perhaps a stabilizer. If eggs are added, the result is *French* ice cream, which frequently also contains tiny specks of ground vanilla in it. Vanilla ice cream must contain at least 10 percent milkfat, but if fruit, chocolate, nuts, or other ingredients are added—usually constituting about 2 percent of the entire ice cream—the milkfat content can be no less than 8 percent. Mixtures used for milkshakes and malts can include less than 8 percent milkfat.

An operation that makes its own soft ice cream usually purchases appropriate mixes prepared by a dairy firm. A special machine is needed to make soft ice cream. This is true also of malts and milkshakes: a special mix is purchased, and a special machine produces the malt or milkshake. Servers need careful instruction on how to operate, care for, and sanitize such machinery. Safety precautions must also be observed in using them.

When a liquid freezes, it usually expands. This happens to a slight degree with frozen dessert mixes. After a mixture is frozen to a thick, ribbony stage, however, the mixer is turned on to whip the mixture at full speed, putting a lot of air into it and making it a much lighter and more delicate product. The federal government allows ice cream to be whipped until the volume of the original mix is doubled. This is called a *100 percent overrun*. The better ice creams have about an 80 percent overrun.

It is important in dishing ice cream to preserve the overrun of the ice cream so that the dessert retains a light, pleasant texture. If scooping results in pushing this air out, a pasty product is obtained. A poor scooping technique also gives far fewer portions per gallon. Normally, scooping loss due to packing is 40 to 45 percent. If the temperature of the ice cream is below 12°F (− 9°C), the mix is too hard and one has to press very hard to get a full scoop. Such pressure increases packing. On the other hand, if the ice cream is above 15°F (− 11°C), the mix is so soft that it packs as it is being scooped, again resulting in a loss of overrun.

It is desirable to use a rolling motion in scooping to allow the ice cream to roll up in the scoop. Scoops with a release device do not roll well and pack more ice cream. Good scooping technique is evidenced by an even top in the ice cream container, as shown in Figure 8-4. The number on the handle of the scoop indicates the number of scoops that one should get per quart of solid product. However, because there is a 40 to 45 percent loss in good scooping, this is never achieved in fountain work. The only way to get full overrun is to obtain prepackaged ice cream and to deliver this to the patron without scooping it. Thus, slicing bricks and serving these also gives more portions per quart, because relatively little packing occurs during slicing—especially if the ice cream is kept at a good slicing temperature.

Table 8-1 indicates the usual scoop size and number of scoops to use for various fountain items. Scoops should be kept in clean water. Make sure that the edges are sharp and smooth. If the scoop is too cold, the frozen dessert will stick to it and pack. Figures 8-5, 8-6, 8-7, and 8-8 illustrate how to make various fountain items.

☐ Handling Patrons

The job of the short order cook changes when serving is part of the job—not only in terms of the work done, but in some of the attendant responsibilities. Chief among these is handling the public properly and

FIGURE 8-4. The proper way to scoop ice cream. Note the evenness of the top and the lack of packing that results by using such a rolling method. (*Photo by Michael Upright*)

TABLE 8-1. Scoop Sizes and Quantities for Fountain Items

Fountain Item	Scoop Size	Scoops per Portion
banana split	30	3
bowl of ice cream	30	4
parfait	30	3
ice cream soda, malt, or milkshake	24	2
sundae	20	2
pie, cake, or pudding à la mode	20	1
table d'hôte, plain	16	1
sundae, meal portion	12	1
à la carte portion	10	1

well. Serving the public is not easy: it requires an individual who has special talents and abilities. Patrons are people, and of course there are all kinds. In fact, each individual is different and special. Some may be easy to serve, while others may be difficult. The server must accept that the difficult ones are an unavoidable part of the day's work, sprinkled among patrons who are a delight to serve and those who are no bother.

1. ½ oz. topping
2. Ice cream
   2 dippers
3. 1 oz. topping
4. Nuts?
5. Whipped cream
6. Cherry

FIGURE 8-5. How to make a standard sundae. The topping may be hot fudge or any number of different syrups.

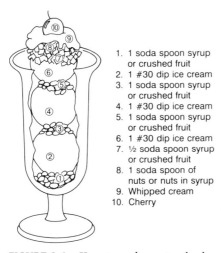

1. 1 soda spoon syrup
   or crushed fruit
2. 1 #30 dip ice cream
3. 1 soda spoon syrup
   or crushed fruit
4. 1 #30 dip ice cream
5. 1 soda spoon syrup
   or crushed fruit
6. 1 #30 dip ice cream
7. ½ soda spoon syrup
   or crushed fruit
8. 1 soda spoon of
   nuts or nuts in syrup
9. Whipped cream
10. Cherry

FIGURE 8-6. How to make a standard parfait.

Some patrons carry their problems with them, and they may often let this show. Food is a very personal thing to everyone. People learn as babies to interpret their environment through food; and even mother love is said to be developed by food, because it is the mother who gives the infant its food. When very young, babies cry when they are hungry, but as they grow older, people learn to submerge this emotional reaction. Still, at times of emotional upset, they may fall back on their original reaction and take it out on the food. Often a "bad cup of coffee," an

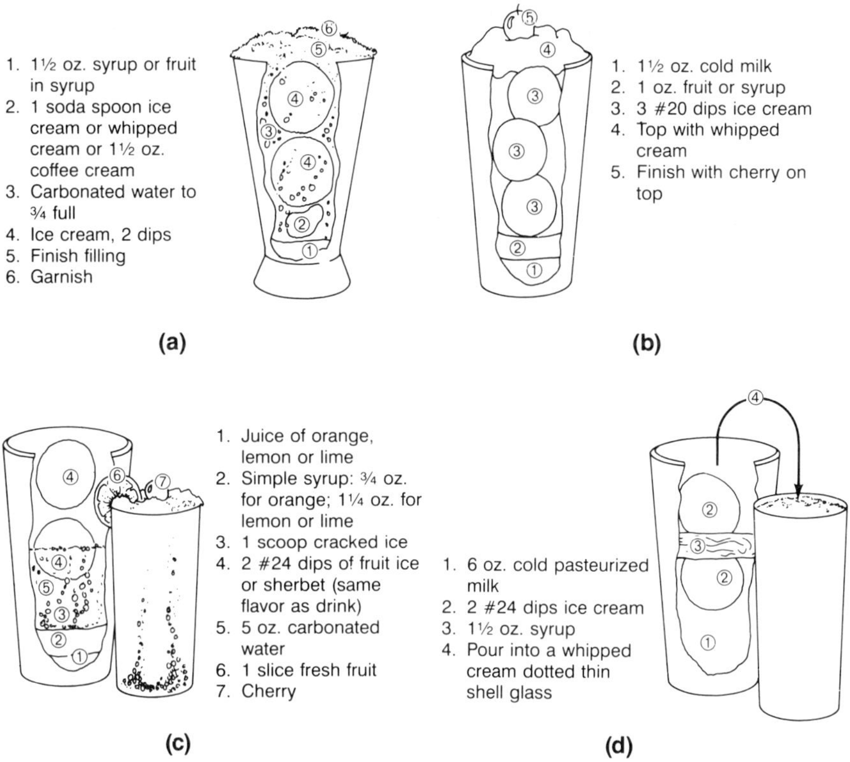

1. 1½ oz. syrup or fruit in syrup
2. 1 soda spoon ice cream or whipped cream or 1½ oz. coffee cream
3. Carbonated water to ¾ full
4. Ice cream, 2 dips
5. Finish filling
6. Garnish

(a)

1. 1½ oz. cold milk
2. 1 oz. fruit or syrup
3. 3 #20 dips ice cream
4. Top with whipped cream
5. Finish with cherry on top

(b)

1. Juice of orange, lemon or lime
2. Simple syrup: ¾ oz. for orange; 1¼ oz. for lemon or lime
3. 1 scoop cracked ice
4. 2 #24 dips of fruit ice or sherbet (same flavor as drink)
5. 5 oz. carbonated water
6. 1 slice fresh fruit
7. Cherry

(c)

1. 6 oz. cold pasteurized milk
2. 2 #24 dips ice cream
3. 1½ oz. syrup
4. Pour into a whipped cream dotted thin shell glass

(d)

FIGURE 8-7. How to make various standard fountain drinks: (a) An ice cream soda. (b) A frappe. (c) A freeze or float. (d) A milkshake. A malted milk is made in exactly the same way as a milkshake, except that 3 heaping teaspoons of malt are added to the concoction immediately after step 1.

"overcooked steak," or a "cold bowl of soup" is nothing more than a patron's reaction to something upsetting that occurred elsewhere. Under these circumstances it takes a very small provocation at the service counter to set the patron off. One may be slow in taking an order or may fail to see that the patron needs a coffee refill, a fork, or butter, and suddenly the patron raises a rather vigorous objection to the situation.

Of course, servers can make mistakes, and when rushed they have many chances to do so. For example, the server may take an order and in the rush fail to prepare and serve it; the customer finally explodes after waiting "hours." Knowing how to handle such problems can help the server get through such tight situations at least somewhat gracefully.

First, it is essential to know the problem. A server who is in the wrong should admit it without trying to make excuses. Apologize and

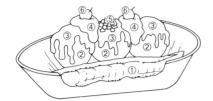

1. Medium ripe banana
2. 3 #24 dips ice cream, assorted flavors
3. ½ oz. each of 3 toppings
4. Whipped cream
5. Ground nuts
6. Cherry or garnish

FIGURE 8-8. How to make a standard banana split.

explain sincerely what happened. Tell the patron that the situation will be corrected immediately, and *then do it*. Admitting a mistake and then taking care of it with alacrity and sincerity is the best way to mend the situation. And once again, a good sense of humor can carry one a long way.

The main thing in serving the public is to keep things going and to keep the patrons happy; everything the server does should be based on this principle. Patrons do not want to be made to feel unimportant because the server forgot their order or embarrassed because the server cannot do the job properly. Servers have to stand out as competent, knowledgeable people who can take care of a multitude of situations and can handle things correctly.

One point servers need to remember is never to argue with a patron. If the patron says hot coffee is cold, take it back and get some more hot coffee—this time in a well-preheated cup. Be cooperative. Thus, if management allows it, offer to exchange a dish a patron does not like or to take it back and redo it in a way the patron finds acceptable. Perhaps a patron has objected to an order of basted eggs because they were basted with hot fat instead of being steam-coated. Take the eggs away, and prepare new ones the way the patron wants them. Even when patrons are wrong, try to satisfy them. Kindness and sincerity can sometimes overcome the most difficult patron. Be cheerful in spite of gloom emanating from the other side of the counter. It can pay off. One may find that, after struggling seemingly in vain to satisfy an unappeasable customer, the patron has left a very sizable tip behind. As a matter of fact, some patrons can get a guilty conscience about how they have acted, and the tip sometimes shows it.

Obviously it is difficult—if one has taken the order, prepared it, and served it—to blame someone else for its failings, but this never should be done anyway. It is permissible and sometimes sensible to camouflage a mistake, but not to blame someone else for it. Admit the mistake, apologize, do something about it, and keep the patron as happy as possible thereafter. Furthermore, there should be a limit to the number of mistakes that occur. Some individuals are just not suited to serving the public, and it is better for them to have other kinds of jobs. Making a lot of mistakes on a job creates a lot of hard work. It puts the counter server under additional stress, and there is already enough of that to go around. More just adds to the level of one's blood pressure.

Giving good service starts with one's attitude. A server must like people in order to serve them well. Patrons want to walk into a clean, neat place where they can get good food and good service from friendly, smiling, warm servers. It is a part of the job of a server to make the person served feel good. Thus, when a patron walks into a place, it should be like a friend coming to visit.

Taking care of a patron's needs is one of the first ways to make that person happy. Good counter servers learn to know when a patron wants to order. Toying with an empty coffee cup or looking up questioningly means, "Please give me a refill." A closed menu means the patron no longer wants to read it and is ready to order. Learning to anticipate patrons' needs is the single best way to earn larger tips, since the amount of a tip is tied to the satisfaction of the customer. Good servers make good tips.

Being attentive to a patron's needs does not mean being obtrusive or annoying the patron with attention. Patrons who are talking together do not want to be interrupted. Other people are loners and may put up a paper and read, thereby cutting themselves off from the entire place. Being too attentive interferes with a patron's desire for some privacy. The patron knows that the server must be there to serve but not to interfere with the meal. It is also important to maintain service at an impersonal, efficient serving distance. Avoid exceeding the boundary of familiarity unless the patron is a friend or unless the patron leads up to it. It might be a grandmother seated with her grandson having a sundae. If she wants to talk about the little boy and praise him, go along with it, even adding something like "He sits there so straight and is eating so well. Yes, he is a nice, little boy." However, do not get caught up in a long conversation; finish serving and slip away as soon and as gracefully as possible.

There are certain typical kinds of problem patrons that a cook-server encounters all the time. While all problem types require the same general kind of treatment, each must be handled in a special manner. It is essential to size up the situation quickly, in order to ascertain what must be done. Each case is individual and unique. Remember also that this is a part of the job: while such trouble may not be a common occurrence, it is bound to arise now and then.

Perhaps the worst patrons to try to serve are ones who are drunk or under the influence of drugs. They have lost normal control of themselves and often can have unexpected reactions to things that are said or done to them. One must handle such individuals carefully. Typically, the night shift personnel encounter most of these problem people. Some of them can be lulled into a sort of stuporous complacency by firm but warm handling. Others can be brought to attention by a firm voice that indicates one is in full possession of one's faculties, whether the patron is or not. In cases of belligerence, sleeping, or making a disturbance, the first thing to do is to ask the individual to leave. If the person refuses, call the manager or someone who might assist in seeing that the person leaves—by force, if necessary. It is also wise for an operation's staff to know how and where to get hold of the police or other help quickly.

Both server and patron should not overstep the bounds of common courtesy, but at times the server must cut annoying patrons off. It is best to do this gently and perhaps in a joking fashion, such as by saying, "Yes, I'd like to have a date with you. I'll bring along my boyfriend." However, if the annoyance becomes a real problem, one should ask the person to leave, or should call the manager, or should ask someone to help get rid of the troublemaker.

Counter operations are busy places. Some patrons come in to have some simple thing such as a cup of coffee and then sit and take up the seat for a long time. The trouble is that these people often have nothing else to do. They come in off the street to "get a load off their feet" and rest. When one encounters such a loafer, one should explain gently that the operation has a policy of allowing a patron to hold a seat for only a certain time and that the seat is needed by other patrons. Ask if any further service is desired, but be sure to imply clearly that the patron has already stayed too long and should now go. Be respectful, but also be firm.

One of the most exasperating problem patrons is the person who cannot decide what to order. The cook-server stands and waits and waits, while the patron sort of muses out loud. Having legitimate questions about specific foods on the menu—how it is served, what is normally served with it, or whether some substitution is possible—is perfectly reasonable, but where it is just a case of complete indecision, the order taker should say, "I'll come back to you later, when you've made up your mind. You will find a lot of good things there"—and then leave. Wait until the patron folds the menu and looks around questioningly, indicating that a decision *might* have been made.

Some patrons change their mind after giving an order. They may wait until the order is about half prepared before completely changing their order to something else. Operations usually either have a policy on what to do in this case or have a policy that, when one brings the order as placed, it is fixed and cannot be changed. If so, the server should explain the policy and say "I'm sorry but I have to go by the policies set here." Occasionally one might let the patron get by with such a change, especially if the item can be salvaged. Generally, if a patron can be kept happy without too much loss, one should make the change. Patrons sometimes back off from changing their mind if told, "Well, we can take it back but it will have to be thrown away. It's just a loss to us." Of course, if the patron has found something legitimately wrong with the order, one should take the item away as quickly as possible. In this case, the fault is with the operation. However, some patrons will find something wrong just to exercise a mind change, and this situation is even more difficult to handle. In most such cases, one simply says nothing and lets the patron get by with it. Again, the worst approach is to argue with a patron.

Another type of problem patron is the critic. This individual feels superior to everyone and also happens to be an infallible authority on everything. The soup is piping hot, but if the critic says it is cold, it is cold. Similarly, french fries may be "too soft" despite being nicely browned and crisp, and the tuna fish sandwich may be "tainted," even though it was made from a freshly opened can of tuna. These patrons may also criticize the way one serves or even the way one looks or is dressed. They are the traditional dissatisfied critics who go around trying to correct everything they see as wrong in the world—and there is a lot they see as wrong.

The way to handle such a patron is to be patient. The patron might actually be trying to cover up an inferiority complex. Thus, by striking out at someone and criticizing, the individual may actually be covering up. Be firm, but gentle and kind. Try to respond to every criticism as though it were valid, constructive, and helpful. Give extra careful and attentive service. Even overdo it a bit, if that makes the patron happy (and it might). Such patron may appreciate the attention and take pleasure in the thought that their criticisms are being given credence. On the other hand, it may just be that the person has a pessimistic outlook, seeing everything in a negative way. In such a case, try to cheer the individual up. Offer a few pleasantries and even joke a bit, if the person is not offended. Again, this is just a matter of keeping patrons happy and is part of one's everyday job. Not all patrons know the rules and follow them.

☐ Personal Hygiene

Individuals who meet and serve the public need to maintain the highest standards of personal hygiene. Patrons want to feel and know that the food they are served is sanitary and safe to eat; and when one is served by a person who has a clean appearance, a clean uniform, and grooming that bespeaks impeccable cleanliness, one feels more assured that this is occurring. The server's appearance can be a major influence on how patrons feel about the operation as a whole, the service, and the food. A sloppy appearance, straggly, unkempt hair, and a soiled uniform can drive patrons away.

Clean appearance begins with high standards of daily hygiene. One should bathe regularly and use a good deodorant. The hands and fingernails should be spotless, and the nails clean and neatly trimmed. Only pale-colored nail polish (if any) should be used, and jewelry should be minimal and in good taste. In other words, flashy and gaudy stuff is out. The teeth should be clean and sparkling. The uniform should fit well, be of good style and color, and be neatly pressed. Wearing too tight a uniform or too short a skirt is highly inappropriate and should not be permitted. Shoes should be polished and should fit well. Open-toed shoes or other casual types should not be worn. Avoid "far out" hairdos. Hair that is well groomed, clean, and tastefully styled is an asset. Beards should be well trimmed and neat. It is better in working around food not to have them. A hair net or a cap should be worn so that the hair is controlled.

☐ Summary

Short order work sometimes involves not only cooking but serving as well. Counter service provides a good way to take care of a large number of patrons in a short time. Usually the service must be fast because patrons are in a hurry. One must be well organized to handle both cooking and serving. A maximum of about fifteen people is all one can handle at one time, and many of the orders must be very simple, if even this many are to be accommodated.

The job of short order cook-server can be divided into a number of parts: preliminary opening-up preparation, side work, taking orders, preparing orders, serving orders, giving checks, taking cash and making change, and closing down for the night. Thus, it is a varied job with quite different subtasks. Serving the public involves special demands, and special talents and abilities are needed to do it properly.

Closing up is a highly specialized job. The place must be put into order and readied for the morning shift. Besides cleaning up and putting things away, the closing personnel need to account for cash, see that the proper reports are completed, and put cash away in a secure place. The job of morning opening is much simplified when the night crew leaves the place in good order.

Serving people and meeting the public take special talents and attributes. Often serving the public is difficult. One of the first things one must have is a knowledge of the job and how to do it to the satisfaction of patrons. This knowledge covers many things, including how to pick up a napkin and silverware in serving a guest. Servers should also learn to read people, noting their moods and attempting to please them. Patrons want courteous, friendly, and cheerful service. Finally, servers should know how to handle the various kinds of problem patrons.

Good personal hygiene is also required of those who meet and serve the public. Clean, well-groomed servers in clean uniforms help convey a feeling of sanitation and safety about the food served. Unclean and poorly groomed servers drive patrons away. Good grooming begins with high standards of hygiene, which covers personal cleanliness; neat, clean, well-styled uniforms; good shoes; and a winning personality.

Fountain items may be served in association with the short-order section. Good, clean, well-maintained equipment should be used. The equipment should keep the frozen desserts at a proper serving temperature. Fountains are also equipped with a carbonation system, and servers should know how to use it and how to replace carbon dioxide tanks.

Most operations that make their own ice cream or soft ice cream purchase premade mixes. Philadelphia ice cream consists of milk, cream, sugar, flavoring, and perhaps a stabilizer. If eggs are added, it becomes French ice cream. It is important that the correct scoops and the proper techniques be used in scooping ice cream and in putting together the various fountain items.

□ CHAPTER REVIEW □

1. What are the advantages of having counter service?
2. What kind of patrons are usually served, and what are their needs?
3. If a patron comes in with a glower on his face, plunks himself on a stool, grabs for the menu without greeting anyone or looking to the right or left, and then begins giving the server a hard time, how should the server handle the customer?
4. How should one handle a flirtatious patron?
5. If a server makes a mistake, how should the server handle it?
6. Is it permissible for a server to try to camouflage a mistake? Is it permissible for the server to blame someone else?

7. Indicate some of the things servers can do to keep patrons happy.
8. Answer True or False: If a patron is wrong, argue with him and point out why he is mistaken.
9. Answer True or False: After a certain length of time, it is legitimate for the server to ask the loafer to leave.
10. What attributes should a server have to do a good job of meeting the public?
11. How should a server dress?
12. What are some of the things the first person on the job in the morning should do to be a short order cook-server?
13. How should a server put silver and napkins before a patron?
14. What is side work?
15. What is a tote box? What is its use?
16. At closing time, the cook-server may have the responsibility to close up the cash register, count the money, put it in a bag, and put it in the safe. What other duties must be handled?
17. What is "sandbagging"? What is "going up a tree"? What is arm work?
18. What are the two kinds of checks used? Why are checks serially numbered?
19. How should an order be taken from a patron?
20. What should be done when a patron enters the place and sits down?
21. How should one handle silverware? dishes in serving?
22. How should a server present a check to a patron?
23. How should one accept payment at the cash register from a patron when the amount tendered is greater than the check?
24. What does *tips* mean, and why do employees have to report them as income?
25. What are the ingredients in Philadelphia ice cream? French ice cream?
26. How does one get soda water at a fountain?
27. Why do some kinds of fountain syrups need refrigeration?
28. What is overrun?
29. What is the proper way to scoop ice cream?
30. At what temperature should ice cream be held to dish up well and preserve overrun?
31. How does one make a chocolate sundae? a banana split?

Recipes

This appendix consists of recipes for common items produced in the short order section. It is divided by meal period (breakfast, lunch, and dinner). Refer to Chapter 5 for further discussion of the types of cookery involved in producing these items.

□ Breakfast

Batter Items

□ Supreme Waffles

Yield: Twenty-five waffles   **Portion:** One waffle (½ c batter)
    (6 lb or 3 qt batter)

Ingredients	Weight	Measure	Procedure
Flour, pastry sifted	1½ lb	1½ qt	1. Sift dry ingredients together.
Baking powder	1½ oz	3 T	
Salt	½ oz	1 T	
Sugar, granulated	4 oz	½ c	
Egg yolks (about 10)	½ lb	1 c	2. Combine yolks and milk.
Milk	2½ lb	1¼ qt	Add butter, and then add this
Clarified butter, melted	½ lb	1 c	mixture to the dry ingredients; mix only until they are blended.
Egg whites (about 10)	½ lb	1 c	3. Beat egg whites until stiff but moist (tops peak but fold over), and fold into the mixture carefully so that the air in the whites is not lost. (This is the secret of making a light, crisp delicate waffle.)

Variations: For all bran waffles, add 2 oz (½ c) all bran; for bacon waffles, add ½ lb (1 c packed) lightly broiled, chopped bacon, and use bacon grease for the fat; for cornmeal waffles, substitute 6 oz cornmeal for 8 oz (2 c) flour; for nut waffles add 3 oz (¾ c) chopped nut meats; for cheese waffles, add 1¼ c (10 oz) grated cheddar cheese (these may stick, and the baker may have to be greased before each new waffle is baked).

☐ Buttermilk Waffles

Yield: Twenty-five waffles (3 qt batter)   **Portion:** One waffle (½ c batter)

Ingredients	Weight	Measure	Procedure
Flour, pastry	1½ lb	1½ qt	1. Sift dry ingredients together.
Baking powder	½ oz	1½ T	
Soda	¼ oz	2 t	
Salt	½ oz	1 T	
Sugar, granulated	2 oz	¼ c	
Egg yolks (about 10)	½ lb	1 c	2. Combine egg yolks, fat, and
Buttermilk	2¼ lb	1¼ qt	buttermilk, and add to the dry
Clarified butter, oil, etc.	½ lb	1 c	mixture. Blend until dry ingredients are just moistened.
Egg whites (about 10)	½ lb	1 c	3. Beat egg whites until stiff but still moist. Fold into the mixture carefully.

☐ Plain Waffles

Yield: Twenty-five waffles (3 + qt batter)   **Portion:** One waffle (½ c batter)

Ingredients	Weight	Measure	Procedure
Flour, pastry	1½ lb	1½ qt	1. Sift dry ingredients together.
Baking powder	1½ oz	3 T	
Salt	½ oz	1 T	
Sugar, granulated	4 oz	½ c	
Milk, dry, nonfat	9 oz	4¼ c	2. Combine milk and water;
Water, cool	2¼ lb	1¼ qt	then add yolks, and blend them
Egg yolks (about 10)	½ lb	1 c	in. Mix this blend into the dry ingredients.
Melted clarified butter, margarine, or fat, or oil	8 oz	1 c	3. Stir fat into the mixture.
Egg whites (about 8 or 9)	½ lb	1 c	4. Beat egg whites until tops peak and fold over; fold into the mixture carefully so that the air in the whites is not lost.

☐ Griddle Cakes (Pancakes, Hotcakes)

Yield: Twenty-five portions
    (7½ lb batter)

Portion: Two large cakes
    (6 oz batter)

Ingredients	Weight	Measure	Procedure
Flour, pastry	2¼ lb	2¼ qt	1. Sift dry ingredients together.
Baking powder	2 oz	6 T	
Salt	½ oz	1 T	
Sugar, granulated	6 oz	¾ c	
Eggs, beaten	12 oz	1½ c	2. Blend milk and water; add
Milk, dry, instant	12 oz	4½ c	eggs. Add oil, and then add
Water, cool	4 lb	2 qt	liquid mixture to dry
Oil or melted	9 oz	1 c +	ingredients; mix well.
butter or		2 T	
margarine			

Note: For dry instant milk, one can substitute 2 qt sour milk or buttermilk; if this is done, one should use 1 T each of baking soda and baking powder in place of 2 oz baking powder.

☐ Buckwheat Griddle Cakes

Yield: Twenty-five portions (6½ pt)

Portion: Two large cakes (½ c)

	Weight	Measure	Procedure
Flour, buckwheat	1¾ lb	5½ c	1. Sift dry ingredients together.
Flour, bread	4 oz	1 c	
Soda, baking		1 t	
Baking powder	½ oz	1 T	
Sugar, granulated	3 oz	6 T	
Eggs, beaten	½ lb	5 eggs	2. Blend eggs and oil into
Oil	4 oz	½ c	buttermilk and add this to dry
Buttermilk	3¾ lb	7½ c	ingredients, making a smooth
			batter.

☐ Crepes or Blinis

Yield: Twenty-five portions

Portion: Three cakes

	Weight	Measure	Procedure
Flour, pastry	1 lb	1 qt	1. Blend all ingredients together
Milk	3½ lb	3½ pt	to make a smooth batter that
Eggs	12 oz	1½ c	resembles heavy cream.
Butter, melted	4 oz	½ c	

☐ *Plättar* (Swedish Pancakes)

Yield: Twenty-five portions

Portion: Three cakes

Ingredients	Weight	Measure	Procedure
Flour, pastry	1 lb	4 c	1. Sift dry ingredients together.
Salt	½ oz	1 T	
Sugar, granulated	4 oz	½ c	
Eggs	1¼ lb	2½ c	2. Blend eggs into milk. Add dry ingredients, and blend into a smooth batter.
Milk	3 lb	3 pt	
Butter, melted	4 oz	½ c	3. Add butter, and blend well. Let batter stand for two hours under refrigeration; cover to prevent it from drying out.

☐ **French Toast**

Yield: Twenty-five portions

Portion: Three slices

	Weight	Measure	Procedure
Eggs, beaten	4 lb	4 pt	1. Blend eggs well into milk. Add salt and sugar, and mix well.
Milk	1 lb	1 pt	
Salt	½ oz	1 T	
Sugar, granulated	6 oz	¾ c	
Bread, sliced		75 slices	2. Cut slices diagonally in half; dip these into the batter so that they are completely covered; fry on a well-oiled griddle or in a deep-fryer until golden brown.

Note: In step 1, 1 c of pastry flour may be blended in.

Potatoes

□ **Hash Browns**

Yield: Twenty-five portions (8¼ lb) **Portion:** 5 oz (¾ c)

Ingredients	Weight	Measure
Potatoes, pared, boiled, and finely chopped	7½ lb	5 qt
Oil or clarified butter	12 oz	1½ c
Salt	as needed	
Pepper, white	as needed	

Procedure

1. For a portion, select a well-seasoned sauté pan; put a thin layer of oil in the pan, and heat it well. Add about 4½ oz (¾ c) of potatoes. Shake and toss the potatoes to prevent them from sticking. When they are well browned on the bottom, turn them with an offset spatula. Season with salt and pepper.

2. When the second side is well browned, tilt the pan to drain off any excess fat for reuse. Then slide the potatoes onto a warm plate.

3. Repeat until all potatoes are prepared.

4. A larger pan can be used for multiple portions. The potatoes may also be browned on a griddle.

Note: To prepare the whole batch at one time, select a large roasting pan, and put in the oil or butter; add the potatoes, mix well, and add salt and pepper; then place the pan in a 375° to 400°F (191° to 204°C) oven. Turn the potatoes from time to time allowing them to brown.

Variation: For lyonnaise potatoes, sauté 1½ lb (about 4 c) finely chopped onions until soft, and blend these with the potatoes before browning. Sometimes lyonnaise potatoes may be sliced instead of chopped.

□ Lunch

Salads

□ Fruit Salad

Yield: Twenty-five portions (1 gal)

Portion: No. 10 dipper
(about 3½ oz)

Ingredients	Weight	Measure	Procedure
Pineapple, cubed	2 lb	4 c	1. Drain fruit well, and mix as
Cherries, Royal Anne (seeded)	1 lb	2 c	little as possible; serve on a bed of shredded lettuce.
Peaches, cubed	3½ lb	3½ pt	
Pears, cubed	2 lb	2 pt	

Note: This recipe is for a small dinner salad; double the recipe for twenty-five large salads.

□ Cole Slaw (Cabbage Slaw)

Yield: Twenty-five portions
(1½ gal)

Portion: About 1 cup (4 oz)

Ingredient	Weight	Measure	Procedure
Cabbage, finely shredded	4½ lb	1½ gal	1. Mix all ingredients together; serve chilled, garnished with paprika.
Salad dressing	14 oz	1¾ c	
Vinegar	3 oz	⅜ c	
Evaporated milk	8 oz	1 c	
Salt	1 oz	2 T	
Pepper, white	⅛ oz	1½ t	
Sugar, granulated	2 oz	¼ c	

[*SOURCE:* U.S. Navy Recipe Service]

□ Carrot-Raisin Salad

Yield: Twenty-five portions (3½ qt)

Portion: ½ c (4 oz)

Ingredient	Weight	Measure	Procedure
Carrots, grated	4¼ lb	3¼ qt	1. Toss all together; chill before serving.
Raisins, seeded	6 oz	1 c	
Salt	½ oz	1 T	
Mayonnaise or boiled dressing	1¼ lb	2½ c	

Note: Some cooks like to presoak the raisins to make them more tender; the weight specified here is the weight before soaking.

□ Mixed Green Salad

Yield: Twenty-five portions (3 gal)   **Portion:** About 1½ c (3 oz)

Ingredients	Weight	Measure	Procedure
Spinach leaves, cut	1 lb	1¼ gal	1. Mix all together lightly.
Cabbage, shredded, or other tender greens	1 lb	1 gal	
Lettuce, cut	2½ lb	1½ gal	

□ Vegetable Salad

Yield: Twenty-five portions (2 gal)   **Portion:** About 1 c (5 oz)

Cucumbers, peeled, diced	2½ lb	2½ qt	1. Lightly toss all together.
Celery, chopped	2¼ lb	2¼ qt	
Tomato wedges	3 lb	1½ qt	
Lettuce, iceberg, chopped	1 lb	2 qt	

□ Potato Salad

Yield: Twenty-five portions (5 qt)   **Portion:** ¾ c (6 oz)

Potatoes, cooked, diced	6¼ lb	3½ qt	1. Mix oil, vinegar, onions, salt, pepper, sugar, cayenne, mustard, and paprika and pour over potatoes; allow potatoes to marinate for an hour or more.
Salad oil	4 oz	½ c	
Vinegar	4 oz	½ c	
Onions, green, sliced with tops	8 oz	2 c	
Pepper, white		1 T	
Salt	1 oz	2 T	
Cayenne		½ t	
Sugar	1 oz	2 T	
Mustard, dry		1 t	
Paprika		1 t	
Celery, chopped	8 oz	2 c	2. Blend celery, parsley, boiled dressing, and evaporated milk. Mix lightly.
Parsley, chopped	¼ oz	¼ c	
Boiled dressing	1½ lb	1½ pt	
Evaporated milk	10 oz	1¼ c	
Eggs, hard-cooked, sliced	8 oz	1½ c	3. Mix eggs into salad, trying not to break them up.
			4. Chill and serve.

[*SOURCE:* Terrell and Headlund, *Large Quantity Recipes*, p. 295]

☐ Fish Salad (Crab, Shrimp, Salmon, Tuna)

Yield: Twenty-five portions

Portion: About 1 c (6 oz) on shredded lettuce

Ingredients	Weight	Measure	Procedure
Fish item	4 lb	2 qt	1. Flake fish item, if needed;
Celery, diced	2 lb	2 qt	add celery and cucumbers, and
Cucumbers, diced	12 oz	2 c	mix lightly.
Eggs, hard-cooked, sliced	1 lb	3 c	2. Add eggs and mayonnaise, and mix lightly.
Mayonnaise	1 lb	1 pt	
Lettuce, shredded	1½ lb	3 qt	3. Place a 6-oz scoop of salad on ½ c lettuce. Garnish with olives, tomato wedges, sweet pickles, etc.

☐ Meat Salad (Chicken, Beef, Veal, Ham)

Yield: Twenty-five portions

Portion: About 6 oz (1 c)

Ingredients	Weight	Measure	Procedure
Meat item, diced	6 lb	3 qt	1. Mix all ingredients together
Celery, diced	1¾ lb	1¾ qt	lightly.
Pimiento, chopped	3 oz	½ c	
Mayonnaise	10 oz	2½ c	
Pickles, sweet, chopped	2 oz	½ c	

Sandwich Spreads and Fillings

☐ Savory Butter

Yield: 1 pt (1 lb)

Portion: 1 t

Ingredients	Weight	Measure	Procedure
Butter or margarine	12 oz	1½ c	1. Cream butter or margarine,
Lemon juice	1 oz	2 T	and add lemon juice slowly, blending it in.
Prepared mustard		1 t	2. Blend in other seasonings,
Prepared horseradish		1 t	and beat until light and fluffy.

[*SOURCE:* Terrell and Headlund, *Large Quantity Recipes*, p. 320]

□ Egg Salad Sandwich

Yield: Twenty-five sandwiches
    (2 qt)

Portion: 2 oz

Ingredients	Weight	Measure	Procedure
Eggs, hard-cooked, chopped	2 lb	1½ qt	1. Combine ingredients, and blend thoroughly.
Sweet relish	6 oz	¾ c	
Pimiento, minced	6 oz	¼ c	
Prepared mustard	1 oz	2 T	
Boiled dressing or mayonnaise	6 oz	¾ c	

[*Source:* Terrell and Headlund, *Large Quantity Recipes*, pp. 322, 323]

□ Ham Salad Sandwich

Yield: Twenty-five sandwiches

Portion: 2 oz

Ham, cooked, chopped	1½ lb	5 c	1. Blend ingredients together well.
Eggs, cooked, chopped	8 oz	1½ c	
Celery, finely chopped	4 oz	1 c	
Sweet pickles, chopped	4 oz	½ c	
Prepared mustard	½ oz	1 T	
Boiled dressing or mayonnaise	12 oz	1½ c	

[*Source:* Terrell and Headlund, *Large Quantity Recipes*, p. 327]

□ Meat Salad Sandwich

Yield: Twenty-five sandwiches
    (2 qt)

Portion: 2 oz

Meat, chopped	1¾ lb	1 qt	1. Blend all ingredients well.
Pickle relish	4 oz	¾ c	
Celery, chopped	4 oz	1 c	
Mayonnaise or boiled dressing	8 oz	1 c	
Eggs, cooked, chopped	6 oz	1 c	
Prepared mustard	1 oz	2 T	

Note: For chicken salad, use ½ oz or 1 T lemon juice.

☐ Toasted Cheese Sandwich

Yield: Twenty five sandwiches
    (3 lb)

Portion: 2 oz

Ingredients	Weight	Measure	Procedure
Cheese, ground	2½ lb	2½ qt	1. Blend all ingredients well.
Dry mustard	1 oz	¼ c	
Worcestershire sauce	1 oz	2 T	
Buttermilk	10 oz	1 c 2 T	
Pepper, white		½ t	

2. Spread on slices of fresh dry toast, and broil under a broiler until the cheese bubbles.

3. Some cooks like to place a slice of tomato on the broiling cheese and warm it through.

Note: If two slices are used per portion, only about twelve to fourteen orders can be made.

[SOURCE: Terrell and Headlund, Large Quantity Recipes, p. 333]

☐ Tuna Salad Sandwich

Yield: Twenty-five sandwiches
    (2½ lb)

Portion: 1⅔ oz

	Weight	Measure	Procedure
Tuna, drained, flaked	18 oz	2½ c	1. Mix ingredients thoroughly.
Celery, chopped	4 oz	1 c	
Pickles, chopped	3 oz	1 c	
Prepared mustard	1 oz	2 T	
Lemon juice	1 oz	2 T	
Boiled dressing or mayonnaise	18 oz	2¼ c	

[SOURCE: Terrell and Headlund, Large Quantity Recipes, p. 321]

☐ Grilled Hamburger

Yield: One hamburger

Portion: One hamburger in bun

Hamburger	2 to 4 oz	1. Shape meat into a thin patty about 4 in. in diameter. Fry on a 360°F (182°C) griddle until slightly browned. Turn with an offset spatula, and cook the other side similarly.

Bun, split

2. While the meat is cooking, butter the griddle in a small area and place the cut sides of the bun down on the griddle, pressing them down lightly; lightly toast.

☐ Hot Dog

Yield: One hot dog in bun

Portion: One hot dog in bun

Ingredients	Weight	Measure	Procedure
Hot dog	usually 2 oz		1. Place hot dog in a small quantity of simmering water, and simmer for 8 minutes.
Weiner bun, warmed			2. Place hot dog in warmed bun.

☐ Barbecued Beef on Bun

Yield: Twenty-five sandwiches

Portion: One bun + 4 oz beef mixture

Ingredients	Weight	Measure	Procedure
Oil or shortening	4 oz	1½ c	1. Add oil or shortening to pan and place over burner; add onions and green pepper, and fry about 5 minutes or until tender.
Onions, chopped	12 oz	2 c	
Green pepper, chopped	6 oz	1 c	
Hamburger, lean	3 lb	1½ qt	2. Add hamburger and fry, separating while cooking.
Catsup	1½ lb	3 c	3. Add remaining ingredients, and cook on low heat for 15 to 20 minutes.
Salt	½ oz	1 T	
Pepper, white		1 t	
Barbecue seasoning	1 oz	3 T	
Sugar, granulated	2 oz	¼ c	
Buns, split		25	4. Lightly toast buns on the griddle. Place both halves of bun on a plate, with cut side up, and spread beef mixture over bun.

☐ Hot Beef Sandwich

Yield: One sandwich   **Portion:** One sandwich

Ingredients	Weight	Measure	Procedure
Roast beef, sliced thin	2 to 2½ oz		1. Cut one slice of bread in half diagonally. Place the whole slice in the center of the plate, with the two diagonal slices on either side. Cover the bread with the meat, and cover this with beef gravy. Often a No. 8 or No. 10 dipperful of mashed potatoes is placed next to the sandwich on the plate and served with gravy over it.
Bread		2 slices	
Beef gravy	2 oz	¼ c	

Luncheon Entrées

☐ Spaghetti with Italian Sauce

Yield: Twenty-five orders

Portion: 5 oz sauce on 8 oz cooked spaghetti

Ingredients	Weight	Measure	Procedure
Onions, chopped	8 oz	1¼ c	1. Sauté onions, garlic, and peppers in oil until wilted.
Garlic, minced		2 cloves	
Green pepper, chopped	6 oz	1 c	
Olive oil	4 oz	½ c	
Beef, ground	4 lb	2 qt	2. Add beef, and sauté until cooked; separate the meat as it cooks.
Water	1 lb	1 pt	3. Add other ingredients, and cook over low heat for about 1 hour, stirring frequently. The mixture should be slightly thick.
Tomato purée	6 lb	3 qt	
Vinegar	2 oz	¼ c	
Sugar	2 oz	¼ c	
Bay leaf		1 leaf	
Thyme		½ t	
Oregano		3 T	
Basil		1 T	
Worcestershire sauce		2 T	

Ingredients	Weight	Measure	Procedure
Spaghetti	3 lb		4. Using 1 gallon of water and 1 T salt for every pound of spaghetti, drop the spaghetti into boiling water and immediately stir with a fork, separating strands from one another. Cook until only just tender. Blanch in cold water, and let stand in cold water, rewarming for service as needed.

5. Place spaghetti in the center of the plate, put sauce over it, and serve with grated Parmesan cheese.

□ Meat Loaf

Yield: Twenty-five portions or 6¼ lb

Portion: 4 oz

Ingredients	Weight	Measure	Procedure
Beef, ground	4 lb	2 qt	1. Mix all ingredients together.
Pork, ground	8 oz	1 c	
Crumbs, bread	5 oz	2½ c	
Eggs	10 oz	1¼ c	
Evaporated milk	2 lb	1 qt	
Salt	1 oz	2 T	
Pepper		1 t	

2. Shape into oblong loaves, and bake for 1½ hours at 300°F (149°C).

3. Cool slightly and slice; serve with beef gravy.

[*SOURCE:* U.S. Navy Recipe Service]

□ Chili con Carne

Yield: Twenty-five servings (1½ gal)

Portion: 1 c (8 oz)

Ingredients	Weight	Measure	Procedure
Beans, red kidney	2¼ lb	1½ qt	1. Examine beans for stones. Wash and soak beans overnight, and then cook them in plenty of water until tender. Drain.

Ingredients	Weight	Measure	Procedure
Green pepper, chopped	1 lb	1 qt	**2.** Sauté garlic, peppers, and onions in fat until tender. Add
Garlic, minced		2 cloves	hamburger and brown, separating it as it cooks.
Onions, chopped	1 lb	1 qt	
Fat (bacon, etc.)	2 oz	¼ c	
Hamburger	4 lb	2 qt	
Tomatoes, canned, chopped	6 lb	3 qt	**3.** Add cooked items to a stockpot with these ingredients
Chili powder	1 oz	2½ T	and simmer for 3 hours. Add
Cumin	¼ oz	1 T	water as needed.
Salt	1½ oz	2 T	
Sugar	2 oz	¼ c	
Cayenne		½ t	
			4. Add beans, and heat to proper temperature. Serve in a warm bowl with soda crackers on the side.

[*Source:* Terrell and Headlund, *Large Quantity Recipes*, p. 120]

□ Baked Beef Hash

Yield: Twenty-five portions (5 qt)   **Portion:** ¾ c (6 oz)

Beef, cooked, chopped	5 lb	15 c	**1.** Mix all ingredients together; place in baking dish so that the
Beef stock	8 oz	1 c	hash is 2 in. thick, and bake at
Potatoes, diced	5 lb	3¼ qt	350°F (177°C) for 1¼ hours.
Onions, chopped	1½ lb	3¼ c	Serve with beef gravy.
Salt	1 oz	2 T	
Pepper		2 t	

□ Mixed Grill

Yield: Twenty-five portions   **Portion:** 1 chop, 1 sausage, 1 liver slice with tomato slice

Lamb chops, rib	5 lb	25	**1.** Brown chops and sausage on
Sausages, breakfast links	2 lb 2 oz	25	both sides. Season chops.
Liver, sliced	4¼ lb	25	**2.** Dip liver slices in seasoned flour, and fry until browned on both sides.

Ingredients	Weight	Measure	Procedure
Tomato, 1 in. slice	2½–3 lb		**3.** Dip tomatoes in bread
Bread crumbs	1 lb	1 qt	crumbs, and fry until both sides are lightly browned.

[*SOURCE:* Terrell and Headlund, *Large Quantity Recipes*, p. 175]

☐ Barbecued Spareribs

Yield: Twenty-five portions (6¼ lb)   **Portion:** 8 oz

Ingredient	Weight	Measure	Procedure
Vinegar	12 oz	1½ c	**1.** Mix all ingredients together.
Sugar, brown	6 oz	¾ c	
Catsup	3½ lb	3½ pt	
Salt	2 oz	3 T	
Onion, grated	2 oz	¼ c	
Spareribs	10–12 lb		**2.** Brown ribs in oven; pour off fat.
			3. Cover ribs with sauce and bake for 1½ hour at 350°F (177°C). Baste with sauce while baking.

[*SOURCE:* U.S. Navy Recipe Service]

☐ Turkey à la King

Yield: Twenty-five servings (1¼ gal)   **Portion:** 1 c (8 oz)

Ingredient	Weight	Measure	Procedure
Butter or margarine	5 oz	⅔ c	**1.** Make a roux of the flour and fat, and add cool milk. Blend well and cook in a double boiler until thickened, stirring constantly. Add seasonings.
Flour	6 oz	1½ c	
Milk	4 lb	2 qt	
Salt	½ oz	1 T	
Pepper, white		½ t	
Pepper, green, chopped	12 oz	3 c	**2.** Boil pepper in water for 4 minutes. Drain.
Pimiento, chopped	4 oz	½ c	**3.** Put sauce, pepper, pimiento, and turkey together.
Turkey, diced	3½ lb	5 pt	
Cream, heavy, hot	1 lb	1 pt	**4.** Add cream to mixture, and stir well.
			5. Serve with light, fluffy rice.

[*SOURCE:* U.S. Navy Recipe Service]

□ Beef (Brown) Gravy

Yield: 2¼ qt   **Portion:** 2 oz or ¼ c

Ingredients	Weight	Measure	Procedure
Beef roast pan drippings or fat	8 oz	1 c	1. Stir flour into melted drippings. Brown lightly, while stirring.
Flour, pastry	6 oz	¾ c	
Beef stock	4 lb	2 qt	2. Add stock slowly to roux while stirring. Cook until thickened.
			3. Season lightly with salt and pepper.

Notes: If a browner gravy is needed, add a bit of brown coloring such as Kitchen Bouquet. If the flour has been browned considerably, more will be needed to give the desired amount of thickening.

□ Dinner

Griddled or Sautéed Items

□ Country Fried Steak

Yield: Twenty-five portions   **Portion:** 7 to 8 oz steak

Steak, round	11–12 lb	1. Pound steaks thoroughly, and dredge well with seasoned flour.
Flour, dredging*	as required	
		2. Brown steaks well on both sides. Do not overcook.
		3. Place on a hot plate, and lightly brush with *maître d'hôtel* butter.

Note: After browning, the steaks can be put on a rack in a roasting pan with a small amount of water on the bottom, and placed in a 325°F (161°C) oven for 1½ hours to tenderize.

*Use 2 oz salt and 1 t white pepper for every pound of flour.

□ Grilled Liver and Onions

Yield: Twenty-five portions

Portion: About 4 oz cooked liver and 2 oz onions

Ingredients	Weight	Measure	Procedure
Onions, sliced	3½ lb	3½ qt	1. Parboil onions in a small amount of water until nearly done; then drain and set aside.
Liver, calf	8 lb		2. Salt and pepper the flour to season the liver. Dredge the liver in flour, shaking off any excess. Fry the liver at 350°F (177°C), and place a hammer on it so that it does not curl during frying.
Flour, pastry	as needed		
Salt	as needed		
Pepper, white	as needed		

3. Place onions in pan or griddle and add some oil. Turn onions and liver as needed. Do not overcook either.

4. When done, place liver on a warm plate and cover with onions.

Note: Frying the onions in butter gives a better-tasting product.

Variations: For braised liver and onions, use the same recipe but fry only the liver. Then place the liver in a pan, cover it with the onions, and add a bit of water or stock; cover and braise in a 300°F (149°C) oven for about an hour. Beef or pork liver may be prepared in these ways, too.

□ Sautéed Fish

Yield: Twenty-five portions

Portion: 5 oz

Ingredients	Weight	Measure	Procedure
Cornmeal	1 lb	3½ c	1. Blend cornmeal with salt.
Salt	2 oz	3 T	
Eggs, beaten	5 oz	3 eggs	2. Blend eggs and milk together.
Milk	8 oz	1 c	
Fish fillets	8 to 9 lb		3. Dip 6-oz portions of fish into milk and egg mixture and drain; then dredge in cornmeal mixture for a good coating.

Ingredients	Weight	Measure	Procedure
			4. Oil a 350°F (177°C) griddle liberally, and fry fish fillets lightly until golden brown. Turn and fry on the other side until golden brown.
			5. Dish fillets onto hot plates and serve with lemon slices.

□ Pan-Fried (Sautéed) Chicken

Yield: Twenty-five portions

Portion: ¼ chicken or two pieces

Ingredients	Weight	Measure	Procedure
Chicken, cut up	15 lb		**1.** Dredge pieces thoroughly in flour and seasonings, and pat to remove any excess.
Flour, pastry	1 lb	2 c	
Salt	1 oz	2 T	
Pepper, white		1 t	
Oil	2 lb	1 qt	**2.** Cover bottom of sauté pan with about ¾ in. oil. Place pan over moderate heat, and heat oil to about 360°F (212°C). Slide chicken pieces into the oil, letting them move away from the hand, to prevent hot oil from splashing on it. Fry until golden brown on the skin side; then turn with tongs, and do the same to the other side. Lower the heat and fry until the chicken is tender, reversing frying sides as needed.
			3. Remove from the pan and drain well.

[*Source:* U.S. Navy Recipe Service]

□ Breaded Veal Cutlet

Yield: Twenty-five 4-oz cutlets

Portion: 1 cutlet

Ingredients	Weight	Measure	Procedure
Seasoning mix:			
Flour, pastry	6 oz	¾ c	**1.** Mix flour and seasonings well.
Salt	½ oz	1 T	
Pepper		1 t	
Paprika, ground		1½ T	

Ingredients	Weight	Measure	Procedure
Eggs (about 4)	7 oz	⅔ c	**2.** Blend eggs and milk together, and use the liquid to make a smooth batter with the dry ingredients.*
Milk	½ lb	1 c	
Veal cutlets	7 lb	25	**3.** Dip cutlets into the batter and then into the crumbs, covering them thoroughly.
Bread crumbs, dry	1 lb	5 c	
			4. Sauté in a pan liberally supplied with oil or clarified butter or margarine, or deep-fry until a light tan.
			5. Serve with an appropriate sauce.

*The flour may be used for dredging, and then the cutlets may be dipped into the egg and milk liquid and then crumbed.

☐ Salisbury Steak

Yield: Twenty-five portions   **Portion:** 1 steak

Ingredients	Weight	Measure	Procedure
Beef, ground	10 lb	2½ qt	**1.** Blend ingredients together, and shape into oval cakes about 7–8 oz and 1 in. thick.
Salt	1½ oz	3 T	
Pepper		2 t	
Milk, evaporated	1 lb	2 c	
Onions, minced	5 oz	¾ c	
Bread crumbs, fresh	10 oz	5 c	**2.** Coat each cake with crumbs.
			3. Griddle fry or sauté in a pan.
			4. Serve with about 2 T of rich *jus* over the meat.

Broiled Items

□ **Broiled Steak**

Yield: 1 steak

Portion: One steak

Ingredients	Weight	Measure	Procedure
Steak		one	1. Dip into seasoned oil and place on a preheated broiler grid, pressing down firmly. Set the grid about 5 in. from the flame, and broil until the steak is about half done. Turn the steak over and finish broiling.
			2. Season and dress (brush) with *maître d'hôtel butter*.

□ **Broiled Chicken**

Yield: Twenty-five portions

Portion: Half, quarter, or two pieces

Chicken, cut up	15 lb		1. Divide the chicken as desired.
Butter or margarine, melted	8 oz	1 c	2. Dip each piece in melted fat, and place each on a broiler, skin-side down. Set the rack about 5 to 8 in. from the flame. When the chicken is well browned and about half done, turn it with tongs and broil it until done.
			3. Serve brushed with melted butter.

□ **London Broil**

Yield: Twenty-five portions

Portion: About 5 oz

Oil, vegetable	8 oz	1 c	1. Blend oil, vinegar or red wine, salt, pepper, and thyme to make a marinade.
Salt	1 oz	1½ T	
Pepper, white		1 t	
Thyme		1 t	
Vinegar or red wine	2 oz	¼ c	

Ingredients	Weight	Measure	Procedure
Steak, flank (Choice grade)	9 lb		2. Marinate the flanks for at least 2 hours, turning occasionally. Remove them from the marinade, place them on a preheated broiler grid, and broil them at high heat for about 3 to 6 minutes per side. *Do not overcook: the meat must be rare.*
			3. Remove from the broiler and allow the meat to rest for several minutes; then slice it diagonally into *thin* slices.
			4. Place slices on a warm plate and serve with *jus* or mushroom gravy on the side.

□ Broiled Lamb Chops

Yield: Twenty-five portions (50 chops)

Portion: Two 3-oz chops

Lamb chops, rib or loin	12½ lb	1. Dip each chop into oil, and place on a preheated grid. Adjust the grid to a proper distance from the flame. Broil on one side until the chops are half done. Then turn and finish broiling.
		2. Place two chops on a warm plate, and serve with a proper garnish. Mint jelly is often served as an accompaniment.

Steamed, Simmered, and Poached Items

□ **Steamed Clams**

Yield: Twenty-five portions

Portion: 1½ qt steamed clams
+ ½ c clam nectar

Ingredients	Weight	Measure	Procedure
Clams, well cleaned	25 lb	25 qt	**1.** Cook in single order batches. Place 1 qt of clams in each sauce pan, cover, and steam for about 10 minutes or until the clams are open about ½ in.
			2. Remove from fire. Strain the juice (nectar) into a small cup. Place clams into a large bowl. Serve with the nectar and a small ramekin filled with clarified butter. Garnish with lemon and parsley. Use hard-crusted bread as an accompaniment.

Notes: Clams are best steamed in small quantity—probably not more than five orders at a time. To eat, remove the clam from its shell with a fork, dip into butter, and eat. The tough end is usually not eaten. Sip the nectar from the cup; it is also proper to sip the nectar from the shell upon removal of the clam.

□ **Sechuan Spicy Steamed Chicken**

Yield: Twenty-five portions

Portion: 1 c

Ingredients	Weight	Measure	Procedure
Chicken	12 lb		**1.** Cut chicken into 1½- to 2-in.
Vinegar	2 oz	½ c	pieces, and let the pieces
Ginger root, minced		2 T	marinate in the mixed
Sesame oil	2 oz	¼ c	ingredients for at least an hour.
Sugar	2 oz	¼ c	Then steam for 30 minutes over
Salt	1 oz	2 T	1½ qt chicken stock.
Garlic, minced	1 oz	¼ c	
Sherry, dry	2 oz	¼ c	
Green onion	8 oz	1 c	**2.** Julienne the onion and red
Red pepper pods, hot		4	pepper, and fry the strips in
Oil, peanut	2 oz	¼ c	peanut oil at high heat for 1 minute.

Ingredients	*Weight*	*Measure*	*Procedure*
Cornstarch	2 oz	5 T	**3.** Mix cornstarch and water, and add this to the stock left from steaming. There should be 1½ qt thickened stock. Then add the chicken and fried items. Mix well.

4. Serve with each order 1 c hot, fluffy rice.

□ Corned Beef and Cabbage

Yield: Twenty-five portions

Portion: 4 oz corned beef and 3-oz cabbage

Corned beef brisket	12 lb		**1.** Start briskets in cold water. Cover pot and simmer for about 1½ hours.
Onions, chopped	8 oz	2 c	**2.** Add *mirepoix* and spices and cook until the briskets are tender when tested with a fork (about 2 to 3 hours).
Carrots, chopped	4 oz	1 c	
Celery, chopped	4 oz	1 c	
Bay leaves		2	
Cloves, whole		5	
Peppercorns		2 T	

3. Place briskets and some of their stock in a steam table or bain-marie to keep warm.

Cabbage wedges	5 lb		**4.** Steam cabbage for 6 minutes, or simmer it in corned beef stock for the 6 minutes.

5. Slice the corned beef diagonally across the grain into thin slices. Portion, add a cabbage wedge, and spoon about 2 T of the corned beef stock over the meat.

6. Serve with boiled potatoes.

□ Simmered Fowl

Yield: 9 to 10 lb clear meat

Ingredients	Weight	Measure	Procedure
Chickens, fowl		6 hens	1. Clean and wash fowl; place into stock pot.
Onions, chopped	8 oz	2 c	2. Add *mirepoix* and spices; cover
Carrots, chopped	4 oz	1 c	with water and simmer about
Celery, chopped	4 oz	1 c	2½ hours.
Bay leaves		2	
Parsley stems		12	
Peppercorns		1 T	
Cloves, whole		6	
Salt	1 oz	2 T	

3. Place stock pot and chickens in a sink in a bath of cold running water. When the chickens and stock are cool, remove the chickens and place them in pans; cover and refrigerate. Strain stock and refrigerate.

□ Court Bouillon

Yield: 1 gallon

Ingredients	Weight	Measure	Procedure
Water	8 lb	1 gal	1. Put all ingredients in a
Vinegar	8 oz	1 c	stockpot, and simmer for 1 to 2
Onions, sliced	8 oz	1½ c	hours. Remove from the fire and
Celery, sliced	4 oz	1 c	strain.
Carrots, sliced	4 oz	1 c	
Salt	1 oz	2 T	
Peppercorns, crushed		½ t	
Bay leaf		1	
Thyme, ground		½ t	
Parsley stems		dozen	
Fishbones, heads, or skin	5 lb		

□ Poached Fish

Yield: Twenty-five portions

Portion: About 6 oz

Ingredients	Weight	Measure
Fish	9 to 15 lb*	

Procedure

1. Oil a fish poacher rack, and lay the fish on it. Cover with court bouillon. Set the poacher over low heat and simmer 5 to 20 minutes, until just done.

2. Lift the poacher by its handles, and drain fish. Serve at once with tomato, hollandaise, lemon butter, mousseline, beurre noisette, or lemon-wine sauce.

3. If the fish is to be served cold, let it cool in the court bouillon. Drain, wrap well to prevent it from drying out, and refrigerate. Cold fish is often served with mayonnaise, tartar sauce, etc.

*Fillets for the 9 lb, and boney fish for the maximum.

Deep-Fried Items

□ Batter-Fried Fish

Yield: Twenty-five portions

Portion: About 5 oz cooked

Ingredient	Weight	Measure
Flour, pastry	12 oz	3 c
Baking powder	½ oz	1 T
Salt		1½ t
Milk	1 lb	2 c
Eggs, beaten	8 oz	1 c

1. Mix flour, baking powder, salt, milk, and eggs into a smooth batter.

Ingredients	Weight	Measure	Procedure
Fish, fillets	10–11 lb		**2.** Cut fillets into 6 to 7 oz portions. Dip fillets into batter; then remove and allow excess batter to drain. Lower the empty fryer basket, slide fillets into 370°F (188°C) fat, and fry for 4 to 6 minutes or until golden brown.
			3. Lift the basket. Shake to remove excess fat. Dump contents onto absorbent paper and serve at once.

Note: If the fish is put into an unlowered basket and then lowered, it sticks to the basket after frying and some of the batter is torn away.

□ Cod Cakes

Yield: Twenty-five portions

Portion: Two cakes about 3 oz each

	Weight	Measure	Procedure
Cod, cooked, flaked	5 lb		**1.** Combine cod, potato, egg, and egg yolk, mixing well.
Eggs	8 oz	1 c	
Egg yolks	4 oz	½ c	
Potato, mashed	5 lb	2½ qt	
Worcestershire sauce	1 oz	2 T	**2.** Add Worcestershire sauce, and season with salt, ginger, and pepper.
Salt	1½ oz	2 T	
Ginger		½ t	
Pepper, white		2 t	

3. Using a rounded No. 16 scoop, make the mixture into round balls; shape these into flat, round cakes.

4. Bread the cakes.

5. Deep-fry at 350°F (177°C). When golden brown, remove from the fryer and drain well.

6. Serve two cakes per portion, with 2 oz (¼ c) tomato or tartar sauce.

[*SOURCE:* Terrell and Headlund, *Large Quantity Recipes*, p. 131]

□ Deep-Fried Chicken

Yield: Twenty-five portions

Portion: Two pieces or ¼ chicken

Ingredients	Weight	Measure	Procedure
Chicken, fryer, cut up	15 lb		1. Coat pieces thoroughly with the flouring mixture; pat to remove excess.
Flour, pastry	12 oz	3 c	
Salt	½ oz	2 t	
Pepper, white		1 t	
Milk	1¾ lb	3½ c	2. Dip pieces into liquid mixture and remove, letting excess drain off.
Eggs, beaten	5 oz	3 eggs	
Bread crumbs, dry	12 oz	3 c	3. Cover pieces with bread crumbs, and shake to remove excess. Place pieces on rack to dry for about 30 minutes.
			4. Bring fat to 350° to 375°F (177° to 190°C). Lower the empty basket, and then slide pieces singly into fat. Fry until golden brown and cooked through.
			5. Remove from the fat, drain well, and serve.

Note: Set up a breading procedure in which the work flows from chicken to flour, to wash, to crumbs, to rack. Flour acts as a binding agent for the egg and milk mixture, so crumbs can adhere. The more egg in the wash (liquid portion), the better the binding power. The finer the crumbs, the greater the breading adherence and the less the grease absorption.

Variations: Cracker meal, cornmeal, crushed cornflakes, or soft bread crumbs are somtimes used instead of dry bread crumbs.

□ Batter-Fried Chicken

Yield: Twenty-five portions   **Portion:** About 10 oz chicken

Ingredients	Weight	Measure	Procedure
Chicken, cut up broilers or fryers	18 lb		1. Dip each piece of chicken into batter made from the flour, baking powder, salt, milk, and eggs.
Flour, pastry	6 oz	1½ c	
Salt	½ oz	2 t	
Baking powder		2 t	
Milk	8 oz	1 c	
Eggs	5 oz	⅔ c	
			2. Drain and fry in deep-fat at 360°F (180°C) until lightly browned and cooked through— at least 15 to 20 minutes.

Roasted and Baked Items

□ Baked Chicken

Yield: Twenty-five portions   **Portion:** Quarter chicken + 2 oz gravy

Ingredients	Weight	Measure	Procedure
Chicken, ready to cook	20 lb	about 6	1. Have chickens cleaned, washed, and drained. Season inside and out with salt and pepper. Place breast-side down on a rack in a roasting pan. Add *mirepoix*. Roast for 45 to 60 minutes in a 325°F (165°C) oven. Then turn breast-side up, and bake for another 15 to 30 minutes. The leg should break easily away from the side when done.
Onions, chopped	6 oz	1 c	
Carrots, chopped	3 oz	¾ c	
Celery, chopped	3 oz	¾ c	
Salt	as needed		
Pepper, white	as needed		
Stock, chicken	3 lb	1½ qt	2. Remove chickens. Pour off and set aside fat. Deglaze pan, using chicken stock. Strain.
Flour, pastry	4 oz	1 c	3. Use chicken fat to make a roux with the flour. Add this roux to the liquid above, and cook until thickened. Season with salt and pepper.

☐ Baked Stuffed Pork Chop

Yield: Twenty-five portions

Portion: One stuffed chop,
2½ oz gravy

Ingredients	Weight	Measure	Procedure
Onion, chopped	1 lb	2½ c	1. Sauté onion and celery in fat
Celery, diced	½ lb	2 c	until tender.
Bacon, chicken or other fat	½ lb	1 c	
Bread, dry, diced	1 lb	9 c	2. Add vegetables and fat to
Sage, ground	1 oz	½ c	bread; add seasonings and stock,
Thyme, ground		2 t	and toss lightly.* (If a more
Pepper, white		1 t	moist dressing is desired, add
Salt	1 oz	2 T	more stock.)
Stock	1½ lb	3 c	
Apple wedges		25 wedges (3 apples)	3. Pare apples, and cut wedges ½ in. thick.
Pork chops	10 lb	25 chops	4. Fill pockets in chops* with 2–4 T dressing; then close with skewers or toothpicks. Lay chops loosely in oiled baking pan, and bake in a 350°F (177°C) oven for 30 to 45 minutes or until done. Remove chops.
Water or white wine	8 oz	1 c	5. Add water or wine to baking
Stock or brown sauce	3½ lb	3½ pt	pan, and deglaze. Strain into a sauce pan; add stock or brown
Roux	as needed		sauce; heat and add roux as needed to make into medium thick gravy.

Variations:

Sausage dressing: Cook 1 lb pork sausage, separating it while cooking. Drain and add to the dressing. Some of the fat can be used for fat in this recipe.

Oyster dressing: Add 1 qt oysters, cut into large pieces.

Mushroom dressing: Sauté 2 lb sliced fresh mushrooms with the onions and celery.

Giblet dressing: Add finely chopped well-cooked turkey or chicken hearts and gizzards.

Cornbread dressing: Substitute cornbread for bread.

*This quantity is sufficient for twenty-five 4-oz portions, which may be more than needed for these chops. Reduce quantities if necessary.

Note: At times a short order cook may find that the pork chops have no pocket. Figure A-1 shows how such a pocket can be made: Insert the knife into the chop

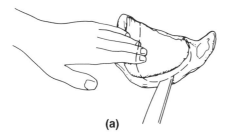
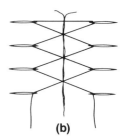

(a)   (b)

FIGURE A-1.

and with a twisting motion cut in a circle upper inside. Reverse the knife and do the same on the lower part of the chop. The dotted line shows the way the cut is made inside. Thus one has a small hole but a large pocket to hold stuffing. Using toothpicks and butcher's cord one can seal the hole so the dressing is not forced out in baking. Such trussing can also be done for poultry, if stuffed, and other items.

□ Roast Rib of Beef

Yield: Twenty five portions (10–12 lb cooked meat)

Portion: 6½ to 8 oz beef + 1½ oz *jus*

Ingredients	Weight	Measure	Procedure
Beef rib, oven-ready	25 lb		1. Place roast on a rack in roasting pan; insert a thermometer in the deep part of the rib, not touching bone or fat. Add *mirepoix*.
Onions, chopped	8 oz	1½ c	
Celery, chopped	4 oz	1 c	
Carrots, chopped	4 oz	1 c	

2. Roast in a 300°F (150°C) oven for 3 to 4 hours. Remove at about 125°F (52°C) for rare and at about 145°F (63°C) for medium. Let stand to firm up before carving.

□ Au Jus

Yield: Twenty-five portions (2½ pt)

Portion: 1½ oz or 3 T

Stock, brown	2½ lb	2½ pt	1. Deglaze roasting pan in which rib was roasted, using brown stock. Strain through china cap. Season with salt and pepper.

Note: A bit of red wine can be used, if desired, with the stock.

Bibliography

Bennion, Marion, *Introduction to Foods*, 7th ed. New York: Macmillan, 1980.

Coffman, James P., *Introduction to Professional Food Service*. Hyde Park, N.Y.: Culinary Institute of America, 1968.

Culinary Institute of America, *The Professional Chef*, 4th ed. New York: Van Nostrand Reinhold, 1974.

Cummings, Leslie E., and Kotschevar, Lendal H., *Nutrition Management in Foodservices*. Albany, N.Y.: Delmar, 1989.

Dunn, M.D., *Fundamentals of Nutrition*. New York: Van Nostrand Reinhold, 1983.

Folsom, LeRoy, *Professional Chef*, 4th ed. New York: Van Nostrand Reinhold, 1983.

Glissen, Wayne, *Professional Cooking*. New York: John Wiley, 1983.

Knight, John, and Kotschevar, Lendal H., *Quantity Food Production: Planning and Management*, 2nd ed. New York: Van Nostrand Reinhold, 1988.

Kotschevar, Lendal H., *Standards, Principles, and Techniques in Quantity Food Production*, 3d ed. Boston: Cahners Books, 1974.

Kotschevar, Lendal H., *Standards, Principles, and Techniques in Quantity Food Production*, 4th ed. New York: Van Nostrand Reinhold, 1988.

Kotschevar, Lendal H., and Levinson, Charles, *Quantity Food Purchasing*, 3d ed. New York: Macmillan, 1986.

Kotschevar, Lendal H., and Terrell, Margaret, *Food Service Planning: Layout and Equipment*, 3d ed. New York: Macmillan, 1985.

Lillicrop, D.R., *Food and Beverage Service*. London: Edward Arnold, 1971.

Longagree, Karla, *Quantity Food Sanitation*, 2d ed. New York: John Wiley, 1983.

Lundberg, Donald, and Kotschevar, Lendal H., *Understanding Cooking*, 4th ed. Holyoke, Mass.: Marcus Printing, 1986.

Mario, Thomas, *Quantity Cooking*. New York: Van Nostrand Reinhold, 1978.

Mizer, David A., and Porter, Mary, *Food Preparation for the Professional*. San Francisco: Canfield Press, 1978.

Morgan, William J., Jr., *Supervision and Management of Quantity Food Preparation: Principles and Procedures*, 2d ed. Berkeley, Calif.: McCutchan, 1981.

National Restaurant Association, "Consumer Nutrition Concerns and Restaurant Choices." Washington, D.C.: NRA, 1986.

Still, Jean, *Food Selection and Preparation*. New York: Macmillan, 1981.

Terrell, Margaret, and Headlund, Dorothea, *Large Quantity Recipes*, 4th ed. New York: Van Nostrand Reinhold, 1989.

U.S. Navy Recipe Service. Bayonne, N.J.: U.S. Navy Supply and Research Center, 1952.

West, Bessie, Hager, Grace, and Wilson, Fay, *Food for Fifty*, 6th ed. New York: Wiley & Sons, 1979.

Whitney, Eleanor, and Hamilton, Eva, *Nutrition: Concerns and Controversies*, 3d ed. St. Paul, Minn.: West Publishing, 1987.

Wood, Henry F., *An Approach to Professional Cookery*. London: Hodder & Stoughton, 1972.

Index